1978

MIKHAIL SHOLOKHOV

A Critical Introduction

Mikhail Sholokhov
A Critical Introduction

D. H. Stewart

Ann Arbor

THE UNIVERSITY OF MICHIGAN PRESS

Preface

My plan in this book is to provide a sketch of Mikhail A. Sholokhov's world and then a series of commentaries on his major
work. I first examine some of the central concerns in his early
short fiction. Next are two studies of his masterpiece, *The
Quiet Don,* in terms of origins, possibilities of interpretation,
and finally epic resemblances. In the last chapter I examine
Sholokhov's novel about collectivization, *Virgin Soil Upturned.*
Because his most recent novel, *They Fought for Their Country,*
remains unfinished, it is not considered. The important matter
of establishing a valid text occupies Appendix B. I have con-
signed the survey of Sholokhov's career to Appendix A because
biographical information about Soviet writers poses special
problems. A friend of his wrote in 1965: "As a writer
[Sholokhov] is well known to Soviet people. Unfortunately,
of Sholokhov the man we know very little."[1]

My general aim is to show that, at his best, Sholokhov's
work invites the same careful scrutiny that serious novelists
in the West do. One would expect this of a book as "primitive"
yet as original and comprehensive as *The Quiet Don,* but it has
not yet elicited extensive serious criticism. Of the many who
have read it with pleasure, few are moved to explain their
response. One is reminded of Professor Gleb Struve's solicita-
tion of Western books on individual Soviet authors to supplement general surveys.[2] My purpose is to discuss Sholokhov
in terms substantially different from those that might appeal

to Soviet readers or to professional students of Soviet literature, who are all necessarily interested in historical, ideological, and political matters. Because he is, first of all, a writer of fiction, I have sought *literary* approaches that would exhibit his works to good advantage. The enabling act of criticism may, I hope, alert readers to literary experiences rarely available in modern literature.

This emphasis is justified because Sholokhov's reputation, indeed the public image he cultivates for himself as a Communist and man of the people, tend to devalue his work in Western eyes. More than twenty books about his work have appeared in the Soviet Union since V. Goffenshefer's pioneer volume, *Mikhail Sholokhov* (1940); only one (in East Germany) has been published outside. He is, to be sure, emphatically Soviet—unlike Boris Pasternak. He devotes as much time to public service as to writing, without any apparent regrets. He told a visitor in 1961: "My guests may think I haven't time left for my main work because so many people are always coming to see me, and in addition there are my responsibilities as a deputy [of the Supreme Soviet] to be fulfilled. Of course this takes time, but if I were to isolate myself, if I were to live beneath a glass bell, then the heroes of my books would also be all glass or plastic, not living people."[3]

Sholokhov bears slight resemblance to the familiar image of a writer as recluse or eccentric. A man of affairs, he has little patience with Western writers who, he believes, have overemphasized individualism and the lonely isolation to which it leads. In his Nobel Prize address, he emphatically dissociated himself from them: ". . . Mankind is not a crowd of disoriented individuals floating, as it were, in a state of weightlessness, like cosmonauts who have escaped the bounds of the earth's gravity. We live on the earth, we are subject to the law of the earth and, as the Gospel says, sufficient unto the day is the evil thereof, its concerns and demands, its hope for a better tomorrow."[4] He sees himself as a man of the people, not of the intelligentsia; and he likes to remind the world of this role by apologizing in public for his crude but candid speech. At solemn writers' congresses, others discourse while he often jests. He has, nonetheless, managed to compose one masterpiece and other notable works, distributed in over sixty languages and uncounted millions of copies—probably more than 50 million.

Lest we mistake him merely for a Russian writer of adventure stories, it should be remembered that over the years letters to him from every corner of the earth have testified to the revolutionary fervor or the human compassion his works inspire. Moreover, Soviet readers as well as Communist critics tend to demand of authors good stories first of all. Displays of technical virtuosity, of the kind provided in the West by Joyce or Faulkner, might be welcomed by Russian intellectuals with appropriate academic training; but they are no better received by Average Ivan than by Plain John—and Average Ivan, armed with Communist ideology, is a far more effective censor than Plain John wielding his purse. Finally, it seems fair to observe that Soviet literature reflects a people struggling with environment while much Western literature since 1917 reflects a people brooding over it. Stated oversimply: one does; the other thinks. A paradoxical literary result of this is the affinity between recent Western and early Soviet fiction. Beckett and Robbe-Grillet conscientiously peel off meanings to reach mere deeds and things; Fadeev and Sholokhov register deeds and things that grope toward meaning.

This is the characteristic of his work that troubled Russian intellectuals before Stalin's purges silenced them. For example in 1930 a critic, Andrei Lezhnev (Gorelov), complained about Sholokhov's indiscriminate piling up of mere childhood impressions as a waste of talent.[5] Sholokhov's anti-intellectualism, together with an unyielding Party allegiance, perhaps also explains the antagonism of post-Stalinist intellectuals and leads, for example, to Valery Tarsis's acrimonious exclamation in *Ward 7*: ". . . The Russian way of life has gone down the drain and so has Russian literature. Who is there nowadays? A drab peasant of a Sholokhov and two-a-penny scribblers like Lebedev-Kumach!"[6] As greater security leads to improved Soviet education and a more sophisticated public, Sholokhov's heroic tales about the nation's founders inevitably lose their immediacy; and when literary bureaucrats hold him up as a model, younger writers justifiably feel coerced and resentful.

In keeping with my intention to be suggestive rather than definitive, I have reduced documentation to the minimum, and I have disregarded such problems as the critical reception of Sholokhov or the use of his books for educational or propagandistic purposes, except where these have biographic relevance. In addition, I have assumed that my reader has read Sholokhov's fiction, hence there are few summaries or condensations of the events he narrates. These are to be found in Ernest Simmons's *Russian Fiction and Soviet Ideology* (1958), Vera Alexandrova's *A History of Soviet Literature* (1963), or other surveys.

For reasons explained more fully in Appendix B and the notes, I have used Soviet translations into English of Sholokhov's novels, altering them slightly where Russian texts justified changes. I am grateful to Alfred A. Knopf, Inc. for permission to quote from *Tales from the Don,* translated by H. C. Stevens (New York, 1967). Although some of the transliteration inconsistencies (e.g., Cyrillic "double i" appears as "y" and "ii") are sanctioned by English custom, some are my own.

I am indebted for assistance through Sholokhov's idiomatic Russian to Professor Assya Humesky, for a great deal of information and guidance to Mr. Henry C. Stevens, and for courteous advice to Mr. Konstantin Priima. Grants from the Center for Russian Studies and the Horace H. Rackham School of Graduate Studies of The University of Michigan enabled me to visit the Soviet Union in the spring of 1966 in order to examine materials not available in the United States. Also I am grateful to the editors of the following journals for permission to use material previously published: *The Slavic Review, Queen's Quarterly,* and *The Soviet and East European Journal.*

D. H. S.

Contents

Chapter I

Sholokhov's Cossack World.

Sholokhov's land is steppe land, limitless and tempest-ridden; so that it seems to scorn and dwarf all human inhabitants except those whose expansiveness and explosive temper can rival its own. Especially before the advent of rural mechanization, only the loudest voice commanded ears; only the strongest fist provoked respect; only the most poignant emotion touched hearts. Medieval flyting and the thunderous braggadocio of the American frontier would ring familiarly on the Don, where ferocity and sentimentality walked hand in hand.

Had one been born, as Sholokhov was, before the 1917 Revolution in the Don Cossack Military Region of southern Russia, he would have absorbed from his earliest years a hostility not only toward the two Russian capitals and city life generally but also toward the sleepy, dull-witted Russian peasant. He would have been encouraged to see himself as one of the Chosen to whom proletarian strikes and peasant revolts were equally alien. Saint Petersburg's imperial splendor or the glitter and noise of Russia's awakening bourgeoisie could scarcely outshine the steppe sun or outsound the steppe wind.

For most people, including most Russians, Sholokhov's Cossack homeland was a distant, exotic place, a spacious land populated by descendants of a race of giants: Yermak, the sixteenth-century conqueror of Siberia; Razin and Pugachyov, rebels who, in the seventeenth and eighteenth centuries, shook the throne of the empire and thus became legendary symbols

1

of popular opposition to gentry oppression. Those who thought about it at all associated the Cossack steppe with Gogol's and Tolstoy's partly romanticized pictures on the one hand and pogroms or raids against workingmen or students on the other. The Cossack was either a dashing primitive or a monstrous barbarian, and mothers terrified their children with visions of the wild horseman with his shock of hair, his scarlet (Kuban) or blue (Don) ornamented dress, and his bloody knout. Before Sholokhov, one could view him either fancifully as a free eagle of the steppe or realistically as a soldier (with homicidal tendencies) in the czar's loyal army.

This stereotype accounts for the surprise that many Russian readers experienced when, in 1928, they read the first parts of Sholokhov's *Quiet Don*—a surprise shared by readers in all nations over the past thirty-five years as they come upon this work for the first time. One Russian critic recorded his response as follows:

> And suddenly came a novel describing Cossack life, describing it in detail, richly, with a beautiful knowledge of material.
>
> Cossacks? The reader began to recall what he had read before about them. There was almost nothing: Gogol's Zaporozh Cossacks, Tolstoy's *Cossacks* and some stories and essays by pre-Revolutionary second-raters. In addition the reader recalled a number of episodes from Soviet books and films on pre-Revolutionary life . . . in which Cossacks always persecuted revolutionaries with knout and sabre. . . .
>
> Hence the odd sound of *The Quiet Don* . . . especially to readers who did not yet know that volume one, dealing with pre-war life, was only the first part of an epic on Cossacks in the Revolution. . . .[1]

Thus we see why the novel was an educational experience for readers—why, indeed, it has been used as an anthropology text in some universities of the United States.

What we obtain from *The Quiet Don* is a picture of the

Cossack that differs radically from the popular image, either of the steppe eagle or the Hun. We learn that the Cossacks enjoyed a superficially stable social order with definite characteristics. Theirs was a society based on tradition and held together by pride. From the sixteenth through the eighteenth centuries, Cossacks were Russians, frequently serfs, who had escaped oppression by fleeing southward along the waterways. Thus, the traditions which they developed in the course of their odyssey were all that distinguished them from the original stock whence they came, though frequent intermarriage with native Tatars in time made them leaner and darker than their peasant cousins.

One of their greatest leaders, Ataman Platov, pointed out early in the nineteenth century that those who wanted to change the "old frontier ways" were wrong because "it was only their military organization which differentiated the Cossacks from the surrounding peasant population, whose abject condition they all despised."[2]

The Cossacks were adventurous and courageous men with the initial fortitude to strike out in search of a better life, even if this meant fighting both the Russian masters whom they had escaped and the Tatar tribesmen upon whose lands they encroached. Originally similar in some ways to the men who took the American West, they were self-reliant, hence equalitarian and libertarian, banding together solely for the purpose of protection and submitting only to a leader ("ataman"—or "hetman," in Ukranian) freely elected from their own people. They referred to themselves, originally, as "The Society of Free People" and received into their ranks any man, on the sole conditions that he was Orthodox and opposed to serfdom. No racial barrier existed. The traditional hatred for Turks, Tatars, Jews and Poles derives from religious, not racial, antagonism. Cossacks wed Mongol or Caucasian women with a fine indiscrimination, providing they were attractive. Indeed, their esteem for individual bravery so far exceeded even their loyalty to Orthodoxy that by Tolstoy's time they often preferred the friendship of an infidel warrior to that of a Christian Russian.

A sense of the fanatical rigidity of the codes by which these people governed themselves can be obtained from a story told about Cossack justice by Alexandre Dumas. An old Cossack and his twenty-year-old son were bear hunting when a leopard attacked them. The father dispatched him, but the son ran away in fright. When he returned home, the father helped the son dig a grave in the frozen earth, then shot him through the head and buried him. Apprehended by the authorities, the father explained, "I have performed an act of justice, as God would have me do." He is convicted, but the magistrate is doubtful about punishment and suggests that "for three days and nights the father shall sit holding on his knees the head of his son, severed from the trunk. If the ordeal kills him or drives him mad, that will be the judgment of God. But if he remains unmoved, it can only be because he acted not in anger but as a conscientious father performing a duty, in which case he is not guilty of murder." A copy of this sentence is sent to Czar Alexander II who confirms it as just. The father endures the three day ordeal without batting an eye, is set free, and lives to be eighty.[3]

It is a curious twist of history that the same Cossacks who produced such men as Razin and Pugachyov should have grown finally into the czar's most loyal police; yet the change is not so hard to understand when one remembers that from Peter's time onward the Russian state gained more and more control over Cossack leaders. As early as 1718 the ataman was given to understand that the continuation of his title depended absolutely on the czar's pleasure, and in 1723 Ataman Lopatin was appointed directly by Peter. It was not, however, until 1848 that the first non-Cossack, General Chomutov, was made ataman.[4]

The change in the Cossack's role during the nineteenth century is also explicable when we remember that the Russian state learned to exploit the inevitable resistance to newcomers that occurred with the increase of population in Cossack areas. A day came when the Cossack, for self-preservation, had to keep the land for himself, which meant that newcomers, far from finding the freedom they sought, became a class of indigents whose status assured the retention of their original peasant mentality. The Cossack found himself between the millstones of autocratic tyranny and peasant misery, and the autocrat was clever enough to preserve the Cossack's loyalty by declining to crush him into the peasant mass. Thus, the Cossack had no chance to become a "yeoman farmer" or to follow the evolutionary pattern of rural America. Russian classes were too inflexible for that.

If, at first, Cossacks' dislike of the peasant was the logical negative expression of their positive sense of freedom and achievement, it later became a custom to which they clung passionately as a compensation, perhaps, for the freedom which they slowly lost in the eighteenth and nineteenth centuries. So strong was the traditional contempt for the peasant that it persisted even when the Cossacks, who first lived by plunder and commerce up and down Russia's southern rivers, had become almost completely agricultural. In other words, what the Cossack held to was the mere husk of a glorious past. He came to have something in common with Scottish Highlanders of the eighteenth century, even to their Jacobite infatuations. His resplendent, half-oriental uniform (though off duty or on weekdays he wore homespun), his horsemanship (though at home he walked behind oxen tilling the land), his sabre and knout (though in the fields he brandished a simple switch), his sacrosanct Cossack earth, a tiny bag of which he wore in the service round his neck with his miniature icon (though at home he bartered it, haggled over it, and exhausted it by overuse), even his cherished Orthodoxy (the spirit of which he evidently ignored); these were the things to which he was almost obsessively attached. The Don River itself became the central symbol of the tradition, as Sholokhov explains in *The Quiet Don*:

In the old days when the Cossacks of the Ataman's Regiment had served their time they'd be equipped to go back home. They'd load their chests, their horses and goods into the train. The train would set out, and just by Voronezh, where the line crosses the Don for the

first time, the engine-driver would go slow, as slow as he
could . . . he knew what was coming. And as soon as
the train got on to the bridge . . . my grandfathers! What
a scene! The Cossacks would go quite mad: "The Don!
The quiet Don! Our father, our own! Hurrah!" and
through the windows, over the bridge straight into the
water would go caps, old tunics, trousers, shirts, and
the Lord knows what else! They would give presents to the
Don on their return from service. Sometimes as you looked
at the water you would see blue ataman caps floating
along like swans or flowers. . . . It was a very old custom (Part v, Chap. 10).

So strong was the hold of tradition upon the Cossack
that in 1918 at one of the congresses held in Petrograd, a
delegate from the Ural Cossacks proposed that their ancient
name, "Cossacks of the Yaik," be restored. The old name
had been abolished by imperial edict in the eighteenth century as a punishment for participation by Cossacks of that
region in the Pugachyov revolt against gentry exploitation.
For a century and a half, they had kept the suppressed name
alive.[5]

Empress Catherine's destruction of Cossack autonomy
after the Pugachyov revolt dates from her manifesto, issued
August 5, 1775. In succeeding years, the Cossacks were even
more rigidly controlled. The reorganization in 1835 gave the
Don Army its final form as a totally separate caste into which
one who entered and all his descendants had to remain for all
time. Non-Cossacks within the army area might no longer
hold real estate. The entire male population was conscripted
for military service. As the top of every branch of administra-
tion stood officers, usually non-Cossacks, whose influence was
so comprehensive that the Cossacks retained only a very
limited freedom. Not only had they to stand the cost of
equipping themselves for induction,[6] they had no right to say
whether they would serve. At the same time the gentry and
czarist state virtually confiscated great tracts of common
land. This blocked Cossack expansion and prepared for the

day when sufficient parcels of new land would not be available for expanding population, though the effects of this were not fully recognized by the time of the Revolution.

But if freedom disappeared, the sense of being a chosen or unique people remained. The extent to which the delusion of exclusiveness was carried is best indicated by the fact that for years true Don Cossacks constituted a minority of the population in the area, yet they continued to conceive of themselves as absolute masters of the Don. By 1916 the total population was 3.4 million, of which the Cossacks numbered 1.6 million, or 47 percent.[7] Under the czar's protection, they preyed cruelly upon the peasants and "outlanders" who shared their land, converting them into day laborers whose future was as hopeless as that of any working man in Russia.

It was the combination of subservience to tradition, of pride, and of exclusiveness that perhaps explains another curious paradox, namely, Cossack individualism. No doubt the main source of this individualism was Cossack tradition itself, but there were other contributing factors. First, all Cossack areas had a disproportionately high percentage of religious schismatics, "Old Believers" as Russians call them. Statistical proof of this assertion is wanting because the czarist government always suppressed figures, yet most investigators concur.[8] In the Russian Orthodox church, under the last Romanovs, the annual practice of pronouncing a solemn curse against religious and political heretics, of whom three of the five singled out by name are Cossacks, demonstrates that recalcitrant elements were never fully assimilated. It would seem reasonable to assume that the presence of these Schismatics accounts not only for Cossack separatism but for the curious appeal that Protestant sects of all kinds have in Cossack areas even to the present time.

Another source of individualism is economic. No doubt the Cossack maintained much of the traditional Russian sense of community, seen especially in his religious and military life and in his practice of periodic partitioning of common lands —distributed in terms of family size, not private property rights. Yet, not only did he remember his heritage of escape from the Russian commune, where less and less land could be privately owned with each passing generation; he was able, as a result of the Don land's abundance and fertility and his own hard work, to sustain himself apart from the community far more successfully than his peasant cousins to the north. By the time of the First World War, his landholding, livestock, and general inventory were still more than twice that of other peasants.

Despite contradictions in their traditions, the public dash and splendor but the private hardship and ignorance, the public camaraderie but the private isolation, czarist favor guaranteed the Cossacks an uneasy synthesis that permitted them to keep the old illusions.

The capital of the area, Novocherkassk, built on a new site in 1805 and demolished by the Germans in February 1943, was a monument to the reconciliation of opposed traditions living in the hearts of the people. Homes resembled citadels. Many streets were negotiable only by horsemen because they were too narrow and steep for vehicles. On the highest hill stood the cathedral, a warlike shrine surrounded by cannon and other captured war trophies. In front stood the statue of Yermak, conqueror of Siberia during the reign of Ivan Groznyi.[9]

Little wonder that we should discover in Sholokhov pictures of stable, static community life and at the same time considerable evidence of the isolation of individuals. The world beyond the Don, and especially the large city (symbol of twentieth-century "progress" and of all the forces inimical to the coherent rural society), is alien or unknown. And, of course, along with this isolation comes ignorance, sometimes amusing but sometimes sinister because of the superstition, sorcery, and the tendency toward self-delusion to which ignorance leads. Even religion is often barely distinguishable from pagan ritual, and one is not surprised to learn that some Cossacks believed they had a divine mandate to slaughter their enemies.

A great deal that is unattractive in Cossack society can be attributed to a deficient educational system. Despite Ataman

Platov's endeavors early in the nineteenth century to make Novocherkassk an intellectual center and to raise the literacy rate by endowing schools liberally, the fact remains that by the turn of the twentieth century, seventy-seven out of every hundred Cossacks were illiterate. Moreover, there was a sharp distinction in literacy between well-off Cossacks and workers and peasants, between men and women, and between city and rural dwellers. Thus, for example, among landholders and government officials literacy reached 74.4 percent, but among Cossack and peasant women, only 7.7 percent. According to the 1897 census, there was only one man per thousand with a collegiate education; among women, one per ten thousand.[10] Before World War I there was only one college in the area—the Don Polytechnical Academy in Novocherkassk.

The color, the courage and freedom of Cossack life were everywhere soiled by a hate-ridden ignorance. The peasant, the *khokhol* (a derogatory name for Ukrainian), the Jew, indeed whatever was non-Cossack had to be despised as inferior. Peasant, *khokhol,* and Jew became terms of reproach exceeded in virulence only by the term "Red," which in Cossack eyes combined all three. But to consider ignorance the sole cause for the limitless contempt which seemed at times to animate the entire society would be erroneous, since it also appears to arise from a compensatory effort to make up for the absence of a positive faith. The Cossacks' daily life constantly refuted many of the ideals and institutions in which they professed to believe (freedom, cavalier ostentation, Orthodoxy), so that all that remained to bind them together and to remind them of their identity was a blind rage at anything which threatened their illusions. Contrary to appearances, there is a sense in which the Cossack was afraid and, at least in a few isolated cases, defensive or uncertain.

The story of how a society with the outward appearance of stability and with an apparently vigorous tradition suddenly reveals its inner emptiness under pressure is one of the most interesting and tragic in *The Quiet Don.* As long as a society exists in its vacuum of isolation, it is relatively secure and impervious to any recognition of its own defects, though even here traces prognosticating the future begin to appear. Senseless pogroms and unprovoked attacks on Ukrainian farmers indicate that the Cossacks sought scapegoats to conceal from themselves the objective historical reasons for their frustrations. The young Cossack, taught to believe in his superior blood, imagined he was the peer of any gentleman's son and supposed that rich merchants would happily give him their daughters to wed. When reality failed to match his expectations, his restlessness heightened tensions already straining the community.

But the most fertile seeds of dissension existed less often among Cossacks themselves, at least before the First World War, than among the men and ideas living, as it were, on the edges of the old Cossack community or outside it entirely. Merchants, whose ancestors followed the wake of Cossack expansion southward and eastward, developed trading posts into thriving businesses. Cossacks distrusted them, partly because of their early reputation of being spies for the Russian state and partly because they visibly enriched themselves at Cossack expense. Closely associated with them were landed aristocrats, the officer caste, men superimposed upon Cossack society by imperial edict. Great Russian interests together with the personal advantage of these two classes developed the non-Cossack city, Rostov, near the mouth of the Don. Indeed Novocherkassk ("New Cherkassk") was established as a military and administrative center by the imperial government to reduce the importance and psychological appeal for Cossacks of Starocherkassk ("Old Cherkassk"), their island stronghold in the Don River. Many refused to accept the change. The Cossack was, all the same, trapped inside a rectangle roughly described by the cities Voronezh, Kharkov, Rostov, and Tsaritsyn. Growing up round him were centers of commerce and industry that he scarcely understood.

This situation, as Sholokhov himself explains, led to the introduction of a third alien force into Cossack life—working-class ideology. It is personified in *The Quiet Don* by a Russian Bolshevik of Lettish extraction named Stockman. It is he who reaches the heartstrings of Cossack life by exposing the contradictory illusions of the Cossack mentality: "He laid the cocoon of discontent. And who could know that within four years the larva of the strong, vital foetus would break out of its decrepit walls."

Perhaps a combination of geography and history accounts for the Cossacks' inability to establish a society strong enough to resist incursion from the north. They occupied a vulnerable area, subject for centuries to the migration of peoples and the passage of armies. They themselves came to it, like the Scyths and Mongols before them, as marauders; they took it and became, as it were, merely the first thrust of a tidal wave, pouring down from Muscovy, which was destined to overwhelm them. However antagonistic they became toward the empire or the Russian, they thought of themselves as Russians, somehow linked to the parent nation. During times of insurrection in the seventeenth and eighteenth centuries, they willingly accepted dissident Russian peasants as allies. Secessionist sentiment was never widespread. That they maintained their identity as long as they did testifies to their strength; that they were marked for destruction from the first yet continued to resist testifies to their tenacity.

It is not hard to understand why the Cossacks' world begins to crumble under the impact of the First World War, just as Russian society as a whole crumbled. Unlike the workers and the peasants, unlike the middle class and intelligentsia who all anticipated radical social change and in many cases welcomed it, the Cossacks' flirtation with revolution remained superficial. Their deepest instincts told them that any break in the continuity of their tradition, any disruption of blood lines would be fatal. Their social and psychological impregnability to the winds of change that swept Russia created higher resistance to the general disintegration of 1917 and almost universal hostility to Communist reintegration afterward. They were strong enough to oppose the inevitable heroically. This is why their story is uniquely interesting—and tragic.

To be sure, they entered the First World War full of illusions that were rapidly dispelled when they came to see themselves as a people living under the heel of a czarist-imposed caste of officers, as a people whose substance was drained constantly into the coffers of merchants. Little wonder that Bolshevik ideas so easily ate into the hearts of front line men and sent them home bewildered and angry, only to find moral erosion in the homeland. Decent householders had grown rapacious; wives and sweethearts proved faithless. But if Bolshevism exposed the duplicity of upper class behavior and destroyed the Cossacks' allegiance to czardom, it quickly betrayed its own duplicity toward them. With czarist perfidy, they could at least go on living; with Bolshevism, they could not. This is why after 1917 they were thrown back on their own material and spiritual resources. Without honorable allies, they had to look backward to their legacy of tradition and finally inward to a reservoir of fortitude and integrity that was purely individual.

Well over half of *The Quiet Don* is devoted to revolution. The March Revolution is announced in Part iv, Chapter 8, and the October Revolution in Chapter 19. Since we know that Sholokhov began the actual composition of the book with what is now Part iv,[11] which takes up the action in October 1916, we can judge it likely that he wrote the entire first volume (Parts i-iii) as a kind of prologue calculated to provide historical perspective for and to render more intelligible the chaotic events of the Revolution. It summarizes and typifies the entire history of the Cossacks, whose social order was almost as feudal just prior to the First World War as it had been three centuries earlier. Without the first three parts, the remainder of the book covering the period from 1917 to 1922 might seem extremely difficult and confusing, but with them we are prepared not only for the anarchy during the months after the October Revolution (Part v) but also for the complex series of Cossack rebellions beginning in the spring of 1918. We understand, in short, why Sholokhov began Part vi as he did:

> In April 1918 there was a great cleavage in the Don province. . . . Only in 1918 was this great cleavage accomplished. Yet it had had its beginnings hundreds of

years previously, when the poorer Cossacks of the north, who had neither rich land nor vineyards nor valuable hunting and fishing grounds, from time to time broke away from Cherkassk, made arbitrary descents upon the districts of Great Russia and were the main stronghold of all rebels from the time of Stenka Razin onward.

Even in later days, when the entire province, crushed by the tsarist autocracy, was seething with unrest, it was the Cossacks of the upper districts who openly rose and, led by their atamans, shook the tsarist system to its foundations, fighting the Imperial troops, plundering caravans of barges on the Don, ranging as far as the Volga, and rousing the downtrodden Cossacks of Zaporozhye to insurrection (Part vi, Chap. 1).

Into this society, characterized by the "great cleavage," Sholokhov was born. Into this world of the "great cleavage" Sholokhov presently brought his literary heroes.

Before the middle of the last century, Sholokhov's grandfather moved from Ryazan Province in Russia to Veshenskaya, a village in the Don Cossack Military Region. He worked in the shop of a local merchant who was also an "outlander." In time the young salesman wedded his employer's daughter and became a merchant himself. He had a large family, four sons and four daughters. The second son, Alexander Mikhailovich, was the author's father.[12]

His mother, Anastasiya Danilovna Chernikova, belonged to the so-called "native peasantry," former serfs long since established on the Don. She was born near the hamlet of Kruzhilin in a community called Yasenovka, which was populated by peasants over whom proprietary right was held by a landowner, Dmitri Evgrafovich Popov—a name prominent in Cossack history. Anastasiya Danilovna's parents died early, and she was taken into the home of the old landowner as a maid. Later she moved to Veshenskaya and was employed in the Sholokhov home.

There young Alexander fell in love with her, and she became pregnant. In order to prevent a disadvantageous marriage, the parents sought a more suitable bride for him; and in accordance with local custom, they married the maid to a retired noncommissioned Cossack officer.

Such solicitude from the older Sholokhovs provoked a protest from the son. Alexander Mikhailovich declined the bride chosen for him and demanded his portion. When he received it, he took Anastasiya Danilovna into his own home as a domestic servant—as if her elderly husband did not exist.

Alexander Mikhailovich finished only the parish church school; but he read a good deal, was attracted to cultural life and, by the standards prevailing at the time, was considered a well-informed man by people of his class. Lacking a profession, he tried his hand at farming, salesmanship, and various schemes that promised quick profits. Anastasiya Danilovna, on the other hand, was illiterate. When people asked Alexander how he could marry a simple peasant, he answered, "You know nothing; she's not a woman, she's a picture!" She learned to read and write only when her son went off to school and began to send home letters which she was ashamed to be unable to read.

Mikhail Alexandrovich Sholokhov was born May 24, 1905, an only child with peculiar legal status. His mother's first husband (whose name Soviet critics have not disclosed) was a Cossack, which meant that Sholokhov inherited all Cossack rights and privileges. When this husband died and Sholokhov's father wed Anastasiya Danilovna in 1912, his birth was thereby legitimitized, but this meant the forfeiture of a cultural heritage considered to be all-important in the area. What problems this may have caused a seven-year-old boy we do not know, though echoes of traumatic discomfiture can be detected in Sholokhov's early stories about children. The crucial fact is that Sholokhov lacked full Cossack status.

One of his cousins recalls that "he grew like all children and was lively like them all. But he was very proud. God preserve me, but when some outsider caressed him, he put on an awful scowl. You couldn't coax him with sweets—he was incorruptible. Sholokhov's father spoiled him, excused his pranks; but his mother punished him at times. Then he'd come running to our place, to hide 'with Auntie Oli' [Olga Mikhailovna Sergina, his father's sister]. She pacified him with stories."

Another cousin (Olga's son Alexander, who acted as nursemaid to young Sholokhov) tells the story of their childhood games:

> In those times after the Russo-Japanese war and the heroic defense of Port Arthur, the favorite game of the village kids, little Cossacks, was called "The Battle under the walls of Port Arthur." Sometimes we gathered in a gully with a stream at the bottom, and we divided into "detachments"—one on one side of the gully, one on the other. I commanded one detachment of eighteen men, and my brother Volodya commanded the other with twenty-five men. Everyone pranced about on sticks of wood, that is "high-spirited horses." The "Russian cavalry" would attack the Japanese firing pebbles and rocks until somebody got "shot" in the head. Then there'd be a quarrel. Little Misha was in my "detachment." I put him in a small trench whence he threw pebbles no worse than others—indeed he pitched in a very military fashion and with warlike fury.[13]

In 1911, six-year-old Sholokhov was tutored by one Timofei Timofeevich Mrykhin, who remembered him as a diligent boy, good at assimilating material but deficient in writing. He was already a passionate fisherman. At that age he wanted to be an officer, but Mrykhin reminded him of the more permanent contribution of great scientists, of the joys of learning; and little Misha said to him, "Then I shall be a student."

In 1912 Sholokhov's teacher was Mikhail Grigorevich Kopylov, who is mentioned in *The Quiet Don* (Part vii, Chaps. 9-11). Concerning Kopylov, Mrykhin said:

He was the son of a local Kargin medical assistant; he was involved before the revolution in a student organization and was expelled in czarist times from teachers' college for political unreliability. During the Civil War when the Whites evacuated Karginskaya and Soviet rule was established, he remained. But then the memorable Upper-Don revolt behind the Red Army lines began, and Kopylov was involved. He vacillated and procrastinated— procrastinated no worse than Grigory Melekhov. After the regrouping of insurrectionary units, Kopylov, together with other rebels, went over to the Whites and was killed in battle.[14]

Late in the summer of 1914, just after the beginning of World War I, Sholokhov's father sent him to Moscow for eye treatments. He stayed several months, wearing dark green glasses, and began school there in 1915. The expense of journeys home and the high cost of living in the capital embarrassed his father financially, and Sholokhov was transferred to a boys' eight-year gymnasium in Boguchar (Voronezh Province) where he was not so far away and could receive parcels of food. It was at this time, apparently, that he wrote some poems. "Who doesn't write poetry in the gymnasium?" he asked years later.[15]

But Sholokhov had finished only the fourth class in school when, in 1918, the Germans occupied Boguchar and he had to return home because of the Revolution. During the Civil War he lived with his family in several communities: first there was Pleshakov near Elanskaya, where his father worked in a steam grist mill. In 1919 the family moved to Rubezhnyi, where Sholokhov learned to know Yakov Fomin, who played an important role during the Revolution, first as a Bolshevik sympathizer, then as an independent bandit chieftain. In the same year they moved once more, to Karginskaya. Here fourteen-year-old Sholokhov's revolutionary sentiments provoked a Cossack to come searching for him and to abuse his mother when she refused to disclose his hiding place.[16] He was, therefore, from 1918 to the beginning of 1920, in an area controlled by the Whites. His reading, if not his formal education, continued. His father subscribed to various journals, constantly bought books, and created a small library for his son, which the boy read through several times. One of his favorite writers during this early period was Jack London. He preferred books to movies and later admitted that for him "a book substituted for any movie or theatrical production."

In 1920, when scarcely fifteen years old, Sholokhov went to work for the Revolutionary Committee (the new civil administrative unit that emerged from the Revolution—usually designated by its abbreviation, Revcom) in Karginskaya. He helped in educational work, gave readings, played the guitar, harmonica, and piano, composed and took part in plays—especially comic roles. In one play, which was adapted from Fonvizin's *Young Hopeful*, Sholokhov did a parody of young Mitrofan: he came on stage smeared with jam. Years later when friends asked whether he wrote this play or others equally crude, "he didn't deny it but wouldn't confirm it either —he just laughed." He did assist in establishing a collective youth theater at Veshenskaya and a Cossack theater for the Don Region which featured choral groups and instrumental ensembles.[17]

In addition to this kind of work, Sholokhov also served for a time with grain requisitioning detachments, often a dangerous and brutal occupation, especially after the crop failures of 1921. To seize grain from irate peasants was dangerous enough, but there was a greater peril: the region was infested with armed bands of brigands and disaffected remnants of anti-Soviet forces who executed Communist sympathizers with alacrity. On one occasion Sholokhov avoided hanging at the hands of the Ukrainian nationalist and anti-Bolshevik, Nestor Makhno, only because he was thought to be too young to know what he was doing. Elements of this adventure are probably incorporated in his short story, "The Way of the Road."

At this time too, Sholokhov began writing, though his first stories were invariably rejected. In addition, he fell in love with a grammar-school teacher, Maria Petrovna Gromoslavskaya, whom he met at the grain-requisitioning office. The girl's father, Pyotr Yakovlevich, was a well-to-do Cossack and colorful figure. A native of Bukanovskaya, he was sacristan of the church and, for several years before 1916, village ataman. At the beginning of the Civil War in 1918, when the Whites retreated, there was an order for Gromoslavsky to join the departing troops; but he evaded it and joined the Reds. He served for a time as a Communist official, but in 1923 he again became sacristan; and, quite naturally, we hear no more about him from Soviet sources until his death in the spring of 1939. Likewise, we know little about Sholokhov's wife except that she bore his four children and became the ideal Soviet feminine "comrade" who accompanies her man on hunting expeditions and unobtrusively shares his fortune.

In the careless manner so characteristic of first generation Soviet writers, Sholokhov wrote a thumbnail autobiography of his first seventeen years which was printed as a preface to *Azure Steppe* (1931), a collection of his stories:

> I was born in 1905 in Kruzhilin hamlet, Veshenskaya *stanitsa*, Donets region (formerly the Don Military Territory).
>
> My father was a middle class citizen from Ryazan who changed professions up until his death (1925). In succession he was a "fast dealer" (livestock buyer), he planted grain on leased Cossack land, he served as a salesman in a small-scale commercial enterprise, he was a manager of a steam grain mill, etc.
>
> My mother was half Cossack, half peasant. She became literate when my father sent me to the gymnasium, in order to write letters to me herself without begging father's assistance. Until 1912 both she and I owned land, she as a Cossack widow and I as a Cossack's son; but in 1912 my father, Sholokhov, adopted me (up to this time he was not married to my mother), and I began to be reckoned a "*meshchanin's* [petty bourgeois] son."
>
> I studied in various gymnasia until 1918. I was on the Don at the time of the Civil War.

From 1920 I was in service and knocked around the Don area. For a while I was a grain collector. We chased the bands [of brigands] who controlled the Don until 1922 and they chased us. Everything went as might be expected. There were many close scrapes but now all this is forgotten. . . .

Sholokhov's serious commitment to literature apparently began when he moved to Moscow in 1922 and joined a group of young writers who called themselves Young Guards and obtained for their quarters one floor of a third-rate hotel. To be sure, he had tried his hand at writing earlier. As early as the summer of 1922 he spoke to friends about a large novel on the life of the Don Cossacks during the Civil War. He cannot, however, be called a true apprentice until he began attending "seminars" for young writers. One for poets was conducted by Nikolai Aseev, a "Futurist" closely associated with Vladimir Mayakovsky; one for prose writers was supervised alternately by Osip Brik and Viktor Shklovsky in the apartment of Mark Kolosov, a friend of Sholokhov and one of his first editors.[18] Sholokhov's exposure to the instruction of Brik and Shklovsky, brief as it was, must have been invaluable because of their emphasis on the *craft* of writing, the forms and techniques of fiction, rather than exclusively on content. They were, after all, two leading exponents of literary "formalism," later anathematized by the Communist Party. On one occasion Sholokhov's group was assigned the task of modeling a story about Soviet life after Chekhov's plot device in "Over-salted" (*Peresolil*), and Kolosov reports that Sholokhov "fulfilled the task more exactly and assiduously than the others; his approximation was closest of all." On another occasion, Osip Brik gave a talk on plotting and then asked for stories with a "reverse effect" (surprise ending). Sholokhov's effort made an impression on the group. Not only was his story "keenly plotted, but rich in language, with memorable characters and nobility of conception."

Such exaggerated praise is, no doubt, the product of a friend's enthusiasm, yet Sholokhov was learning. The staccato

style, hyperbolic imagery, and "chronological displacement"
that appear in early portions of *The Quiet Don* mark the extent of formalist training. His first published work, which
he signed "M. Sholokh," was a feuilleton called "The Test"
that appeared September 19, 1923. Despite its unnatural
language and clumsy imagery, it exhibits a Chekhovian
concern for precise physical detail and for meiotic rather
than climactic resolutions.

One of the most striking features of this story is Sholokhov's concern with "internal conspiracy"—the fact that the
party itself has been infiltrated by unsavory characters who
plague loyal members. This concern was commonplace during
the NEP period, and as we shall see, the problem became
crucial for Sholokhov himself during the first Five-Year Plan,
very nearly costing him his career.

But Sholokhov was not satisfied in Moscow. Progress
was slow. He labored at various menial jobs to pay his keep,
talked a great deal about literature but wrote little of merit.
Only at the end of 1924 (December 14), over two years after
he arrived in the capital, was his first story, "The Birthmark,"
published in *The Young Leninist*. New stories appeared in
rapid succession during the spring of 1925. As one result, he
was able to meet his first major literary celebrity, A. S. Serafimovich, who had achieved prominence for his fiction before
the Revolution and received Soviet acclaim in 1924 for his
novel *The Iron Flood*. The meeting was important because
Serafimovich took a personal interest in his "fellow countryman" (he too came from the Cossack region). Sensing genuine
talent in Sholokhov, the older author not only encouraged him
but extended to him his patronage by writing a preface to
the first collection of his stories, reviewing enthusiastically the
opening volume of *The Quiet Don* and becoming his most
stalwart defender against those who attacked him later on.
Sholokhov recorded his gratitude in numerous tributes. It
was, apparently, after their first meeting that Serafimovich
"dashed off" a brief word portrait of the twenty-year-old
Sholokhov:

Sholokhov threw himself back; he had a broad white forehead, unnaturally prominent, and light, curly hair. His face was tanned. Sharp, precisely outlined asiatically-elongated, blue-gray eyes looked straight, almost smiling, from beneath thin brows raised like a girl's. Then the eyes spoke and the lips almost smiled as if he were saying, "I know, I know, brother; I see you through and through."[19]

Here, then, was a tough, young Russian-Cossack. Through these searching eyes, he had watched a primitive world collapse into outright savagery without relinquishing his longing for culture and decency. With these eyes as his guide, he would discover in the life he knew a paradigm of all Russian and Soviet history. When his vision blurred, he would resort to the best corrective lens available to him at the time—the lens of Marx modified by Lenin and called Bolshevism. The result was a socialist interpretation of Cossack history and the Russian Revolution qualified by a ruralized and regionalized Bolshevism. Most of the time, however, he needed no lens because he had the light of the steppe sun for illumination and the sound of steppe wind filled with song and legend to give his prose its music.

Chapter II

Sholokhov's Early Fiction

The quality of Sholokhov's early fiction is not uniformly high. Rarely does he achieve Isaac Babel's level of craftsmanship and only occasionally do his studies of a minority people, the Cossacks, justify comparison with Babel's of the Jews. This is not to say, however, that the Don tales deserve attention merely as a "prehistory" of *The Quiet Don*. Sholokhov himself explicitly repudiated such an approach when it became fashionable among Soviet critics:

> Don't you see that from the viewpoint of artistic mastery, the accumulation of a writer's experience, the *Tales of the Don* were, to all intents and purposes, trials of the pen, tests of literary strength, and therefore they preceded *The Quiet Don*. But it is impossible to see "prehistory" where it doesn't exist. Certain critics lift from the text words, analogous settings, and expressions; they seek coincidences. What they offer in proof, however, has actually no significance in the creative history of the writing of *The Quiet Don*. The person who calls the *Tales of the Don* an artistic "pre-history" can't distinguish day from night. Some critics spin the plot of *The Quiet Don* out of the stories "Crooked Path," "Doubly Wed," or "Azure Steppe"; and then again "Doubly Wed" and "Crooked Path." This gets you a cold soup [*okroshka*] but not creativity. Had I written *The Quiet Don* that way,

with the help of scissors and paste, then I would never have gone further than "Crooked Path"—one of the weakest of my stories.[1]

We can, then, examine the stories as experiments that stand or fall independently, though at the same time we may identify stylistic and thematic elements that are characteristically Sholokhovian.

The early stories are adventures in a revolutionary setting. Most of them occur in 1921-22 when bands of armed marauders, not White armies, were the besetting evil in the Don area. Emphasis in every case is on the deeds of people not on their thoughts. Hence our minds are rarely engaged. We simply watch—amazed, appalled, helpless—as the Cossack horsemen race in and out of our vision, laughing, weeping, sometimes falling dead at our feet.

Conceivably, Sholokhov chose his subject matter not only from life, as he and the Soviet critics always insist, but in response to directives by Party activists. Yury Libedinsky, for example, speaking in 1923 for the "Octobrist" faction with which Sholokhov was allied, proclaimed that writers should depict living men in contemporary situations, and he suggested three thematic cycles that deserved treatment: new forms of social life supplanting old, worker participation in building a socialist economy, and working-class endeavors in political affairs.[2] Elements of all three can be found in Sholokhov's stories, though he had to search assiduously for "workers," as Communism formally defined them, in a Cossack setting.

Not subjects, however, but Sholokhov's own method of presenting them is necessarily our first concern. What he was trying to convey, apparently, was the *immediacy* of the events narrated. His teachers, it should be remembered, encouraged him to use Chekhov as a model and insisted on the importance

of "significant incident" and concrete imagery. Many of the
stories are narrated in the present tense. Frequently Sholokhov
invents a narrator in order to relate events from a first-person-
singular point of view. His descriptions at times become
telegraphic as well as clumsily impressionistic:

> Sultry heat. Silence. The only sound to be heard was
> the shuffling of feet along the wattle fences, stirring up
> the dust, and the tapping of old men's sticks over the
> hummocks as they felt for the road.
> The bell was ringing to summon a village meeting.
> The business before the meeting was the hiring of a
> herdsman.
> A hum of voices in the Executive Committee Office.
> Tobacco smoke. ("The Herdsman")[3]

While sometimes effective, the practice of writing one-
word sentences all too often betrays a writer into mistaking
words for things. Pasternak parodied this kind of writing in
Doctor Zhivago (Chap. iv, Sec. 12) and observed that "facts
don't exist until man puts into them something of his own,
some element of willed human genius." The artist must make
language live in the reader's mind first; and then afterward
the words may point outside to facts in reality. Somewhat like
John Dos Passos and a number of young Russian writers in
the twenties, Sholokhov mistakenly assumed that the fact
and the word were simultaneous; if the facts were right, the
words would take care of themselves. In his mature work
this "*démeublé* style" functions well (for example, in the
opening of "A Word on Our Country"); earlier it often
obtrudes.

The imagery in Sholokhov's stories is often extravagant
and unnatural, as when a bullet "kisses" a man who then
"cocks his head to the side like a bird, bristles up and dies,"
while nearby a machine gun "spits" into the steppe toward a
haystack, but "its spittle fell to the right. . . ." He had yet to
learn that thrift and congruency are ultimate virtues for the
writer.

In many of the stories, children play a major role; indeed they become "centers of consciousness" who define the significance of the story for the reader. In "The Outrage"[4] a peasant is robbed of his seed grain so that he cannot plant in the spring and must watch his children starve. The following fall he recognizes one of the thieves and kills him with a pitchfork, while the murdered man's three-year-old son burrows into a wagonload of hay. The murderer digs him out, pleading with him to leave off screaming for his father; he intends to raise the boy himself. While the child's role is wholly passive, he is the crucial witness of the story's climactic event, and we recall the story as if we had seen it all through his eyes. Both the horror of the situation and the irony of the new relationship are heightened by the child's innocent vision.

Sholokhov's objectivity and detachment, qualities for which he has been both praised and blamed by critics, depending whether they were preoccupied with the inclusion or exclusion of ideology in fiction, were probably not conscious devices at first. Rather they resulted from the straightforward rendering of his own experience during the Revolution. He reproduces what he saw at an age when any comprehensive judgment was impossible. His senses were at once innocent and preternaturally acute, hence the accuracy of detail. When his stories fail, the fault will generally be found in some deficiency of language or in an unhappy tendency to adopt formal contrivances such as the accumulation of gruesome trivia. For example, in "The Brat" a boy looks at his father's sabre-slashed face and notes that on "one bulging eye, floating and swaying in blood, was a large green fly."

Insufficiently discriminating in his search for significant detail, Sholokhov will multiply particulars and use four words where one would do better. Anyone who has examined an author's revisions of his early texts (and Sholokhov is no exception)[5] sees at once the marks of an impatient pencil, scoring out superfluous verbiage. Pretentious imagery goes next and elegant elaborations close behind, as if directness and simplicity were the final tests in most cases.

Sholokhov's stories everywhere bear signs of experiment.

He was seeking not only an idiom but a perspective from which to render the life he knew. This explains why he will use the Tolstoyan omniscient narrator in one story, first-person-singular in the next (usually a child or an old man who are, of course, repositories of the native, local idiom), or a combination in the third, for example the framed narrative in "Family Man" and "Azure Steppe," where we have stories narrated by a character within a story.

Sholokhov's first published short story, "The Birthmark," contains, stylistically and thematically, many characteristics that come to typify his work. The title itself announces a problem as old as literature, namely the problem of recognition. Sholokhov treats the birthmark exclusively as an identifying blemish; it is not treated symbolically, as Nathaniel Hawthorne treats it in a story by the same name. Sholokhov uses the mark to dramatize a situation that derives its relevance from an historical period when time itself is out of joint, the community dislocated, and the people scattered. Recognitions are fundamental. Aristotle, writing in a sophisticated age, prefers the subtle version of the recognition story in which a man loses and discovers himself, as does Oedipus; yet, I suspect that the most dramatic and moving versions involve loss and discovery among kindred, since "we" is more human and more profound than "I," especially when the "we" are united by blood. This is why the *Odyssey* contains more great recognitions than the *Iliad*, why the Orestian cycle stands as high as its Oedipal peer. In the Slavic folk epos the legend becomes, as in Sholokhov's version, both hyperbolic and bloody. Ilya Murometz, having recognized his illegitimate son, Sokolnichek, tears him into two pieces.

To be sure, "The Birthmark" is an amateurish sketch, but the concept of recognition is both present and powerful. An eighteen-year-old Red commander (his name, Koshevoi, signifies his rank as chieftain in Russian), who lost his father during the First World War, feels lonely and insecure. He is ashamed of his age, sensitive to jokes by the men of his squadron. He believes that his political commissar is ashamed of him because he is ignorant. The commissar, in whom he seeks a surrogate father, proves unsatisfactory because he was a war casualty who stutters and has tics. In a passage that would interest Freudian critics, the commissar insists, while they are bathing in the Don, that Koshevoi's birthmark, "the size of a pigeon's egg on his left leg above the ankle," is a sign of luck. This provokes Koshevoi to retort: " 'I've been an orphan ever since I was a kid, all my life has gone in work, and you tell me I'm lucky.' And he swam off to a yellow sandbank which embraced the river."

Sick of his violent life, young Koshevoi wants to go to school in the city; but a courier, who has ridden his horse to death, arrives with news that a band of brigands has burst into the district for plunder. They steal grain from an old peasant and humiliate him by forcing him to eat earth. Then Koshevoi, squadron commander and protector of the aged, traps the marauders but is killed by their leader, who pulls off Koshevoi's boots and recognizes his son by the birthmark. Having kissed his boy's hands, the father shoots himself.

Virtually every detail in this story has the authentic Sholokhovian flavor. Its substance is the dislocation caused by revolution. Father and son do battle. Dogs howl mournfully, gazing at horses whom men, scurrying on their urgent business, have ridden to death and left lying with a "black ribbon of blood oozing from the dusty nostrils." Even in sleep there is no peace: Koshevoi lay abed at night listening to the Don in spring flood and imagined "the waters stealthily creeping through the cracks in the floorboards, rising till they carried off the hut." You pursue or you are pursued. Something always hunts you out.

In addition, the story is so completely rural that the city exists only as a dream. For young Koshevoi the city signifies his ambition for prestige through education. To the father it means an odyssean nostalgia, for he has wandered seven years: prison in Germany, then Wrangel, Constantinople dissolving in the sunlight, then another prison camp and a Turkish felucca, and finally home to the steppe. Their world is defined by the flowing river Don and the tears of a suffering people: even the dewy grass is "tear-stained" and the home-brewed vodka "clearer than a maiden's tears." The city lies somewhere beyond the horizon beckoning the hopeful.

The final and strongest impression made by "The Birthmark" is of *waste*. Strong men, promising boys, valuable horses perish uselessly. People dump precious grain on the earth where livestock trample what they cannot eat. Men have perverted not only the natural order but the social order as well: they till bits of sterile soil in order to make illicit vodka

> because it had always been so; their grandfathers and great-grandfathers sowed and drank. It was not for nothing that the arms of the Don Cossack Army depicted a drunken cossack straddling a wine barrel. In the autumn the villages and district centres wade through a heavy and deep intoxication, the crimson crowns of the Cossacks' fur caps nod tipsily above the osier wattle fences.

In other words, the entire tradition that governs the lives of the people is moribund. Human life itself is crazed, and the wolves and kites move surreptitiously about the steppe watching men, feeding on corpses, waiting. And well they can, for man seems determined to waste his own substance and commit collective suicide.

For a ten-page short story, "The Birthmark" has impressive features. It is, nonetheless, defective. Descriptions sag beneath the weight of trivial adjectives. Characters remain vague. The detail is keen but not always functional. Why, we may ask, does mist come in "milky shreds"; why must "warm sticky spittle dribble" down the sleeping father's beard?

These are the deficiencies that keep Sholokhov's stories from equalling Babel's. The two authors share the eye for detail, but Babel makes better use of what he sees. There is this difference too: where Babel's stories are self-contained and terminal, Sholokhov's leave one dissatisfied precisely because they seem to be fragments of some invisible whole work. One remains inquisitive as to how and why the events he has witnessed came to happen, so that the stories read at times as if they were journalistic accounts rather than self-contained, unified works of art. In this deficiency, however, there is one advantage: Sholokhov had to keep working on ever larger canvases to illuminate the how and why of his episodes, while Babel never could, or at least never had to, hence the scope of his work remains limited.[6] There is no sense of reaching out.

In every word that he wrote, Babel presupposes the city (the universal "ghetto" of modernity) as the driving force behind revolution and the instigator of measures aimed at destroying Russia's immense rural inertia. He takes cities completely for granted in his fiction, though he complains bitterly about them in his private correspondence. Sholokhov, on the other hand, had not, in his stories, even begun to understand the city. It remains an attractive but unreal alternative to rurality. And the interesting consequence of this fact is that it restores to Sholokhov a measure of the legitimacy as a Russian writer that he lost by foregoing membership among the cosmopolitan intelligentsia. It associates him with the classical Russian pantheon in literature, where not a single major figure found urbanism comfortable and where virtually every writer made cities hallucinatory—including even such true-born urbanites as Ostrovsky. Sholokhov had still to enlarge his canvas to include cities, albeit minimally, in *The Quiet Don*.

The two years during which he composed most of his stories witness marked improvement. If he did not yet extend his concern to the city or learn to control his linguistic exuberance, he did begin to gain a detachment that was more than stylistic. His anecdotal quality begins to subside. He begins to see meaning in violent events where before he registered only numb horror. For example, in "The Farm Labourers" an orphan boy, who has been exploited and brutally treated by a kulak, at last discovers comradeship in the Komsomol and realizes that ". . . only a little while ago I thought there was nothing but sorrow in the world and all people were strangers." And in the story "Alien Blood" Sholokhov records for the first time one of the hallmarks of his mature work: the formality of Cossack behavior that attempts to ritualize human joy or pain and thus make them bearable. The hero is an old man, Gavrila, whose son vanished fighting for the Whites. The son's comrade, Prokhor, comes home from Turkey and visits Gavrila in order to inform him of the son's death. An impregnable courtesy reigns. The formal welcome followed by conventional inquiries about the weather and the guest's affairs constrain Gavrila's excruciating desire to learn the truth; he controls himself and twice reproves his wife for blubbering an inquiry:

Prokhor kneaded the dirty fringe of the tablecloth with his fingers and didn't answer at once. "It was in January, I think. . . . Well, yes, it was in January. Our company was quartered not far from Novorossisk. There's a town of that name down on the coast. . . . Well, we were just quartered there as usual. . . ."

"Tell me, was he killed?" Gavrila asked in a low whisper, leaning forward.

Prokhor didn't raise his eyes, and didn't reply; perhaps he didn't hear the question. "We were quartered there, but the Reds broke through to the hills, to join up with the Greens. Our company commander sent your Pyotr out in charge of a reconnaissance. Our commander was a Lieutenant Senin. . . . And something happened . . . you understand?"

At the stove an iron pot fell with a ringing crash. Stretching out her hands, the old woman went over to the bed; a cry tore from her breast.

"Don't howl!" Gavrila barked in a threatening tone and, leaning his elbows on the table, looking Prokhor straight in the eyes, slowly and wearily got out the words: "Well, tell us the rest."

"They sabred him," Prokhor cried, turning pale. He stood up and groped over the table for his cap. "They sabred him to death. The reconnaissance halted close to a forest to give the horses a breather, he loosened the saddle girth, and the Reds came out of the forest. . . ." The words were choking Prokhor, he crumpled his cap with trembling fingers. "Pyotr caught hold of the saddle bow, but the saddle slipped under the horse's belly. . . . It was a

fiery horse, it couldn't stand it, and he was left behind.
... And that's all there is to tell."

"But supposing I don't believe it?" Gavrila said, distinctly articulating every syllable.

Prokhor went hurriedly to the door, and said without
looking back: "As you like, Gavrila Vasilich; but I'm telling the truth. . . . By the true God. . . . The naked truth.
. . . I saw it happen with my own eyes. . . ."

"But supposing I don't wish to believe it?" Gavrila
hoarsely croaked, going livid. His eyes flushed with blood
and tears. Tearing his shirt open at the collar, he advanced
towards Prokhor with his bare, hairy chest exposed, and
groaned, thrusting forward his sweating head: "My only
son killed? Our breadwinner? My little Pyotr? You're
lying, you son of a bitch. D'you hear? You're lying. I
don't believe a word you say."

Here for the first time we see the sustaining power of
tradition. The impact of the passage depends on the etiquette
which first controls the father's emotion and then dramatizes
it by dissolving before our eyes. Moreover, the characters define themselves precisely in terms of the formal etiquette that
governs the scene—the father's willing though apprehensive
restraint which at last breaks into an uncivil profanation of
the guest; and young Prokhor's impatience, betrayed when he
kneads the fringe of the tablecloth and again when he savagely
recounts the details of the son's death, his initial courtesy and
solicitous self-control having been disregarded.

Sholokhov's discovery of the formative power of conven-
tion represents a major step forward, though he did not exploit
it fully until he began writing the first parts of *The Quiet Don.*
It marks his recognition that mere "significant incidents," while
indispensable in a narrative, may be very confining when used
exclusively, because they deprive human actions of the broad
social context which ultimately defines them and gives them
meaning. The miniature and the anecdote may be striking if
exquisitely executed; they can never be profound. The arrival
of a distinctive Cossack way of life in Sholokhov's scenes

signifies his effort to break out of the boundaries of his own limited education in the craft of fiction. His direction will carry him from story writer to chronicler—*bytopisatel*. The Chekhovian incident and the formalist's linguistic preoccupations were not enough: they could produce the kind of perfection we see in Babel; they could not produce the mature Sholokhov.

Perhaps the best illustration of what happens when a "social moment" is incorporated within a story of pure event occurs in "Alien Blood" when just at the moment that a band of Whites routs the Communists "the crimson sound of church bells jangled incessantly over the village. The village idiot had climbed up into the belfry and, acting on his own stupid reasoning, had seized the clapper ropes of all the bells, so that instead of sounding the alarm he was ringing out a merry Eastertide dance."

No doubt the synesthetic "crimson" bells are inept, but the emphatic superimposition of religious ritual upon mere violence creates a context that itself comments meaningfully on the events beheld. That the crazy Easter bells should herald the coming of the powers of darkness instead of the Red angels is both an irony and a comment on the disorder of the times.

What is most impressive about Sholokhov's early stories is not only his growing awareness but the recurrent—perhaps originally subconscious—concerns which help explain the future novelist and which very likely enabled him to understand his own direction better as he came to recognize their power. Three stand out: concern for education, for the meaning of revolution, and for the Cossack land.

The yearning for education is constant. Every child in the book wants it desperately and realizes he must leave the village and go to the city for it. But the desire is always frustrated: education remains a hope, the city a preposterous dream, as we learn from Mishka's nightmare in "The Brat" ("The Shame Child").[7]

In "The Herdsman" a boy obtains a few books and constantly reminds his sister of their need for knowledge. He is killed, and at the end of the story she tries to fulfill his dream:

> Now the miles are retreating behind her. From the steppe ravines comes the howl of wolves furious with life; but Duniatka strides along at the roadside, for she is going to the town where the Soviet government rules, where the proletariat study in order to know how to run their republic in the future.
> So it said in the book Lenin wrote.

Young Fyodor in "The Farm Labourers" was trained by his peasant father who believed he would be no good at books:

> so he had given him grain-sowers' hands, broad in the bones, hairy and unshapely but with an iron strength. All the same, little by little he imbibed the wisdom of books: somehow, crookedly and criss-cross, like a waddling sledge sliding all over a hummocky and rutted road, he could explain what "class" and "party" meant, and what tasks the Bolsheviks were pursuing, and the difference between Bolsheviks and Mensheviks.

Thus, the struggle for knowledge proceeds painfully, perhaps pitifully. Not a single well-educated person appears in Sholokhov's stories. Party functionaries, who know a little revolutionary tactics, are as close as we come to intelligentsia. This is one of the reasons why Sholokhov's fiction sounds both unfamiliar and to a degree "un-Russian." Russian literature is, after all, despite notable exceptions, a literature of the intelligentsia, as are all modern literatures of the West. Sholokhov's stories are not; they are distinctly of the people, which means that the intellectual quotient is low indeed. They are stories of doing, not thinking. The young yearn for ideas to differentiate themselves from the old; they do not yet *have* ideas.

The second recurrent concern has to do with revolution. What is important about it, however, are neither triumphal *journees* nor abstract ideals nor the generalized Russian and world-wide event, but the peculiar aspects which characterize it in a Cossack setting. In the stories, revolution means three things: it means waste, pursuit, and autonomy. We see the waste in a variety of ways. Young men are slain before education can form them or age can ripen them through experience. More illustrative than the horse ridden to death in "The Birthmark" is the pregnant mare in "The Diehard": with her legs broken by shrapnel, she struggles to rise, the halfworn horseshoes glittering on her hoofs. Also typical is the traitorous girl in "Shibalok's Family" kicked by a soldier while she was in labor and then shot after she delivered her child, who is taken by her executioner to be raised as a loyal comrade. Sholokhov seems almost to relish scenes in which young people or animals perish, ripe grain burns or is trampled into the soil, substantial homesteads fall to ruin. The scourge of revolution is a weapon in the hands of the people, but they turn it upon themselves and wield it frenziedly.

With wanton slaughter on every hand, the logical corollary is for men to seek concealment. Nowhere in literature, I think, do pursuit and concealment become so compulsive as in Sholokhov's fiction. I say this knowing that the idea of retreat, socially and psychologically, is a major concern, not only in Soviet literature but in all Western literature in the twentieth century. Examples are ready at hand: Kafka's dream-men burrowing with the moles; O'Casey's characters in rooms into which calamity leaps through the windows and doors; Willa Cather's claustrophiliac professor; Pasternak's Yury Zhivago, who spends a long book searching unsuccessfully for a hiding place. But these are in every case, with the possible exception of O'Casey, examples of sophisticated intellectuals' attempts at evading responsibility—*consciously* evading it while they weigh the pros and cons of commitment. Sartre's *Dirty Hands* is probably as explicit a treatment of the issue as we can find.

Sholokhov's characters, however, are not sophisticated. There is no thought of evasion because there is no conception of reacting one way or the other to an abstraction such as "responsibility." This is precisely what they are only beginning to learn. Inattentiveness to one's horse; surliness to one's elders; habitual malingering: these are patent examples of irresponsibility, and the people are equipped to judge them. But the evasion of responsibility *in general* is unthinkable. They work in the fields and barnyards; they fight and die when the occasion demands. They may work and die well or badly, but they cannot conceive of evading work or death by speculating on the pros and cons of commitment. This trait appears in Grigory Melekhov, a greater hero in a greater book. In the stories, however, toil is as much a part of the characters' existence as the air they breathe.

This is why the savagery of revolution in Sholokhov's stories strikes so powerfully. If brave boys and hard men, who can endure, indeed *have* endured incredible tribulations, begin seeking refuge when they have an instinct for action, we have some measure of the suffering and fear that afflicts them. And when the search for a sanctuary becomes obsessive, we must acknowledge that we are participating vicariously in experiences far beyond the limits of anything that comfortable men are likely to know, perhaps beyond the limits of anything that men *ought* to know.

Little Mishka in "The Brat" conceals himself and his precious possessions beneath a granary. In "The Way and the Road" a father and son hollow out a space for themselves in a stack of dung bricks; later the son seeks refuge in the tunnels of an old stone quarry. He creeps through the freezing clay, water oozing round him, "like a polecat in a warren." The child in the early story "The Outrage" burrows into a load of hay, both to save himself and to reject the cruelty he has witnessed in the world. The hero of "Dry Rot" is a member of the Komsomol who has incurred the hatred of his father and brother.

> Night after night he dreamed the same dream: he was being buried somewhere out in the steppe, under a sandy slope. He was surrounded by strangers, people he didn't know; scrub with dry stalks grew over the slope, and

needle-leafed wild onion. He saw every little twig, every little leaf as clearly as if he were awake.

Then they flung his dead body into a hole, and heaped clay on him with spades. One cold, heavy clod fell on his chest, then another, a third. . . . He woke up; his teeth were chattering, his chest felt tight, and when fully awake he took in deep rapid breaths, as though short of air.

Asleep or awake, one must constantly seek a hole to hide in, fearing, of course, that every hole may be a grave. Yet to emerge from one's hole is to invite worse terrors. Even animals are made to suffer this confrontation with terror, as Sholokhov explains in the first paragraph of "The Foal":

> He emerged from his mother's womb in broad day-light, head foremost, his little forelegs stretched out, by a heap of dung thickly plastered with emerald flies. And the first thing he saw right in front of him was the fine, dove-grey, melting cloud of a shrapnel explosion. A howl-ing roar flung his little wet body under his mother's legs. Terror was the first feeling he experienced on this earth. A stinking hail of grapeshot rattled on the tiled roof of the stable and, sprinkling over the ground, forced the foal's mother—red-bearded Trofim's mare—to jump to her feet and then with a brief neigh to drop her sweating flank against the sheltering dung heap.

To be sure, the foal soon experiences "the unforgettable sweetness of a mother's caresses," and presently a sympathetic soldier dies saving his life. Terror, however, remains the domi-nant emotion in his life. A large part of the story's poignancy derives from the animal's peculiar vulnerability: there is no tunnel or cave for him to retreat to. He remains exposed, and his cry as he is washed down river into a whirlpool "was exactly like the cry of a baby."

For men there is one compensatory aspect to the terrors of exposure in a time of revolution. The exceptionally strong who survive the holocaust mean to persevere by taking things into their own hands and establishing a better way of life for themselves. The desire for autonomy is very strong. Revolution not only destroys the old order, it exhibits to ridicule all doctrinaire efforts to reestablish system, for every system is sooner or later contradicted by the exigencies of immediate violence. When life is at stake, every system becomes irrelevant. System brings the bureaucrat or commissar—than whom nothing is sillier in the face of truly vital issues. The solution of vital issues inevitably devolves upon local authority, ultimately perhaps on the individual. *He* must decide, especially when, during revolution, formal authority breaks down. He must decide because for once he *dares* to decide. Every man is czar presumptive for a little while during revolution. But of course one man or one group soon becomes the true czar, and things go on as usual—perhaps a little more, perhaps a little less efficiently.

Sholokhov describes the centrifugal movement for autonomy more than once in the stories. In one of his few purely comic tales a certain Bogatiryov, entirely on his own initiative, proclaims his small hamlet an independent "republic" in order to mobilize the citizens and repulse a band of anti-Soviet marauders. The community is victorious, but Bogatiryov, who loses a leg in the struggle, almost dies. Later, Communist authorities investigate to learn why he presumed to appoint himself chairman of the revolutionary Soviet and to proclaim a separate republic. This illiterate and overzealous comrade answers straight out:

> "I ask you, comrade, not to start getting so serious, but in regard to the republic I can explain: it was because of the bandits. But now peace has come, our village is called Topchansk. But, bear in mind, if the white hydras and other scum make any more attacks on the Soviet government we'll turn every village into a fortress and a republic, we'll set old men and children on horses, and, although I've lost a leg, I'll categorically be the first to go and shed blood."

He had nothing to answer to that; and, squeezing my hand very hard, he rode off the way he had come.

The story "Farm Laborers" takes place after the Revolution when kulaks have begun to take advantage of impoverished peasants. The sole convinced Communist in the area resolves to form cadres of loyal youths to break the kulak stranglehold, and he advises one lad whose confidence is flagging:

> "Stop talking rot. What you don't know now you'll learn during the winter. We ourselves aren't all that educated. The District Committee tried to treat us high-handedly: no help, no good advice, only instructions to do this, that, and the other. We, brother, will manage everything with our own strength. So there!"

In both examples the zealot is nominally a Communist with excessive "initiative," hence what Sholokhov is describing is not individualist heresy, but "left-wing deviation," in which devotion to the cause becomes potentially anarchic, at least from the viewpoint of established Soviet authority. But in Communism as in Catholicism immoderate zeal is tantamount to heresy. The moment *I* or *we* on a local level presume to "manage everything with our own strength," the principle of "monolithic unity"—whether Muscovite or Roman—has been transgressed, for the result is local or individual autonomy, which is anathema once any single party has consolidated the revolution.

Sholokhov does not develop the idea of autonomy in the stories, but the seed exists and will germinate in *The Quiet Don* and *Virgin Soil Upturned* as one of the most challenging alternatives to the Red and White extremes.

The third recurrent concern in Sholokhov's stories is with the land, the native Cossack steppe. There can be no doubt that for Sholokhov the steppe has a peculiar fascination which he expresses repeatedly in his lyrical digressions or apostrophes. In the early work, however, the steppe, though it already en-

joys an independent existence, is confined within extended
pathetic fallacies; that is, nature and natural phenomena are
made to reflect or contradict human affairs and moods. In "The
Diehard" a Communist is marched out onto the steppe to be
shot:

> The night was starless, wolfish. Beyond the Don the
> lilac-hued steppe was lost in shadows. On the rise, beyond
> the luxuriant shoots of the wheat, in a ravine washed with
> spring water, in a lair made under the heady scent of
> long-lying dead leaves, a wolf bitch was whelping; she
> groaned like a woman in labour, gnawed at the sand under
> her saturated with her blood, and as she licked the first
> wet, shaggy whelp, she pricked up her ears as in the
> scrubby undergrowth not far from her lair she heard two
> muffled rifleshots and a human cry.

The affinities that Sholokhov constantly finds between
nature and human behavior are not primarily literary; they
derive from the impact of the rural environment on the sensitive but equally rural consciousness. Thus they are often coin-
cidental, not contrived, reminiscent of Willa Cather's in *O
Pioneers!*

The important question, however, is what impression does
nature make on the sensitive consciousness? When he stops to
consider his environment, the native immediately senses an
alien or at least an indifferent animism in the land. In "The
Herdsman" a lad, thrilled at the prospect of attending school
in the autumn, lies gazing at a distant hill one scorching noon,
and he

> had the feeling that the steppe was a living thing and was
> finding life difficult under the burden of the innumerable
> settlements, villages, and towns. The ground seemed to be
> rocking with a spasmodic breathing, and somewhere be-
> neath the surface, under the thick layers of strata, another,
> unknown, life was pulsing and throbbing.
> And in the midst of the day he was filled with awe.

That is the impression repeatedly created by the steppe on human consciousness. Man is the intruder and despoiler, hence nature conspires against him. Pestilence decimates a herd of calves which the boy tends, and the superstitious villagers explain the loss as a visitation from the wrathful deity whom the youth has offended because he is a Communist heathen and anti-Christ. But it seems to matter little whether men act crazily or intelligently; nature remains indifferently cruel or benign. Presumably the community could have sent for a veterinarian instead of a priest. Then there would have been no need to kill the boy and stuff his mouth with black earth. But in a sense he provoked retaliation by aligning himself with Communism, with the city, with education; and his murderers become the natural agents of that Spirit beating spasmodically beneath the land's surface.

Certainly, then, the impression in Sholokhov's mind of the steppe's inscrutability is fundamental. It leads him to one of the quaintest observations in modern literature:

> The night gathered awkwardly in the darkness of the alleyways, in the orchards, over the steppe. With a brigand whistle the wind tore along the streets, tousled the bare, frost-bound trees, insolently peered under the eaves of the buildings, ruffled up the feathers of the sleeping sparrows and set them in their sleep recalling the sultry heat of June, ripe, dew-washed cherries, dung maggots and other tasty things which we human beings never dream of in the winter nights.

But something more fundamental than quaint impressions is at stake in Sholokhov's treatment of the steppe and nature. Beyond sensitive responses, Sholokhov was, in the early stories, groping toward a conception of nature which he articulates only rudimentarily at first but will elaborate in *The Quiet Don*. Sholokhov conceives of nature in terms of labor. Nature is a working relationship that includes man and can only be defined functionally. But unlike the traditional Christian definition which explains nature as a proving ground for eternal life, or the two modern Western definitions which explain it either as a vast tract of real estate open to speculative exploitation or a gigantic laboratory for scientific investigation, Sholokhov's definition postulates a workers' world in which toil becomes an end in itself—or a necessary function of nature. One works not for salvation, not for wealth, not for knowledge; one works for the sake of both being and meaning. Take their work away from Sholokhov's characters and they vanish. They are what they do, not what they think or dream. They lack the scientist's objectivity and detachment, the capitalist's authority, and the Christian's assurance. Their hands define them better than their words do, and Sholokhov never allows us to forget their hands for long. One young hero refers to his maimed arm with the epithet "food-giver" (*kormilitsa*).

It is, moreover, nature which controls their actions and thereby determines their awareness. In spring all hands yearn for the plow; in autumn for the scythe. Let man get right with nature and everything goes well. She dominates him utterly. But it is precisely from this domination that Communism tries to liberate men and that they try to liberate themselves by turning instinctively to the city and to education. Thus, Sholokhov's stories are the reverse of, for example, Silone's *Bread and Wine*, which opposes the corrupt cities of the plain to the rural purity of the mountains. In "Alien Blood" old Gavrila, whose son has died a White, adopts a disabled young Communist and the two work together in the fields all spring and summer as the boy convalesces. But then comes a letter from the Urals. The boy's comrades in the foundry call him back to operate the machinery which has stood idle since 1917. His new-found father would gladly level the foundry brick by brick in order to hold him. But the boy frees himself from the siren song of the steppe wind and the Don flood water. Instinct draws him toward a new working relationship with nature whereby he can dominate her with the machine, though he is unaware of this significance. Indeed, Sholokhov himself seems oblivious to the inimical qualities of mechanization. The city is still a good dream.

In the stories neither the power of urban industrialism

nor the charm of rural nature is fully dramatized. The middle class is absent and the proletariat meagerly represented, while descriptions of nature nowhere approach the lyricism of *The Quiet Don*. The lines of conflict are, nonetheless, drawn and irreconcilable. Implicit already are divisive forces that will exalt the minds and break the hearts of stronger men and women than any we see in the short stories. In them we find only a foundation: the young man, ready to be formed by education and experience, caught in a revolutionary world between modern society and primitive nature. It is a simple foundation but strong. To claim more would be a mistake since Sholokhov has expressed his own dissatisfaction with them.[8] He needed still to perfect a language and devise a perspective through which to render his story. This he did in *The Quiet Don*.

Chapter III

The Origins and Direction of *The Quiet Don*

Turning from the stories to *The Quiet Don* is not simply a matter of following tributaries down to the main stream. Sholokhov is perfectly justified in saying that the stories are not a "prehistory" of the novel. The tributaries, to be sure, continue to flow, but the main stream which they feed is already a substantial river before their arrival. I mean not only that Sholokhov, because he had lived longer and thought more carefully about life, was now prepared to annex a larger subject into his literary province, more important, Sholokhov rapidly became aware that he was engaged in a highly traditional profession which draws nourishment from its own past— from the works of other authors, from perennial themes and forms renewed generation after generation by the hands of pen-and-ink craftsmen. This is why anecdotal and journalistic blemishes gradually decrease as the novel progresses and finally vanish altogether. We have moved, in other words, from the trials of an amateur to the craftsmanship of a professional. Confident originality, which consciously uses predecessors, supplants uncertain imitation.

Soviet critics all too often minimize this purely literary aspect of Sholokhov's work—assisted, to be sure, by Sholokhov's reticence. Their emphasis is on the profundity of an author's understanding of human beings and his compassion for them or on his grasp of historical and social forces. What they often forget is that all kinds of men may comprehend people and

43

history but only the writer *records* this comprehension in memorable forms. Thus if we are to judge the artist's performance, we must adopt criteria that will tell us something about his artistry first. To be sure, neither a stupid nor an unfeeling man could become a great artist—he could not become a great anything. Ultimately, greatness of mind will define the dimension and worth of any performance. But the literary mind becomes great only when it masters the medium through which it has chosen to express itself. Sholokhov, in the course of writing *The Quiet Don*, came to see clearly what many Soviet critics have never seen, that he was not only recording events from reality but composing something that had its own laws and that imposed its own exigencies and problems which had to be confronted on their own terms within the created work—not with reference to external events. This is the only way I can interpret his allusion to Gogol's *Taras Bulba* in 1940: "Remember how Taras Bulba said to Andrei, 'I begot you and I will kill you'? . . . All I can say is that the end of [*The Quiet Don*] will disappoint many, very many."[1] The book had an inner logic as well as an outer commitment to reality, and Sholokhov had to attend to both.

Having said this, we find ourselves facing the most difficult problems posed by any unique literary work: What are the distinctive properties of Sholokhov's "professionalism"? In what does his craftsmanship consist? Exactly what is *The Quiet Don* that makes it unique in modern literature? To answer these questions, one is tempted to use a comparative approach, for Sholokhov's book shares features with many forms of fiction. For example, it would be illuminating to compare and contrast *The Quiet Don* not only with Soviet works on the Revolution but with those historical novels in the West that treat similar revolutionary situations: Scott's *Woodstock*, Hugo's *Ninety-three*, France's *The God's Athirst*, Malraux's *Man's Fate*, Hemingway's *For Whom the Bell Tolls*, and Silone's *Bread and Wine* come to mind. Or one might discover profitable analogues with the "regional novels" of Hamsun, Giono, Laxness, or Faulkner. The aristocratic bias and the distinctive linguistic texture of regional fiction alone, to say nothing of content, would justify such comparisons. Or one could attempt to relate Sholokhov's book to the venerable tradition of the "family chronicle," so common in Russian literature, or the *Bildungsroman* which focuses on the maturation process of a youth and exposes him to the typical snares and dilemmas of social life. Or finally, one might derive insights from juxtaposing *The Quiet Don* beside a minor but striking subcategory of fiction that has been labelled *"khurvan"* (or holocaust) literature. This is a Hebrew term signifying the two destructions of the tabernacle in Jerusalem. The term was resurrected to describe books on mass liquidation of Jews but applies equally well an any story of genocide and the desecration of a people's temples.

Numerous insights might accrue from these comparisons if the aim were to demonstrate Sholokhov's position in the many trends of modern literature or to measure him beside his peers. I think, however, that another approach is far more suggestive. If *The Quiet Don* is only a book somewhat like this "chronicle" or that "historical novel" or some "regional romance," then it may be destined for the shelf. But if, as I believe, the novel possesses closer affinities to the folk epic than any book of our time, then it makes special claims for our attention. The question of how this came about obliges us to begin by describing the book's origins.

A manuscript, dated June 10, 1934, and preserved in the Gorky Institute, contains Sholokhov's draft of an introduction to the English translation of the novel:

> I am glad that my novel, *The Quiet Don*, has been warmly received by the English reader and the press. I am especially glad because England is the homeland of great writers who have contributed much of value to the treasury of world literature and who have assisted, through

their immortal works, in developing the taste of English readers.

It is somewhat distressing to me that the novel is received in England as an "exotic" tale. I would be happy if the English reader discerned beyond this depiction of Don Cossack life, so unfamiliar to Europeans, something else: those colossal upheavals in habits, life, and human psychology which occurred as a result of the war and Revolution.

My aim consists not only in describing various social strata on the Don during both the war and Revolution, not only in tracing the tragic fate of individuals swept away by the mighty wave of events that occured from 1914 to 1921 but in showing people in the years of peaceful construction under Soviet rule. To this problem my last novel, *Virgin Soil Upturned*, is devoted.

Finally, I must say that I have often heard the reproach in English reviews against a "cruel" representation of reality. Certain critics also generalized about the "cruelty of the Russian temper."

Granting the first part of the reproach, I think that the writer would be bad indeed who would enhance reality to the direct detriment of truth or spare the reader's feelings from a false desire to conciliate him. My book does not belong to that class which are read after dinner, whose only task is to facilitate placid digestion.

And the cruelty of the Russian temper scarcely exceeds the cruelty of the temper of any other nation. Indeed, were not those cultured nations perhaps more cruel and inhuman who sent their troops in 1918-1920 into my exhausted country and tried to impose their will on the Russian people with an armed hand?[2]

Sholokhov's pugnacious tone scarcely conceals the defensive note that sounds in the first paragraph, where we cannot be certain whether he is grateful to English readers with cultivated taste for accepting his novel or whether he means to remind them that his novel, like those of great English writers, will assist in the further development of their taste. Equally interesting is his deploring the English reader's tendency to see this depiction of Cossack life as an "exotic" adventure. Cossacks were, after all, far from Moscow, hence far from everywhere; thus, Western Europeans perhaps found it possible, for comfort's sake, to disregard them—as Americans find it possible to disregard Indians. But Sholokhov is not content to insist on the importance of this distant people; he means that his *books* are important too, if not as revolutionary events, then at least as literary events.

Overinsistence on this point would be rash, for Sholokhov's own statement is very guarded. Indeed, he wrote it at a time when he was probably not altogether certain of himself, having completed neither of his two major works. This was the time when he hoped his work would be pertinent "for a decade or more." What he clearly wants, nonetheless, is that attention be fairly paid to his books because of their relevance and their truth. Sholokhov was a literary man displaying his handiwork— but markedly unready to divulge the secrets of his craft, either in an introduction or elsewhere.

Another intriguing element in Sholokhov's belligerent introduction is his insistence on "truth." For him, the truth of his book seems to lie between two mistaken alternatives: we can fail to see the truth by misinterpreting *The Quiet Don* as an "exotic" romance; or, what is evidently worse, we can fail to see it by assuming that Sholokhov overemphasizes the "cruel," naturalistic aspects of reality and thus gives us a false picture. There is also the unexpressed distinction, of which every Soviet writer is aware, between truth and propaganda; and Sholokhov wants us to know that, while he certainly understands how propaganda works, he opts for truth.

As a Communist, he would no doubt insist that all truth is propagandistic, though not all propaganda is true. This, I take it, is what he means by his repeated assertion that "each of us [writers] writes according to the teachings of his own heart, but our hearts belong to the Party and the people whom we serve with our art." In other words, *my* truth coincides with *Party* truth; and the Party, aberrations excepted, is the reposi-

tory of *all* truth. When exceptions become the rule, as under
Stalin, right-thinking men go silent or die. They do not tell
harmful lies; they do not wail about the difficulty, relativity, or
inscrutability of truth, for truth has never belonged to trimmers
or weaklings.

The Quiet Don, then, is true in the sense that it is accurate.
But this by no means guarantees its excellence as a work of
art, since there are many kinds of accuracy—*Alice in Wonder-
land*'s or *Madame Bovary*'s. Moreover, every creative writer
(perhaps excluding the commercial) would claim that his
works accurately record some element of reality—Kafka no
less than Arnold Bennett, Gogol no less than Zola. Initially it
is not verisimilitude in this limited sense of "true to" nor even
"true of" reality that defines excellence; it is the vividness and
power with which the created illusion of life captivates our
minds, delights us, moves us, and last of all, perhaps, teaches
us. Whatever else he does, the author must work memorably.
This is the test.

All the same, Sholokhov is a writer of historical fiction,
one measure of which is what an author does with actual
events or persons whom he includes in his fiction.

Except for a few Communists (including Stalin) who
complained thirty years ago that Sholokhov's portrayal of Party
men was inaccurate, the only objection comes from Imperial
Army veterans of the first war who believe that Sholokhov
conveys a slightly exaggerated impression of Cossack engage-
ment in battle. Cossacks were, according to this allegation,
used more for police and patrol duty behind the lines (where
their depredations against civilians made them a nuisance)
than for combat. While Sholokhov makes the point more than
once that Cossacks spend much time "held in reserve," he
engages them in cavalry charges often enough that we recall
them as combat troops, not ill-behaved military police.

As for the fictional use of actual persons, Soviet students
of Sholokhov, notably I. Lezhnev and M. Soifer, have investi-
gated this problem fairly thoroughly and discovered models
for almost every character Sholokhov has described in both
The Quiet Don and *Virgin Soil.*[3] There is, for example, an

actual community in which many citizens believe that their village was the model for Gremyachy Log in *Virgin Soil*. Quixotic individuals often turn up saying, "I was myself just such an Ilyinichna" or "I knew the real Aksinya"—or even a half-dozen Aksinyas. In *The Quiet Don* Sholokhov included living persons without troubling to alter names, for example, Imperial Army officers who led the Whites, and minor Communist functionaries. As for the fictitious characters, Lezhnev observed that the family of Sholokhov's grandmother perhaps served as a model for the Mokhovs, that his mother's life had much in common with both Ilyinichna's and Aksinya's, and that Sholokhov knew two men personally whose careers closely resembled Grigory's, Fyodor Melekhov and Evlampy Ermakov. Lezhnev recorded an interview with Ermakov's daughter in which she claimed Turkish descent, noting that because of their dark complexion, her people were called "gypsies." Except for the fact that he was absent from the Don between 1920 and 1924 and, hence, did not serve with Fomin's band, Ermakov's life is mirrored in great detail by Grigory. Even minor characters have their real life equivalents: Davidka was one David Mikhailovich Babichev; Kotlyarov, Ivan Alexeevich Serdinov, both of whom Sholokhov knew as a boy.

While engaging in the search for prototypes himself, Lezhnev reminded his readers that such an approach to literature had attracted bourgeois critics and was "unsound" because it neglected the role of imagination and violated Gorky's insistence on the author's right to "exaggerate." That Lezhnev adopted an apologetic and defensive tone gives some indication of the low esteem in which creative imagination was held during the 1950's in Soviet criticism. Outside the realms of science fiction and children's tales, the word "fantasy" came to have only a pejorative sense.

Sholokhov's own remarks about invention are quite explicit. While he looks with disfavor on "prototype-hunting," he is the first to admit that there were many Grigory Melekhovs on the Don and many exemplary women to serve as models for his sturdy heroines. This is to be expected from a writer who believes that "Tolstoy always remains in Russian and world literature the grandest, unattainable summit." On another occasion he said:

> On the whole there was no need to tax the imagination. . . .
> In the literal sense, of course, no such situation as described in [*The Quiet Don*] existed in actual life. But in general, village life, life in the Cossack '*stanitsa*,' abounds with such stories. . . . It is generally known that a mere episode, life itself, prompted Tolstoy to write *Anna Karenina*—the same kind of family, the same experience and the same tragic end. The reader, however, is not concerned with that. He knows only of one Anna Karenina, the one described by Tolstoy.[4]

Another measure of *The Quiet Don's* accuracy is that it often sounds more like anti-Bolshevik history than a Communist-sanctioned novel. Sholokhov himself told a group of Rostov workers in 1930 that he was "describing the struggle of the Whites against the Reds, not the struggle of the Reds against the Whites. Therein lies the great difficulty." The distinction is basic. When one reads Wrangel's or Denikin's or Tschebotarioff's histories of the Civil War, he senses immediately the recriminatory tone and the nostalgia for departed grandeur and a lost world. Sholokhov recreates these qualities—which explains why a bad critic or a vindictive enemy might imagine that Sholokhov purloined the manuscript from a White. By his own admission he used foreign and White Guard sources as well as Soviet works as he wrote.[5] *The Quiet Don*, therefore, contains more exciting disclosures about the Revolution in southern Russia than all the yellow journalism that the West has produced in forty-five years.

Among comparable novels on the Revolution, Sholokhov's is unique because, while in them the aim is generally to witness the conflict between Left and Right from a neutral middle-ground which in the end loses its neutrality and becomes Red (Veresaev, A. Tolstoy, Fedin), in *The Quiet Don* the aim is to witness the struggle chiefly from the Right's point of view and thus to display its inadequacy. This explains the difference between *The Quiet Don* and such candidly "Rightist" novels as Troyat's *The Red and the White* and Pasternak's *Doctor Zhivago*. Pasternak's novel adopts the viewpoint, not of a reactionary national minority, but of an instinctively conservative intellectual; and the aim is to vindicate, not discredit, this viewpoint. This leads to a complete qualitative shift. *Doctor Zhivago* is filled with recrimination, self-justification, and nostalgia. It is a quarrelsome, ill-tempered book which the doctrine of transcendental charity cannot sweeten. This, indeed, may be a virtue since Pasternak was vindicating the old Russian intelligentsia's quarrel with Stalinist brutality. But the disadvantage is that his consciousness is wholly contained inside the novel, so that its content, its characters and their ideas define the tone of the novel absolutely. *The Quiet Don* shares much of the content and tone, but they do not circumscribe the narrator's consciousness. He remains free—and therefore the reader remains free. We sympathize with the hero and his viewpoint; we never become his converts. Let him do the best that he can; let him think as hard as he can; we keep our distance.

This detachment is all the more remarkable in Sholokhov because he achieves it even though he was an eyewitness of the Revolution. It is this essential detachment that enables Sholokhov to divulge what I take to be the mainspring motivation in individuals during every revolutionary period and also the precise quality of despair that afflicts the defeated. In major revolutions, every thread in the mammoth web of society either breaks outright or is twisted. A vacuum occurs in which the conventions and laws which regulate our lives vanish—indeed the very men (government administrator, employer, priest, teacher, police officer, soldier, etc.) who pull our strings disappear for a while. The result is that every intelligent man experiences, at least momentarily, a feeling of infinite expansiveness. The possibility exists for a realization of his every potentiality. This is the ultimate emancipation. If I am sufficiently clever and energetic, I can be the policeman, the priest, the boss, the czar, the God!

But when the moment passes and I must admit that I

failed to realize myself, then a proportionate despondency sets in. I failed! I could have become all things, I could have ruled the world; but I missed my chance. Then comes the ultimate despair. I tell myself that evil, stupid men cheated me. My spite knows no bounds. I say to others that the evil, stupid men have destroyed all that was good in the world in order to establish their selfish will and their ridiculous ideas—but what I really mean is that I envy them and that I too would have destroyed much in order to impose my will.

Every revolution leaves an alluvium of self-recrimination, of spite, of illusory alternatives. There is so much frustrated passion in the alluvial remnant that it becomes fertile ground for heresy. We in the West spend perhaps too much time picking about in the mud, while the waters after 1917 tumble along seeking their course, cutting a new one where none exists. We might do better to watch for Augustine and let the Manicheans go!

Sholokhov's detachment enabled him to describe both the water and the mud, but it is important for another reason. In literature it is precisely the criterion by which we distinguish between historical and "antihistorical" writers. The writer who believes that history is both progressive and edifying will strive to create the illusion of detachment so that the mind is free for reflection, for dispassionate analysis which can separate good from evil and thus choose a preferable or advantageous course. This writer's work is an act of faith in history and by implication of faith in man who, he believes, can and will choose wisely between alternative courses. The antihistorical writer (who may, to be sure, write historical novels) believes that history is uninstructive either because it operates cyclically or because some nonhuman power directs it or because, even assuming that it is *potentially* instructive, men are congenitally incapable of learning lessons from it, being either fallible or perverse. Such a writer will do one of two things: he may force upon history the pattern he believes in and then attempt to persuade the reader that the pattern is accurate, or he may strive to create the illusion of timelessness or inescapable repetition. If he chooses the second, his books will emphasize the primacy of *the* moment over the sequence of moments; he will dramatize paralysis, not action; he will insist on eternal verities, metaphysical essences, archetypal recurrences. With his faith defined and circumscribed by postulated forms of the mind, which are by definition fixed, this writer's hero will invariably be *man violated, man betrayed, man alienated* by time. Where he loves being, his opposite loves becoming.

In practice the distinction is never perfect, but the tendency is constant. Where the distinction is extreme, we get Flaubert's *Salammbo* on one hand and Tolstoy's *War and Peace* on the other. More interesting for purposes of analysis is the middling type, for example, the novels of Scott, Dumas, or Hugo. These writers recognize the polarized alternatives but deplore them because of an abiding faith in reconciliation and compromise. Process invites enthusiastic rendering, but only because (and only insofar as) it leads to the restoration of equilibrium. Thus we see why Scott appeared to his contemporaries to be a true historian. They shared his predisposition for compromise, and the reconciliations in his novels seemed not only convincing but objectively accurate. With the passage of time, however, his reconciliations are seen to be unsatisfactory and unworkable—the product of an imposed, static conception rather than of an acceptance of process itself. Sholokhov, on the other hand, is all process, all becoming, all flux. The priority of mental forms has not even begun. He has no criteria by which to judge the violation, betrayal, and alienation of man. These things happen because the human condition predicates them, not because man lapsed out of Eden or forsook the readiest way to return to it. Sholokhov has not yet discovered these hypotheses, these mental forms. His rare allusions to Marxism as the "true way" always seem interpolated and irrelevant.

If the period when he wrote his stories can be called an apprenticeship, then Sholokhov's journeyman years saw the composition of most of *The Quiet Don* and the first volume of *Virgin Soil Upturned*. We can, moreover, see in this second period, four stages of literary development. In the first passages written (Part iv),[6] he depends for material upon firsthand accounts of the Revolution and on written records, probably newspapers, which serve to document his narrative, as if it were for some reason insufficiently authoritative and could not stand on its own merits. One is reminded (though the effect is different) of Cervantes' practice of interpolating traditional tales in the narrative of *Don Quixote*, as if Quixote's personal blend of reality and fantasy needed the reinforcement and perspective supplied by fictions that were part of the conventional mental apparatus of his readers. He "doubles" the fictitiousness. So Sholokhov reinforces his realistic narrative with factual, journalistic accounts of events, thus "doubling" his realism.

This explains why Part iv is probably the least satisfactory of the entire novel. Its central episode, the story of Kornilov's abortive insurrection at the end of August 1917 is the first passage that Sholokhov wrote—approximately Chapters 10 through 21. Most of this narrative records historical events through mechanically polarized groups of characters: Kornilov and other generals on one hand, Communists and their sympathizers—Bunchuk, Podtyolkov, and Koshevoi—on the other.[7] Such a convenient literary device falsifies by oversimplification, though the climactic event, Bunchuk's execution of Kalmykov, dramatizes powerfully the collapse of reactionary as well as liberal opposition to a Bolshevik coup. The most serious defect of Part iv, however, is in the first nine chapters, in which Sholokhov had to compose a transition between the prophetic failure of Kornilov and the lengthy narrative of Cossack life in the first three parts. His solution was to devote a chapter or so to each of his main characters, bringing them up-to-date; so that we can pursue their fortunes immediately after the Kornilov episode. Striking scenes, for example Darya's propositioning her father-in-law, are infrequent.

The moment Sholokhov abandons journalistic immediacy for the reminiscential historical background that occupies

Parts i through iii, he becomes what Russians call a *"bytopi-satel,"* a chronicler, and enters a new phase in which two things happen simultaneously: the narrative becomes self-sufficient and authoritative, obviating the need for interpolated rein-forcement; yet Sholokhov's awareness of literary precedents increases markedly, so that the text becomes, at times, objec-tionably derivative. Folk legend sanctions the unusual birth of Pantelei Melekhov, which prevents us from seeing it merely as a coincidentally violent commencement of one family's fortunes and forces us to remember that mysterious births invariably foreshadow the lives of heroes. Descriptions of the steppe contain verbal echoes of both Cossack folksongs and Gogol's prose. As a "family chronicler," Sholokhov consciously follows Tolstoy. The hunting and horse racing scenes in Part i show this clearly. His treatment of the illicit love between Grigory and Aksinya reflects—indeed, mistakenly imitates in language as well as psychological motivation—Tolstoy's presen-tation of adultery in *Anna Karenina*: Aksinya's fault, like Anna's, is that she refuses to conceal her illicit affair. And the Cossack recruits' initial exposure to battle in World War I verbally and ideologically imitates Nicholas Rostov's in *War and Peace*. Finally, the diary of the dead lover of Liza Mok-hova explicitly recalls Turgenev and Pushkin by noting the young intellectual's inclination to imitate literary models and to adopt even the idiom of fictional heroes.

Imitativeness notwithstanding, it is the first three parts that reveal Sholokhov's discovery of his own regional idiom. This in turn leads to the dilemma that regionalism invariably poses. As his text gained in authenticity through the incorpora-tion of folksongs, saws and jokes which give his prose its distinctive melody, and as the narrative grew authoritative through the inclusion of minute detail about Cossack customs and conventions, so its seemed to lose universal appeal and every hope for communicating abstract doctrine which Com-munist critics expected. Even friendly critics, by way of apology, had to concede that Sholokhov probably erred when he focused his story in southern Russia instead of Moscow or

Petersburg, the "heart and brain" of the Revolution because of
Lenin's or Stalin's presence.

To be sure, this is cant. One cannot deny, however, that
the adoption of regional idioms is symptomatic of an abandon-
ment of highly abstract thought together with the rejection of
standardized, impersonal language—the language, let us say,
of the universities. William Faulkner, for example, no less than
Sholokhov, suffered from linguistic fidelity, as shown by the
quarrels in the margins of his typescripts between himself and
his editor over the use of the word "nigger." He too betrayed
impatience with abstract and systematic thought, thus dis-
qualifying himself as completely as Sholokhov is disqualified
from writing a cosmopolitan novel such as, for example,
Thomas Mann's *Magic Mountain.* For this reason alone it is
easy to see why a Communist critic—or a Catholic or humanist
critic, for that matter—will experience doubts in the presence
of the regional writer, will indeed admonish him to expand his
dimensions. This is what Prince Mirsky did, shortly before his
incarceration, when he complained that Sholokhov's world
was spacious but filled exclusively with *stanitsas.*[8]

What Sholokhov did to generalize Cossack experience was
perhaps not what Communist critics expected. He did not
"Communize" his book; he humanized it. He gave it broader
dimensions than any dogma can circumscribe. In addition he
became his own most exacting taskmaster in the use of language. Already in 1934 he admitted: "Many Soviet writers (and
I am included) err in over-using 'local speech.' To a majority
of us, in one degree or another, this is inherent, as are other
literary deficiencies." As the years went by, he removed many
Cossack words and expressions which earlier appeared in such
profusion that some editions of the novel contained an appended glossary. Thus, by 1951 he could announce to the
Bulgarian Writers Union:

> I consider the misuse of elements of dialect in works
> of literature a weakness. In new editions I am purifying
> my books of local words. Let's take an example. In Soviet
> Russia there are many dialects: in northwestern Siberia

they speak so that many words cannot be understood in the south. I have a friend from Archangel. (I myself am from Rostov.) When he begins to speak rapidly and uses in conversation words of his region, I understand him with difficulty. And it's the same for him when I speak.

Where possible, one ought to dispense with these local words. One ought to write in a widely accepted literary language. For books by Soviet writers are read not only in the area where the writer lives but far beyond its limits, in the entire country. Consider how many problems arise for translators. Let us grant the use of local dialects to a degree, but one must know how to do this in good taste.[9]

What Sholokhov sought and found was an intermediate position between the national and local, the general and specific. Balance evolved—though even his revised and modified language has trouble conveying abstract ideas.

A third phase in Sholokhov's development begins with his return to the story of the Revolution in Parts v and vi. Confidence and facility combine to make this section of *The Quiet Don* perhaps the liveliest of all. Reliance on journalistic accounts increases again but almost never becomes as obtrusive as it is in Part iv. Proclamations, letters and communiques appear frequently, not as superfluous documentation, but as indispensable ingredients in the narrative of a people whose very lives are determined by *ukases* emanating from Red Moscow or White Rostov. Printed paper burns and blows across flat Russia, making a red and white snow that bewilders men and evokes latent hysterias. The nearly endless sequence of violent events which Sholokhov narrates appears to be, in one sense, idiotically repetitious; yet any reader who has caught the spell of revolutionary history hastens entranced through the pages, hypnotized and propelled by the same monotonous dynamic of bloodshed that supplies logic for Shakespeare's *Macbeth*.

The literary echoes of Sholokhov's second phase continue but are integrated and virtually inaudible. They do their work, as they should, behind the reader's conscious participation in vicarious experience. It is in Part vi, for example, that lyrical digressions about the steppe surpass in intensity those of Gogol; it is here that the Slavonic Bible becomes a literary force when Sholokhov uses the fiftieth chapter of *Jeremiah* in his portrayal of old Grishaka; it is here (and this is the surest sign of mastery) that Sholokhov toys with his own idiom by arranging some lines of Chapter 60 into a typographical form reminiscent of Mayakovsky's poetry. In subsequent editions he conventionalized the passage and later told Lezhnev that the "stunt" was a product of the search for new forms of expression which led to extravagances.

We witness the final phase, which includes both Sholokhov's artistic fulfillment and certain transitional elements that indicate decline, in Parts vii and viii of *The Quiet Don*, written (or at least revised) after *Virgin Soil Upturned*. Here the craftsman has mastered his idiom. Language flows effortlessly; action seems to unfold with unpremeditated ease. The governing principle, despite claims by Soviet critics to the contrary, derives not only from "life itself," in the sense of observed phenomena converted in fiction, but from the book's internal logic. It has, at last, an independent existence that is self-determining, so that we understand fully the early parts of the book only in terms of the conclusion. The conclusion articulates a unity in the whole that was probably not conscious at first. Its effect, therefore, is reflexive and appropriately terminal. It rounds off the immense diversity of material and circumscribes all the centrifugal tendencies, making the work self-contained— which is to say artistic instead of formless. As in the first three Parts of the novel, the hero dominates the last two.

No trace of literary imitation remains, yet the book suggests innumerable analogies with prose classics of all nations and with the epic. For example, the consummate simplicity with which Sholokhov describes Natalya Melekhova's last hours reminds one of Tolstoy, yet one would err to call the passage "Tolstoyan" because it contains the distinctive severity and violence of Cossack life and lacks Tolstoy's philosophical brooding.

As cursory a description of Sholokhov's development as

this gives some idea of his growth. We see, I believe, a fairly conventional process of literary development in which the author's first impulse stems from the impact of raw reality upon his consciousness. Then the impulse is disciplined and transformed by a growing awareness of the craft of art and the traditions of the profession which in turn sustain, indeed quicken, the initial impulse; so that the commitment to reality deepens, yet simultaneously the work gains an independent existence, a reality of its own. Stating Sholokhov's position this way enables us to account both for his invariable emphasis on "life itself" as the one true source of art and also for his acknowledged and unacknowledged use of literary models.

Regarding literary influences Sholokhov is not helpful, though perhaps no less so than his peers in Soviet literature. Borrowing from the past frequently provokes the skepticism of Communist ideologues whose fondest wish is to make a clean break with the culture whence they came, or, as they prefer to believe, who wish to preserve only the healthy and progressive. Enlighteners of this kind, however, are notorious for discovering little corruptions almost everywhere they look. In Russia, no one, not even the nineteenth-century "Revolutionary Democrats" Dobrolyubov or Chernyshevsky, quite comes up to the mark. Thus, while obliterating the past entirely is heretical, imitating the past is also dangerous because one may unwittingly fall into reaction. The Soviet novelist Leonid Leonov's fascination with Dostoevskian techniques and themes placed him again and again in vulnerable positions from which retreat was often the only way to salvation. And the poet, for example Pasternak, who was intrigued by the possibilities of imagistic or symbolist language, ran a risk of conviction for decadence. Sholokhov was lucky. He was young and uncommitted. When he had to acknowledge his choice of past models, he had learned a certain astuteness.

Perhaps his most candid remark came in 1937 when,

after admitting his obvious dependence on nineteenth-century
realism, especially Tolstoy, he said:

> There are writers whom Tolstoy and Pushkin did
> not influence. . . . So help me God, all good writers have
> influenced me. Each is good in his own way. Take Che-
> khov, for instance. Would it seem there is anything in
> common between Chekhov and me? But Chekhov too
> has influenced me! And it is my misfortune and that of
> many others that the great writers did not influence us
> more.[10]

Clearly, Sholokhov was trying to dissociate himself to
some degree from Tolstoy, nor is this surprising if we remember that when his Don epic first appeared, he was constantly compared with Tolstoy and found wanting, charged
with being an imitator. Soviet critics continued to rebuke
him until 1940 when the novel was finished and Sholokhov's
originality became more obvious. Western critics, on the
other hand, have been unable or unwilling, up to the present
time, to see him as anything better than a low-grade Tolstoy.

In an interview recorded in France during his visit there
in 1959, Sholokhov was asked about his favorite author:

> "I love and esteem all talented writers equally,
> as a writer should."
> "But have you no personal favorite? Balzac or
> Hugo? Tolstoy or Dostoevski?"
> "This always reminds me of a child's question:
> Who's stronger: a lion or a tiger?"
> "But all the same. . . ."
> "I'm a normal adult and I prefer Gorky. But
> Chekhov isn't bad either. Nor Gogol. Concerning my
> own apprenticeship and the influences which were
> exerted on me, one might say that I learned a little
> from all."[11]

The only conclusion we can reach on the basis of Sholo-

khov's remarks is that he has not the slightest intention of
pinning himself down with one master-model or even with
one literary tradition. If we were so disposed, we could use
discreetly selected parallel passages to demonstrate how
Sholokhov borrowed. We might cite from Gogol, for example,
the hymn to the steppe in the second chapter of *Taras Bulba*,
or the dirge for bereft mothers in the ninth, or the apostrophe
to the Dniepr River in "The Terrible Revenge." From Gorky
we could take the affair between Foma and Pelagea in *Foma
Gordeev* or any of several descriptions of a man's losing his
temper with his wife. Examples of borrowing from Tolstoy
have already been noted.

In every instance, however, the important thing is not
merely that Sholokhov imitated some master while he was a
novice, but that he rapidly achieved independence. Having
comprehended the letter of his predecessors, he was able
to build upon their spirit, maintaining the continuity of a
tradition without being enslaved by it. What one remembers of
Gogol when reading Sholokhov is the Gogolian ecstasy over
Russia's land, so intense that it bursts forth in personal and,
therefore, lyrical apostrophes. But even here there is a difference: Gogol's obsessive concern for stylistic texture and
his constant rewriting force the reader to attend to his verbal
contrivances as well as to his subject or to the emotions he
seeks to evoke. The process of articulation, in a sense, diverts
our attention from the object. In Sholokhov the object stands
out as if the communicative medium were transparent.

What one remembers of Gorky is not some comparable
relationship between characters, nor his sometimes rigid presentation of class stratification; rather, one remembers his
enthusiastic faith in man, his astonishment at the diversity of
human existence, and most of all his pervasive emphasis on
work. The one statement of Gorky's with which Sholokhov
would certainly concur is Gorky's verdict in 1928 on his own
contribution to literature:

If I were a critic and had to write on Maxim Gorky,
I should say that the force which made him what he is,

such as he is here before you, the writer that you love
and appreciate so exaggeratedly, well, I should say that
this force derives from his having been the first among
Russian writers and perhaps the first in general to have
understood, directly and unaided, the tremendous value
of work; work, creator of all that is beautiful, great, and
precious in this world.
      They have said that nature accorded me certain gifts.
I don't think so. I was born just like any one of you. Yes,
that's what I think. And I know, too, that the nature whose
beauty we admire and describe in word, color, music, and
in our culture, that nature was not part of my dreams.
. . . I love it as you do, comrades, but there is another
nature dearer to me, a nature which—let me express it by
a word today in disgrace—a nature which I respect and
venerate as holy. It is the nature issuing from the hands
of men, the second nature that we on earth create, in
standing up to the first.[12]

If Gorky is right that he originated the concern for
work in Russian literature, then Sholokhov concretized it most
successfully by his unfailing attention to the human hand. In
addition, Sholokhov enjoys this advantage: where Gorky
championed work as a result of seeing how urbanization and
industrialization dehumanized labor; where Gorky, therefore,
was responding to a capitalist phenomenon that had long
alarmed Western thinkers (from Saint Simon and Carlyle to
Marx); Sholokhov, on the other hand, sees work in a rural
environment but sees it with eyes liberated precisely by
Gorky's Marxist spectacles. One must never underrate the
similarities between Gorky and Sholokhov. They were, for
example, self-educated men exposed early to inhuman cruelty,
and they both developed an early affection for nature—Gorky
for birds and Sholokhov for both pigeons and horses. At the
same time, one must recognize that Sholokhov's consciousness
was more thoroughly rural. He is more nearly the "primitive,"
coming closer, perhaps, to Tolstoy's ideal of the earthy man
than Gorky ever did. As a result he restores dignity to rural

labor. He neither deifies it, as the Populists did, nor scorns it, as did the urbanized proletariat no less than the urbanized bourgeois. The special charm of rural labor in Sholokhov is that he (and the reader too) take it so completely for granted. Unlike Gorky, Sholokhov retained the "dream of nature." As a result the earth and labor are equally holy.

It is this too that distinguishes Sholokhov from Tolstoy. Western critics err, where Soviet critics usually do not, by setting these two writers side by side in a kind of literary vacuum in which only the narrowest literary criteria obtain. Thus the splendidly educated, Christian *pomeshchik* (landed-gentleman) beats the self-educated rough-neck badly. But this is almost like saying Dante beats Cervantes. Beats him at what? Both authors break any literary vacuum we fashion for them, and the lovely air of extraliterary life blows in, bringing new tests of excellence and new insights—much to the dismay of the absolutists of criticism. In 1941 a Soviet critic, L. Levin, made perhaps the sanest statement about Tolstoy and Sholokhov: "The influence of Tolstoy on Sholokhov can in no way be called copying; it is simply that, reading Sholokhov, you feel that Tolstoy exists too . . . and that Sholokhov knows this well."[13]

Take the narration of similar events and the manner of attributing meaning to events. In *War and Peace* (Part x, Chapters 4 and 5) Yakov Alpatych journeys to beleaguered Smolensk; Prince Andrei visits Bald Hills and observes soldiers bathing in a muddy pond. Sholokhov narrates almost identical events in Miron Korshunov's journey to occupied Millerovo (Part vi, Chap. 1), Grigory's several hasty visits to his home and Yagodnoe, the Listnitsky estate, and his bathing with his brother and other soldiers in a pond (Part iii, Chap. 10). In every case, the great difference is the *social class* of the central character, who colors the event with his particular vision of it. Yakov Alpatych is a servant, not a solvent and independent householder. Andrei is an officer, the purest of aristocrats—educated, philosophical, accustomed to authority. Grigory is a commoner whose sensitivity and perception develop, but whose entire life is precisely the struggle upward toward a disinterested vision of reality that Andrei inherited by birth. The surging male flesh in the pond fascinates Andrei and evokes a scrupulous meditation on dirt and the pathos of living cannon-fodder that echoes later when he arrives at the field hospital near Borodino and sees dismembered limbs and mangled bodies. With Sholokhov, we enter the pool. We *are* pink, vital bodies; we feel the pride and shame of naked male flesh; we know through our very pores the threat of mortality, the terror of a total dismemberment that will fracture our tingling carbon and distribute us back into primal chemistry. We understand the brave miracle of life that Homeric Greeks discovered in the very bone and muscle of man— but also the brave mystery of death that sends man down to darkness in a crash of armor.

Always in Tolstoy, the narrator or a character thinks, surmises, speculates, explains. In Sholokhov this happens only when he imitates Tolstoy. One can recognize imitation when Sholokhov writes that an event results from such-and-such cause or a man acts because of such-and-such motivation. This almost invariably rings false and belies Sholokhov's talent. It short-circuits the immediacy of overt experience that Sholokhov relies upon for his greatest effects. Perhaps the most obvious passages in both writers' works that dramatize this difference are the death scenes. Compare the final days of Count Rostov with those of Pantelei Melekhov. For Tolstoy, death causes sober concern; for Sholokhov, death is neither more nor less than the soberest fact of life—precisely *beyond* concern because it escapes all human understanding.

Sholokhov has in him something of that unquestioning resignation to death that impells Russian soldiers to throw their grenade-laden bodies under the very treads of an enemy tank. It is a resignation that puts him (and many other Russian writers as well) almost beyond the bounds of tragedy. Facing destiny *too* readily impairs tragic exaltation as surely as refusing to face destiny at all. We demand proportion, equilibrium; and Sholokhov achieves these only in the last half of *The Quiet Don.*

Tolstoy was a noble and a gentleman—one of the most

thoroughly civilized men who ever lived. Sholokhov was none of these. Indeed, between the biological fact and the legal sanction of Sholokhov's birth lay a moral, perhaps a psychological lacuna. This difference does not mean that the two authors live mutually exclusive lives. It does mean that Tolstoy must imagine the peasants' inner world as Sholokhov must imagine the aristocrats'. Predictably, both make mistakes, as when, for example, Tolstoy claimed once in *Anna Karenina* that peasants did not care who profited from their labor because they had the joyful satisfaction of the labor itself; or when Sholokhov hits false notes in his otherwise credible description of Eugene Listnitsky's adoration of the czar. Tolstoy could no more create a Melekhov than Sholokhov could a Bolkonsky. But then what would Dante do with Rocinante? We do not judge writers only by what they cannot do but by what they do well.

Tolstoy, we must remember, had to work to see things new. Artifice and sophistication are never absent, no matter how hard he strove to conceal them. By comparison with Sholokhov's poetic, intuitive temperament, Tolstoy's was wholly rational. As his diaries and the autobiographical passages in his fiction testify, he consciously tried to remove the scales from his eyes in order to see life in a new way— not just as a landlord, a Russian, or a Tolstoy. With the better half of his soul, he always strove to reach outside of himself, as Dostoevski always strove to reach in. Sholokhov, on the other hand, was born *between* two fathers; he was born ambiguously and illegitimately a Cossack, *between* a peasant mother and a *meshchanin;* he was born among an elite people caught *between* rural, peasant, autocratic, Orthodox *Rus* and urban, totalitarian, atheist, cosmopolitan Communism; he was born with a cancelled birthright, perhaps no birthright at all. Well may he have seen in the birth of a mere colt, as he describes it in the story "The Colt," his own initiation into the world. For him there were no options and no guarantees. Sholokhov, therefore, entered the world with an innocent eye. There are no scales to remove, hence his pictures of reality seem to contain an instinct for accuracy where in Tolstoy's the accuracy is consciously worked for.

This is one of Sholokhov's major innovations, perhaps the chief feature by which we distinguish him from Tolstoy. In the best analysis in English of the two Russian novelists, Helen Muchnic states:

> . . . To Tolstoy's men and women, action and sensuous perceptions are a testing ground of ideas; all that happens physically corroborates ideas or perturbs the mind. For Sholokhov the opposite is true. Occurrences in the physical realm are primary and most important. The mind like the body, reacts automatically to the blows that overwhelm it. The senses are not subordinate to the imagination. . . .
>
> It is, then, the realm of consciousness, in the role of the mind's debate with itself, that one detects the basic difference between Tolstoy's realism and Sholokhov's. Sholokhov seems to have no quarrel with himself, and the disharmony one notices in his work does not appear to have engaged his consciousness. He has neither the habit nor the need to look inward; he does not have to fight his mind. . . .[14]

To exploit this difference as a derogation of Sholokhov is, however, to misunderstand the literary advantage of freeing the senses from the imagination. What it leads to is a narrative whose meaning seems to derive purely from accumulated random details that reveal their own order rather than having an order imposed. Sholokhov sees reality—and forces us to see it—as Adam saw it or as the modern scientist tries to see it: it exists and works independently of consciousness; indeed *consciousness becomes a function of material reality.*

This is the quality that exasperates not only Western critics but certain Communists too because both like to insist on the priority of mind. For one it is "free" imagination; for the other, "free" will, operating through the Party line. One makes art autonomous; the other makes it didactic. Both oversimplify. Sholokhov, like the epic bards, applied the axiom: "Being determines consciousness." There are those who believe that this idea violates the mind, but perhaps we should claim instead that it merely instructs the mind by reminding it of its origins. Otherwise we risk the supercilious attitude that Sholokhov attributed to the aristocrat Listnitsky, who believed Cossacks were primitive, simple creatures deficient in "moral consciousness." A fairer claim is that in Sholokhov we rediscover *emergent* consciousness.

If in Sholokhov's early stories the narrator's consciousness remains naive because it is childishly impressionable and nothing more, in *The Quiet Don* the narrator's consciousness begins deliberately to suppress itself for long periods and then to step forward for calculated effects, for example in various digressions and elaborate tropes. What is striking is that expressions of this consciousness grow naturally from the materials themselves. This is how Sholokhov creates the illusion that the story tells itself through him rather than that he is telling the story. But to say that Sholokhov "has neither the habit nor the need to look inward" is, it would seem, a serious misrepresentation. Sholokhov did, after all, write *The Quiet Don*; it lived in his mind before it lives in ours. The crucial point is *how he saw* the mind as he watched its operation, not that he declined to look inward.

This impression of the difference between Sholokhov and Tolstoy may be merely a way of describing what 1917 meant in Russia. Before 1917, the world belonged to the czar and the landlord; after 1917 it belonged to Everyman. In Russia, as in the United States in the nineteenth century, many an Everyman took a new look at the land and saw both that it was beautiful and that it was his—to walk upon, to plow and, of course, to name. Thus, peasants plowed roadways as well as untilled fields; they renamed factories, towns, and rivers. The work of assigning names, for modern men as for Adam and Eve, is perhaps the most pleasant work in the world because it is the first work we do that separates us from nature, that makes us ascendant over nature and that places us in a relationship with nature which defines our being and determines our future. In Sholokhov's fiction there are far more new words than in Tolstoy's—not only because Sholokhov invents neologisms but because he was recording Cossack dialect and also because all dialects of Russian changed rapidly under the impact of revolution.

To say that someone has an "innocent eye" is, in a way, to misrepresent the facts. Heredity and environment together preclude the "innocence" of any human eye—a fact which exasperates artists so thoroughly that, in order to neutralize it, they sometimes try to look at the world through the eyes of a horse, as Tolstoy did, or a lunatic, as William Faulkner and Günter Grass have done; or they will even derange their senses with narcotics, alcohol, and self-induced hallucinations. For better or worse, no writer has ever succeeded in becoming anything other than a human being—though many have deluded themselves into believing they were angels or messiahs.

To claim for Sholokhov an innocent eye must not blind us to the fact that he watched the world with Cossack and Communist sentiments. Innocence here means mainly the lack of both formal education and experience with the city. That this puts a modern writer at a disadvantage is obvious, for it retards his facility in articulation and reduces his scope. The initial compensatory advantage is that what the innocent eye records is refreshing to any educated, urbanized reader for whom cosmopolitan excitements have grown tedious. But this is really no advantage for Sholokhov because it leads readers, as he has complained, to seek escape in his novel and to luxuriate in an exotic locale or in the restorative health of rural life. Were this all he had to offer, then he would indeed be a gross sentimentalist, akin to that host of nature-lovers who once worshipped Wordsworth's flower poems. In the person of Prime Minister Khrushchev, Sholokhov had to contend with one of these walkers-in-the-woods who made a soporific of nature. His disapproval of such behavior appears in the warning he uttered to devotees of Mikhail Prishvin—with whom they mistakenly compare him. "The merit and at the same time the inadequacy of this remarkable artist is that he keeps face to face with nature to the exclusion of everything else. But life, especially our Soviet life, is varied and beautiful, and it must be described fully."[15] No single element of existence, be it nature, rural life, war, or what have you, is enough.

The innocent eye alone has little value. Combined with preternatural sensitivity one must have what I would call an instinct for the sanctity of human vision. "Natural" sensitivity is nothing because beasts often sense and see better than men. The only eye worth having not only sees; it works; it composes. It is the mind's tool as the hand is.

Sholokhov's problem was to teach himself to articulate both what he saw and what his mind did to the data gathered by his eyes. The right word for this is "insight" or "discovery." But nothing could be more difficult than to teach the hand to record the eye's labors. Sholokhov, as we have seen, worked by trial and error. He imitated; he borrowed; he failed often. Finally, however, he learned; and from that moment it became irrelevant to speak of the genesis of his work in the limited sense of elaborating antecedents. From that moment his work belongs to the community of monuments in literature whose outstanding common quality is excellence.

Each step in the four-fold process of Sholokhov's development represents the accretion of some traditional form or subject of fiction. As with many other great novels, there is a sense in which *The Quiet Don* rehearses the evolution of the genre. Beginning strictly as a realistic account of events, it does little more than to order, intensify, and thus dramatize what happened. Defoe could be the model. From the very first, however, two superficially contradictory tendencies appear. It seems a little miraculous that a confused, rag-tag mass of Cossack conscripts could successfully oppose the mobilized brain-power and money of traditional vested interest in Russia. Had things followed their expected course, Kornilov's counterrevolution should have won as easily as a Spartan suppression of Helots. But we are dealing with one of those rare moments in history when vested interest proved corrupt and incompetent while the tiny cadres of revolutionists were both keen and resolute. This is what gives a legendary, heroic extravagance to events and enables Sholokhov's narrative to sound "primitive"—comparable to a medieval "history" such as *The Narrative of the Azov Siege of 50,000 Don Cossasks against 300,000 Turks*. As the novel proceeds, the Cossacks' role reverses, placing them in the ranks of counterrevolution; but the legendary quality increases, so that at last they find themselves outnumbered, besieged, and defeated exactly as they were generations before, though now the enemy is Russia rather than Turkey.

The model for the folkish tone and texture that Sholokhov creates in his narrative must be sought in Russian *bylinyi* (folktales). Consider one example:

> For three whole days and nights, for three whole hours, for three whole minutes did our champions continue hewing down the super-natural beings; but without success, their enemies only continued increasing. At last their strength began to fail them, their noble steeds galloped off in all directions, and their steel swords and sharp spears began to break and bend. . . . For some time our heroes would not yield, but when they saw that the more they cut down the supernatural beings, the more they increased, they became greatly alarmed and retreated up high rocks and into dark caverns for safety. But hardly had they reached the top of the rocks, when first one brave champion, then the other, was turned to stone. —And these were the last of the Russian warriors.

Paralleling this growth of archaic legend, the novel follows the history of the genre by becoming both a family chronicle and a *Bildungsroman*. In other words, it moves forward as well as backward from its circumstantial starting point. Here *The Quiet Don* continues in the direction of Sholokhov's early stories with their emphasis on the young man ready to be formed by education and experience but caught in a situation where formal education is unavailable and experience all too frequently fatal. Nonetheless the search for comradeship and then love proceeds apace, while all around the environment which traditionally gave form to the process of maturation disintegrates, making friendship insecure and love compensatorily frantic. This is why love, in *The Quiet Don*, becomes such a terrifying and in many ways destructive force: in the persons of Ilyinichna, Pantelei, and Natalya, maternal, paternal, and connubial love crush their respective victims physically when the son is reported dead and when the husband abandons his wife. In the persons of Grigory and Aksinya, love is not only a passion that burns like a steppe fire, it is a gesture of rebellion against society and a talisman guaranteeing freedom. Love was never meant to carry such a burden as the people in a dying world heap upon it.

Grigory Melekhov's yearning and capacity for knowledge, for "truth," lie at the very root of his personal tragedy and make of him the traditional "ill-starred" hero. His training for life consists of learning to fish, to till the soil and later to murder men. There is a hideous perversion in the ambidextrous sabre-skill he cultivates: with either hand he can split a man in two. Hard hands, black hands, yet tender, as Aksinya or his children know. Even the scythed fledgling knows their caress. All the more poignant, therefore, is that moment at the end of *The Quiet Don* when Grigory reverts to the most primitive and utilitarian artistry and carves wooden spoons, bowls, and dolls, perhaps subconsciously reminding himself that he is not yet an animal though he lives like one.

All the more poignant too are the lost opportunities for acquiring the knowledge which might have saved him. Garanzha had a truth, Izvarin had a truth, even old Grishaka had a truth; but none will do for Grigory because he never has a chance to digest anything, to make it his own, to live by it. Always he is thrown back upon his native resourcefulness and his own private honor. Inborn decency contends inside him with congenital darkness. Both seek mastery of his will and succeed repeatedly in paralyzing him. Theirs is a costly struggle. He is maddened by nightmares, driven at one moment into wanton slaughter, at another into throwing open the doors of a prison, at another into drunken orgies, at still another into vegetable apathy. In the end this inner contention drives him to pass the harshest of all judgments on himself: "I float like dung in a hole in the ice."

Yet, he remains a seeker. We never escape his black, inquisitive eyes which somehow see everything but learn nothing. No sooner does the light of recognition blaze up than he is physically wrenched away from his vision, forced once again to set his foot in the stirrup, to draw out his sabre. There is no finishing school or gymnasium for him. They belonged to the Listnitskys and Mokhovs of the world, hence they would have been useless to him in any case because, given his background and forebears, they would have tried to instill in him the mentality of a lackey or the soul of a clerk.

But Grigory Melekhov was born to be an ataman or prince. He is the exceptional boy, the young man who attracts beautiful women, the winner of decorations, the leader of men; but history catches him in a land-bound family where he dares not assert the full measure of his superiority because the hereditary aristocracy will punish him for presumption and the Bolsheviks for betrayal. Both insist that he remain a tiller of the soil and contract his heroic proportions. They deprive him precisely of his Cossack identity which guaranteed power to the community's best individuals. Somewhat like Prince Hal in Shakespeare's *Henry IV*, Grigory has his unique, personal honor to vindicate. It is his and his alone—unlike Listnitsky's archaic pretentions (Hotspur avows anachronistic self-righteousness) and unlike Prokhor Zykhov's ludicrous, self-pitying esteem (Falstaff democratically asserts, "Honor's but a word. . .").

Here is where Soviet critics go wide of the mark so frequently. If they dislike Grigory Melekhov, they call him a kulak or a confused "middling peasant"—rarely a Junker. If they like him, they say he is a peasant who loves labor and the soil and thus despises the gentry-landlord class like a true revolutionary—rural if not proletarian. But to make a sodbuster of Grigory Melekhov is to ignore his Cossack heritage and the charisma of his personality. While he likes to work in the fields during his furloughs, and while he constantly dreams of rural contentment as an alternative to a soldier's life, he could no more spend a lifetime following teams of oxen than Sholokhov himself could. He is too inquisitive and volatile.

Marx long ago diagnosed the disadvantages of peasant life, but let me cite a more recent and extreme reaction. E. M. Cioran, a Rumanian emigré who has cast his lot in France with the *avant garde* intellectuals, wrote a provocative essay asking, "How can one be a Rumanian?"

> . . . Hating my people, my country, its eternal peasants delighted with their torpor and almost bursting with stupidity, I blushed that I was descended from them, disclaimed them, refused to allow myself to accept their sub-eternity, their petrified larval convictions, their geological dreaming. . . . To be part of it, what humiliation and irony! What a calamity! What leprosy![16]

Cioran's overscrupulous reaction puts the case clearly and enables one to see that Cossacks are not simply peasants, least of all Grigory Melekhov. This is precisely what Russian critics find so difficult to admit.

Grigory is too special for them—perhaps for Sholokhov as well. In 1935 and 1937 he categorically denied that Grigory was a middling peasant, while in 1957 he saw in Grigory "characteristic features not only of a prominent section of Cossacks but of peasants in general. What happened among the Don Cossacks during the Revolution and Civil War happened similarly among the Ural, Kuban, Siberian, Semirechnii, Transbaikal, and Terskii Cossacks and also among the Russian peasantry."[17] No doubt Sholokhov was attuned to the Party line when he qualified his stand. But Grigory is indeed a contradictory man, a kind of Achilles (some might say Thersites) born into a world instructed by Horatio Alger and Demyan Bedny. He becomes a man of honor and even courtesy—the "natural aristocrat" that Willa Cather, William Faulkner, and many other American authors occasionally discovered along the frontier. This is why he is doomed. There is no one to instruct a gentle-man. What would the masters of Soviet culture teach him? A course in Marxism-Leninism? And what would the masters of Western culture offer? Some Freud? Some "direct social action"? Or a little theater of the cruel and absurd?

This is not to say, however, that Grigory is merely a relic miraculously surviving in a changed world. While his problems are not comparable to those of the maturing youth in the West where middle-class attitudes color every stage of the formative process, they are immediately comparable to those of a majority of human beings on earth who are only beginning to develop beyond "primitive" patterns and who are more grievously "under-privileged" in many cases than Grigory. For a majority of readers in the world *The Quiet Don* is an edifying book, not simply because it explains the process of growing up in a backward environment under attack by the "forces of progress," nor because it supplies ready answers. *The Quiet Don* is edifying in the same way that the *Bildungsroman* has always been: it sets forth the crucial issues that one is likely to face and dramatizes vividly the consequences of a variety of responses to them. If it does not tell you what to do, it does tell you what you are in for. This itself assists in enabling one to make decisions or to adopt new kinds of behavior.

Unlike the traditional *Bildungsroman* which carries its hero up to some preconceived ideal of being—a respectable *pater familias*, a solvent executive, or (with increasing frequency as we approach the contemporary period) an artist—*The Quiet Don* brings Grigory to an acceptance, not of being, but of dying. He follows Achilles. Where so many maturation stories end with a confirmation of ego, this one ends with its extinction. If in Dickens, Dostoevski, or Gide penitential suffering leads to atonement and vindicates the "I," in Sholokhov the traditional apparatus of salvation has ceased to function; yet his hero declines to cry out against life's seeming injustice, as, for example, Kafka's passive heroes do. They feel victimized, cowed into submission; and in the hidden recesses of their minds they nourish a conviction of their own supreme worth. Grigory, on the other hand, feels liberated. Having *acted* his part instead of merely *thinking* a dozen roles he might have acted, he sees that a man has, not alternative lives or potential lives, but one life. The only choice he has about this one life is to have it taken or to give it voluntarily. His gesture of submission at the end of *The Quiet Don* is an act of giving, not of being; it is a self-sacrifice on the altar of human history. It is penitential, like Achilles' acceptance of his own death in *The Iliad*. And in both it celebrates the ritual exorcism of barbarism that societies must rehearse again and again: the rash child must be taught death and reconciled to it, lest he behave forever as a brute.

Grigory Melekhov bids to accompany Achilles and Hector. The one thing we can take for granted about him as we watch his development from boyhood to maturity is his lack of pretention to be anything more than a man. No office, rank, or profession makes the least difference. While his family may adore his insignia when he commands a brigade, while fellow Cossacks may envy him, and while aristocratic officers may consider him a boor or a parvenu, the reader watches only the man. When I call him a prince, I mean to describe a capacity he has and a manner, recognizing that technically it would be an odd prince who spoke as ungrammatically or wore his fingernails as dirty as Grigory does. He may pick his nose and button his trousers in public, but in courage and rectitude he has the royal bearing. What one senses, I suppose, is that in a decadent aristocratic or bourgeois world, even a backward Cossack seems regal: Grigory is the man on horseback who has won the right to be there, not merely by inheritance or expediency, but by his own integrity. In his own way he becomes a defender of women's honor, a protector of the aged, and a crusader for the world's old order. If Don Quixote deserves knighthood, so does Grigory Melekhov. He worked his way into the role without having had to invent it first in his imagination. Every day of his life that takes him forward in chronological time takes him back in historical time, first to knighthood and then to the cave—not a cave of Montesinos, but a prosaic hole in the earth. Perhaps this is why he becomes a colossus among the pigmy heroes of modern literature. Who, in the literature of the past century, is Achilles' peer? There is no Hector, and Joyce's version of Odysseus scarcely bears mention.

Sholokhov added nothing to the form of the family chronicle or the *Bildungsroman*. The form was already finished by Tolstoy and Thackeray, so that the only thing left for subsequent authors was to "interiorize" action, as Proust and Joyce did. Sholokhov restored both forms to their original, albeit obsolete, grandeur. He avoided duplication by introducing the kind of family and hero that had not been treated before. Our formal pleasure, therefore, derives not from witnessing an incarnation but a resurrection. I would be reluctant to assign a greater measure of creative energy to either.

What makes Grigory a great hero is that in him we see portrayed the spiritual and mental struggle, not of the intellectual, but of the common man, carrying his immense burden of ignorance, which is to say of human history as perceived by instinct. We see the spiritual and mental struggle for a new life as it occurs in the lowest levels of society. Sholokhov reaches back in time with his hero in order to capture the most common human denominator. Then he smashes his hero through the window of the future. When the hero resists, broken glass cuts him mortally. This is the tragedy. This is the waste and the pity. It is also the hope; for once the window breaks, men with hard hands can extract threatening fragments and climb through. But someone must die first—a sacrifice. Achilles had to die in order to exorcise age-old ignorance that has forever cancelled the conquests of civilization. Orestes must suffer so that Athena can pacify the Eumenides.

Feeling himself to be an heir of the entire tradition of Western fiction and committed to faith in continued human progress, Sholokhov startled no one when he expressed surprise at claims of the novel's obsolescence in his Nobel Prize address:

> . . . The novel best predisposes one . . . to a profound grasp of the vastness around us, rather than to attempts to present one's little "I" as the center of the universe. This genre is by its very nature the broadest springboard for

the realist artist. Many youthful trends in art reject realism, claiming that it has served its purpose. Without fearing reproaches for conservatism, I declare that I hold the opposite views, that I am a confirmed adherent of realist art.[18]

Breadth of vision plus realism in presentation enabled Sholokhov to exercise a great civilizing influence in a nation temporarily reduced almost to barbarism by revolution—and in a world where many nations (East *and* West) must still go through this process.

Chapter IV

The Quiet Don as Epic

The aim of the previous sections has been to observe *The Quiet Don* in terms of its genesis and development. We must now travel an unfrequented road in order to measure the novel's stature and appeal in terms of its similarity to the popular, as distinct from literary, epic.

First, we should remind ourselves that, as the result of an historical accident, conditions existed in the Cossack area amenable to the creation of the epic. Consider, by comparison, William Ker's description of Iceland as an isolated epic-repository:

> The most perfect heroic literature of the Northern nations is to be found in the country where the heroic polity and society had most room and leisure; and in Iceland the heroic ideals of life had conditions more favourable than are to be discovered anywhere else in history. Iceland was a world divided from the rest, outside the orbit of all the states of Europe; what went on there had little more than an ideal relation to the course of the great world; it had no influence on Europe, it was kept separate as much as might be from the European storms and revolutions. What went on in Iceland was the progress in seclusion of the old Germanic life—a life that in the rest of the world had been blended and immersed in other floods

and currents. Iceland had no need of the great movements of European history.[1]

Only after the Revolution was Cossack life pulled into the flood of European history. Cossack society was secluded and anachronistic until then. It enjoyed, moreover, a unique blend of egalitarianism and aristocracy which, according to Ker, presupposes the epic.

> The form of society in an heroic age is aristocratic and magnificent. At the same time, this aristocracy differs from that of later and more specialised forms of civilisation. It does not make an insuperable difference between gentle and simple. There is not the extreme division of labour that produces the contempt of the lord for the villain. The nobles have not yet discovered for themselves any form of occupation or mode of thought in virtue of which they are widely severed from the commons, nor have they invented any such ideal of life or conventional system of conduct as involves an ignorance or depreciation of the common pursuits of those below them.[2]

As we have seen, Great Russia did impose an artificial aristocracy upon the Cossacks, but the Cossack world managed to maintain its identity so that in *The Quiet Don* individual Cossacks viewed Listnitsky or Mokhov as aliens. A purely Cossack esprit survived among the pedigreed, an esprit so strong that the gentry, even the church, had to make allowances for it. This leads, for example, to the relative absence of money as a force in *The Quiet Don*. That many Cossacks practice avarice is obvious enough; yet, in Sholokhov's world (except for merchant Mokhov) money loses much of its miraculous metamorphic power. Aristocrats and Cossacks live by privilege; the lower classes by sufferance and grit—though to be sure, Sholokhov would not be a twentieth-century writer at all if he failed to hear a subterranean, golden trickle everywhere.

Thus, epic materials were indigenous, ready at hand when the right eye came along to recognize them. But availability

of native materials alone cannot account for Sholokhov's performance. There is a second source that supplied epic im-
petus—the rise of socialism and the October Revolution. In his
book, *Reflections on Violence,* Georges Sorel makes a distinction that explains how revolution elicits heroism:

> The Socialist point of view is quite different from
> that of former democratic literature; our fathers believed
> that the nearer man approached Nature the better he was,
> and that a man of the people was a sort of savage; that
> consequently the lower we descend the more virtue we
> find. The democrats have many times, in support of this
> idea, called attention to the fact that during revolutions
> the poorest people have often given the finest examples
> of heroism; they explain this by taking for granted that
> these obscure heroes were true children of Nature. I ex-
> plain it by saying that, these men being engaged in a war
> which was bound to end in their triumph or their enslave-
> ment, the sentiment of sublimity was bound to be
> engendered by the conditions of the struggle.[3]

Now the October Revolution, like the French Revolution,
made heroism and "the sentiment of sublimity" accessible to
every man. Such times demand physical heroism; in addition,
the popular mind spills out of old channels and races in all
directions seeking the new. Heroism appears everywhere,
uncheapened even by the appearance of equal measures of
cowardice and craven self-seeking.

Revolution, then, is the modern epic's antecedent, its
igniting spark. "To make up a heroic age," wrote Constance
Rourke,

> there must be two factors, the new and the old; the young,
> vigorous war-like people must seize on, appropriate, in
> part assimilate, an old and wealthy civilization. It almost
> seems as if we might go a step further and say that for
> every great movement in art or literature we must have

the same conditions, a contact of new and old, of a new spirit seizing or appropriated by an old established order.[4]

We may conclude, therefore, that the essential preconditions for the creation of a popular rather than a literary epic existed by a coincidence in which socialist revolution inundated an isolated, coherent, aristocratic society in which primitive vestiges survived intact. Perhaps this explains why a Soviet-Cossack author wrote a book resembling *The Iliad, Beowulf* or Norse sagas, while an American author, Stephen Benet wrote *John Brown's Body*, a literary epic resembling Milton's or Virgil's more than Homer's.

We can, I think, concur with C. S. Lewis' judgment that "Any return to the *merely* heroic, any lay, however good, that tells merely of brave men fighting to save their lives or to get home or to avenge their kinsmen, will now be an anachronism. You cannot be young twice."[5] The fact is, every nation emerging from the wings onto the stage of history brings its youth along. Too few have a young bard to herald their entrance. But when they do, the "lay" that commemorates their advent is more than "*merely* heroic"; it is historically significant as well.

We can also concur with another student of the epic, Brian Wilkie, who asserts that the epic cannot be satisfactorily defined by generic rules or common characteristics. Rather, one should say that the epic is a matter of accepted *cases*, "a tradition rather than a genre; it operates through propagated family resemblances rather than in obedience to more abstract laws."[6] The epic has, of course, many frequently recurring traits and devices.

To be sure, I use the word "epic" metaphorically, and I am aware that the trick of metaphor is to know how far to carry it. The advantage of the metaphor is that it supplies extensive criteria commensurate with the work, as Sholokhov himself sensed in 1940:

When I began to write *The Quiet Don*, I was convinced that, however desirable, I could not succeed in achieving compositional unity and form, no matter how much I wanted to. I had to mix together an enormous number of events, facts, and people. The breakthrough occurred when I forgot about a person and he stayed outside the sphere of my attention for long periods of time. By comparison. . . , *Virgin Soil Upturned* was easier in compositional arrangement. There were fewer people in it. I didn't have to rush from the Don to the Kuban, to change the scene of action constantly.[7]

What he strove for, despite six hundred characters and innumerable episodes, was to handle his material "so that each event and each detail carried its own weight."[8]

In addition, *The Quiet Don* shares enough "family traits" to warrant comparison with the epic. It is a story of *wrath* that begins with a quarrel between a man and his people over a woman. It is comparable to the epic not only because it embodies the standard motifs of heroic poetry, love, revenge, and personal bravery; it is comparable because of its subject matter and language as well. *The Quiet Don* is strongly reminiscent of the universal folktale about the wanderings and return home of a husband. It is a book about war, prowess, and fame; its action concerns crucial episodes in the history of a homogeneous people; its hero's ambition is to achieve glory through the martial defense of his home. Although his individual pride far surpasses national or family pride, his creator, Sholokhov, infuses the entire work with an impassioned patriotism. In language, we find numerous epic characteristics: if there is little literal repetition, there is surprising attention to the minutiae of formal verbal behavior among members of the dominant Cossack caste, even to the proprieties of receiving and entertaining guests; moreover, the fixed epithet appears with distinction, although it is overshadowed by frequent and memorable epic similes.

That Sholokhov conceived of his work from the beginning in an epic manner is indicated by his first title, *Donshchina*, which he may have discarded because it invited a too literal analogy with the old Russian epic-fragment *Zadonshchina* and because its archaism is somewhat affected and ostentatious. What is important about the initial title is its indication of Sholokhov's awareness of literary antecedents, not only "life itself." The title, *The Quiet Don,* retains the required national and regional flavor and adds to it a quality which announces both the dignified tempo of the work and an implicit thematic attitude.

Traditionally, critics of the epic examine four things: action, character, language, and meaning. Believing these to be sufficiently comprehensive for examining any prose fiction, I shall keep to precedent.

The Quiet Don is the story of the fall of a people, witnessed specifically through the parallel fall of a hero whose rising fortune is dramatically reversed as a result of his fatally vacillatory nature. The central action provides unity for the wide-ranging subject matter and elevates the whole above the level of a mere chronicle. It is richly anagogic because the "fall" can be taken in several senses: it is an Adamic fall as a result of pride, a Cain-ite fall as a result of fratricide, a Christian fall (probably unredeemed) through renunciation of divinity.

The book depends structurally upon a combination of two complementary principles, incremental repetition and symmetrical parallelism in the treatment of action and character. This explains partly the paradoxical response by readers who sense at once the sturdy continuity within the lives of Sholokhov's people, yet also the tumultuous historical chaos seething round them.

To assist in the difficult task of ordering the historical events which occupy the decade that he treats, Sholokhov availed himself of a series of symmetries. First, he places the revolution between periods of relative peace, thus achieving a natural increase and decrease in intensity. Second, he resorts to the standard social class divisions for some of his subplots by delineating on the one hand the story of the aristocracy and bourgeoisie in coalition and on the other the story of the impoverished people, native and alien, who subsist on the lower verge of Cossack society. With the passage of time this symmetry is imperceptibly transmuted into the harsher dialectical triad of revolution when the Cossacks stand squarely between the White forces and the Red.

Another source of secondary narratives is the parallel treatment of individuals within a family. We find frequent references to the similarities and differences between Grigory Melekhov and his father. We have the linked but very different lives of Grigory and his brother, of the sisters-in-law Dunya and Darya Melekhova. Grigory is flanked by a mistress and a wife, each pursuing independent paths through life which are alternately attractive to him. Beyond the family come friends and relatives: Grigory's boyhood chums Koshevoi and Korshunov typify the impoverished and the prosperous extremes within Cossack society; and beyond these are the Communist Stockman and the gentleman Listnitsky whose contact with Melekhov is tenuous, yet ultimately of greatest importance since they symbolize the great forces which first collide in the Revolution.

The numerous parallel and symmetrical subplots are in every case simple—that is, they contain no reversals except in the case of individuals who share the fate of a larger group— and Sholokhov picks them up or drops them as he needs them for comparison or contrast with the central action.

In the early volumes parallelism and contrast are often mechanical, hence, restrictive: Communist Bunchuk's hands are black, aristocratic Yevgeny Listnitsky's, white; the letters that pass between Grigory and his father are fumbling, troubled, half-literate compositions, those between Listnitsky and his father are pompous, decisive, and stilted. In wartime bleeding corpses often lie amid ripe grain or in copses ringing with birds. These juxtapositions are simply too blunt and artificial. Sholokhov misses the Tolstoyan ebb and flow of existence that he was apparently striving to achieve, though often his tragi-comic effects are striking, as when grief-broken Bunchuk lies alone recalling Anna while round him the Cossacks joke merrily. Moreover, his handling of class conflict is at times too schematic, too visibly dependent on academic Marxism.

In the last parts, however, class appears only through living relationships between men and in this way becomes a more dramatic and effective determinant of behavior. In addition, even when Sholokhov deliberately builds a situation externally comparable and parallel to one earlier in the book, the impression conveyed is not of repetition, but change: the sun darkens twice for Grigory and Aksinya Aktakhova; thrice they meet by the Don and each meeting is crucial; time after time they are separated and each parting is more poignant, more portentous than the last. Here is the simple juxtaposition of events from the passing stream of life, but we see them long enough to recognize the pattern; then they blend back into eternal flux. Time and change yawn ahead of the Sholokhovian man at the same instant that they engulf him from behind.

Now the major plot, dealing with the Cossack people and specifically with Grigory Melekhov, reveals a number of turns, each one inspiring first hope and then despair, so that the general movement of the story is comparable to that of *Oedipus Rex*, which rises through a series of minor revelations and obfuscations to a climactic understanding of man's fate. *The Quiet Don* at the end crosses the line between epic and tragedy.

As in all epics, the improbable as well as the probable appears. Because Sholokhov works constantly with historical fact, the probable bulks large; indeed, he at times abandons his fiction and incorporates journalistic accounts of events and reproduces documents in such profusion that they interfere with the flow of the narrative. The improbable occupies a smaller place. We see it in two ways. Since he cannot implicate traditional Gods, pagan or Christian, Sholokhov turns instead to Nature and allows natural phenomena either to foreshadow events or miraculously to participate in and influence them. Thus, steppe fires in the summer, vast accumulations of snow upon the land, or the spring thunder of ice breaking on the Don prophesy coming events or dramatize their meaning. Thus also, a storm collaborates in Natalya's malediction upon her husband, and Grigory himself actually enters and wins a race with a sunbeam during the battle of Klimovka. Most spectacularly, the sun grows dark when Aksinya Astakhova dies.

In the second place, Sholokhov uses folklore and superstition to suggest the miraculous. As the witches in *Macbeth* do not cause events, but, rather, foreshadow them, so in *The Quiet Don* the flight of an owl to the graveyard or the abnormal howling of wolves or the black magic practiced by a village crone only anticipate future calamities instead of causing them, though some members of the community assume the opposite. So Homer has Zeus send an eagle bearing a snake above the battle by the ships. An additional note of mystery sounds in the prophetic melodies and lyrics of the folk songs which occupy such a large place and invariably supply events with a contrapuntal musical accompaniment.

Among countless examples of this, the most obvious is the use of epigraphs at the beginning of Parts i and vi. The first volume begins with two old songs:

> Not by the plough is our glorious earth furrowed. . . .
> Our earth is furrowed by horses' hoofs,
> And sown is our earth with the heads of Cossacks.
> Fair is our quiet Don with young widows,
> Our father, the quiet Don, blossoms with orphans,
> And the waves of the quiet Don are filled with
>   fathers' and mothers' tears.

> Oh thou, our father, the quiet Don!
> Oh why dost thou, our quiet Don, so turbidly flow?
> How should I, the quiet Don, but turbidly flow!
> From my depths the cold springs beat,
> Amid me, the quiet Don, the white fish leap.

The third volume (Part vi) is introduced by one song (untranslated in the British/American version):

> Oh, Father, quiet and glorious Don,
> Don, our father, Don, our keeper,
> Blessed is your name,

Good and great your fame.
But once you swiftly flowed, oh Don,
Swift and clean you flowed.
Yet now, oh Don, you flow so muddily,
Muddy through and through you flow.
And then spoke forth the quiet and glorious Don.
"What but muddy should I be?
Far away my eagles brave are flown,
My eagles—Cossacks of the Don,
And my banks are washed away while they are gone,
While they are gone, my yellow sands grow
    tresses long."

Clearly this last song heralds the tragic conclusion of the epic.

Because of the role of nature in Sholokhov's work, we cannot dismiss it by saying merely that it is instrumental in providing "improbability," for this would falsify its paramount position. Together with farms and villages, "nature" *is* the setting for *The Quiet Don*; it is both so prominent and so engagingly depicted that it constantly attracts the reader's eye, coloring his judgment of people and events. It is dramatic, not pictorial—often as much a part of the action as events themselves. At the same time, nature invariably keeps her distance. Thus, we have a paradox: on one hand, she is constantly personified, both because of her role and because of the Russian language which automatically attributes gender and animates natural phenomena, as for example, "Don Ivanovich," "Dniepr Slovutich," or "Mother Volga." On the other hand, she retains a divine impartiality that tends to belittle human beings by equating them with horses, wheat, even passive snow.

Consider the last paragraph of Part vi, Chapter 44. Grigory has just butchered some Red sailors and then, afflicted by a penitential seizure, fallen into convulsions so that his men must hold him on the snowy ground and disarm him:

Only the grass grows on the earth, indifferently accepting the sun and the rain, feeding on its life-giving juices, humbly bowing under the destructive breath of the storm. And then, scattering its seeds to the wind, it dies as indifferently, with the rustle of its withering stalks welcoming the autumn sun.

One of Sholokhov's best Soviet critics found this passage objectionable because, like some of Gogol's digressions, it leads the reader astray, carries him away from the specific idea or sense of the action portrayed.[9] Grigory is, apparently, like the indifferent grass which accepts sun, scatters seed, and dies. But, as Levin insists, Grigory is not indifferent: he has just slain the Red sailors. Sholokhov, then, is guilty of excessive objectivity for allowing nature to suspend judgment, as it were, upon the hero. The description of nature is functional and dramatic but misleading, virtually immoral.

Western commentators, on the other hand, fancy that, if not this passage, then many others like it are purely ornamental—examples of "purple" writing. Both are mistaken because both tend to isolate such passages from the total context and in this way misunderstand them. As V. Kirpotin has pointed out, the crucial factor in *The Quiet Don* is not nature, but history.[10] Spectacular descriptions of nature appear to be static, like Gogol's, only when we isolate them. The moment we extract a passage, Sholokhov becomes vulnerable to the charge of being both pantheistic and naturalistic. Although he may have deserved the charge when he began to write, he outgrew the limitation by locating descriptions of nature in an historical continuum.

It was Walt Whitman who equated men with blades of grass, not Sholokhov. He does not say that Grigory is like grass. They have only generation and mortality in common. Unlike grass, a man goes questing for his fate, which is determined by his time and place in history. Thus, history supplants the gods in *The Quiet Don* and eclipses the hero as the driving force of the book—as is proper in the epic where the hero's greatness emerges only as he resists "divine" or in this case "historical" necessity.

Time never stops in *The Quiet Don*. No clock defaces the church steeples in Sholokhov's immediate world, though Spassky Tower may chime in far off Moscow. No character wears a watch which he can break when time's passage becomes unendurable—except perhaps an occasional aristocrat. Time moves in the steppe wind and the river; time wears callouses and swollen joints in the hands of Sholokhov's people, plows furrows upon their brows; time is the wind-blown tangle of a horse's mane. This is why Sholokhov's nature becomes so dynamic:

> Across the sky, furrowed with a grey ripple of cloud, the autumn sun rolled over Tatarsky. High up a gentle breeze urged the clouds slowly on towards the west; but over the village, over the dark-green plain of the Don valley, over the bare forest it blew strongly, bending the crowns of the willows and poplars, ruffling the Don, and chasing droves of crimson leaves along the streets. On Christonya's threshing-floor it tousled a badly stacked hayrick, tearing away its top and sending the thin ridge-pole flying. Suddenly snatching up a golden load of hay as if on a pitchfork, it carried the burden out into the yard, sent it whirling across the street, and scattered it munificently over the deserted road, finally throwing the untidy bundle on to the roof of Stepan Astakhov's house. Christonya's wife ran out into the yard without her shawl and stood for a minute or two watching the wind lording it about the threshing-floor, then went in again (Part iv, Chap. 5).

A prodigal wind here plays the tease, laboring to undo man's work and democratically redistributing his accumulated wealth. Nature becomes a kind of celestial music that man hears accompanying the uneven tempo of his own history.

Appropriately, the tempo of events in *The Quiet Don* changes. In the book's final form, action does not begin *in medias res*, although Sholokhov actually began writing at the exact middle point, namely, the narrative of Kornilov's rebellion and attempted coup d'etat in Petrograd, an event that properly introduces the long sequence of revolution and counterrevolution which occupies the largest part of the work.[11] Sholokhov had to commence with background material because it contains information indispensable to an understanding of the subsequent behavior of the Cossack people. Without the early parts of the work, dealing with their history and culture, the Cossacks' unique performance during the Civil War might seem at first unintelligible.

In addition, by placing his study of the pastoral violence of old Cossack life first, Sholokhov is able to contrast its relatively slow and regular tempo with the veritable whirlpool of war and revolution under which the stable Cossack social structure disintegrates; and finally, having passed through the maelstrom, he can introduce the stately, muted movement at the end of the work when the tempo itself emanates and amplifies the sense of exhaustion and emptiness which characterizes postrevolutionary affairs.

What we have, then, is the slow rise and fall of an action whose dimension and variety give it considerable force. The little decade that *The Quiet Don* covers, everywhere flows into channels of time which seem centuries long instead of months. The book carries us from a world of semifeudal collectivism through modern individualism and up to a new collectivism, thus representing the entire historical shift which the West has experienced over the past five hundred years but through which the rest of the world is passing precipitously in the present century. This is what Sholokhov's symmetrical structure communicates; for the parallel events or situations, while they provide a sense of coherence and continuity, serve mainly to emphasize the incredible passage of time and the immeasurable changes wrought by it. Flux is the sole constant.

To the charge that *The Quiet Don* is *too* long and contains too much literal history or too many superfluous episodes (the editors of the original English translation clearly believed this, as their abridgement shows), one may admit that "interpolations" appear here as they do in any popular epic; yet they usually possess an intrinsic interest which justifies their inclusion. Witness, for example, Pantelei Melekhov's drunken journey, the Old Believer's tale of the cruel commissar, the diary of the dead Cossack who lived with Liza Mokhova. To be sure, in the early volumes detailed accounts of the deployment of troops and virtual transcripts of conversations between commanders of armies concerning strategy may seem obtrusive and indicate a servility on the author's part to historical trivialities.

"It is the nature of epic poetry," according to William Ker:

> to be at ease in regard to its subject matter, to be free from the strain and excitement of weaker and more abstract forms of poetry in dealing with heroic subjects. The heroic ideal of epic is not attained by a process of abstraction and separation from the meannesses of familiar things.
>
> . . . The element of history in Sagas, and their close relation to the lives of those for whom they were made, have given them a substance and solidity beyond anything else in the imaginative stories of the Middle Ages. It may be that this advantage is gained rather unfairly. The art of the Sagas . . . is largely indebted to circumstances outside of art. In its rudiments it was always held close to the real and material interests of the people; it was not like some other arts which in their beginning are fanciful, or dependent on myth or legend for their subject matter, as in the medieval schools of painting or sculpture generally, or in the medieval drama. Its imaginative methods were formed through essays in the representation of actual life; its first artists were impelled by historical motives, and by personal and local interests. The art of the Sagas was from the first "immersed in matter"; it had from the first all the advantage that is given by interests stronger and more substantial than those of mere literature. . . .[12]

A more important justification for *The Quiet Don's* length appears when we note that a seemingly irrelevant episode often helps communicate the important sense of passing time, or it renders indispensable service by altering briefly the mood

or atmosphere, relieving the tension of endless scenes of violence—for example, Grigory and Prokhor's goose hunt or Grigory's meeting with the happy, depraved woman with the ox
cart. The directness of the central action permits one, digressions notwithstanding, to retain a comprehensive view of the
whole, to contemplate the beginning, middle, and end in a
single purview.

We are accustomed in Western literature to extreme characters: on the one hand, they are exquisitely sophisticated,
disembodied intellects; on the other, they are mindless brutes
living sensually with the meagerest spark of awareness. This
is inevitable when writers and the intelligentsia for whom they
write are alienated from general society and constrained to
seek satisfaction either in their own elaborate cogitations or
by frantic reconnoitering into the social nether regions where
alienation is equal, though for different reasons. That writer
is most popular who, like Faulkner and D. H. Lawrence, succeeds in exploiting both elements simultaneously.

It was Sholokhov's good fortune to write *The Quiet Don*
in and for a society embarked on a search for "classless"
homogeneity. Communist theory insisted upon the union of art
with life. For many Soviet artists, this had catastrophic results,
but not for Sholokhov. One feels that his work, like Homer's,
is an expression of the national life and culture, that it is
simultaneously great and popular, that its aesthetic and ethical
components are largely indistinguishable—a coincidence almost
never achieved by Western writers in the twentieth century.
Reasons for this may be found in many features of *The Quiet
Don*, but I think its characters explain most clearly the book's
wide appeal.

The hero Grigory Melekhov, for example, although his
contemplative faculty is rudimentary, comes perhaps closer to
conveying the divisive force which makes Hamlet great than
do comparable Soviet or Western literary heroes, despite their

superior intellects. I cannot imagine anyone's claiming for the divided hero of A. Tolstoy's *The Road to Calvary* or Pasternak's *Doctor Zhivago*, let alone the split personalities in the works of Faulkner or Camus, a more potent sense of the agony suffered by individuals caught between colliding social systems or between historical-cultural contradictions which utterly devastate men's loyalties. The explanation for this is that Grigory actually *lives* the contradictions that comprise his world, while others only think about them. His scars from the revolutionary trauma are physical as well as mental and spiritual; theirs are psychic. Thus, Grigory is not only fully realized, he is the most human figure of all, including even those who confront comparable revolutionary situations, as, for example, in Malraux's *Man's Fate*, Silone's *Bread and Wine*, or Hemingway's *For Whom the Bell Tolls*. Sholokhov has succeeded in drawing a hero who is profoundly moving not merely to the intelligentsia, but to every man, as the millions of copies of the book in all languages testify.

The characters of *The Quiet Don* divide queerly into three groups: women, the hero's adversaries, and the hero. Since we know that women "took sides" in the Revolution along with men, this division is all the more difficult to explain, yet it is clear that the women, whatever their social class, are totally apolitical.[13] This is practically true even of the young Jewess, Anna Pogudko, whom we remember primarily as a woman, while her lover and comrade-in-arms is always the Communist Bunchuk. Cossack women, possibly because native tradition barred them from political activity and other "men's business," seem to lack any sense of ideological commitment; therefore, although they exert a tremendous conservative influence, they are never condemned for it on political grounds. Darya Melekhova's murder of Ivan Kotlyarov is an outrage against human decency, not a political crime. Perhaps this explains why Sholokhov's women are among his liveliest creations, though, of course, like all women, their highest sentiments never accompany their greatest actions, and they remain intrinsically less interesting than the hero.

Of the many women in *The Quiet Don*, three are

monumentally drawn: the mother, the wife, and the mistress
of Grigory Melekhov. They form a brilliant constellation
around the hero. Ilyinichna Melekhova is the traditional
Cossack mother, whose prototype we have met in Gogol's
Taras Bulba, where she is less intimately and fully portrayed.
The quality of Ilyinichna that makes her a triumphant character is her reserve of inner strength—which is only partly
revealed in overt action. To be sure, she is strong to accept
the privations and responsibilities of the farm when her
husband leaves to fight; her physical labor alone requires incredible stamina. Yet, a power hitherto unseen begins to mani-
fest itself toward the end of her life when we listen to her
memories of youth or of her first days of marriage and realize
that beneath the burden of cruelty, injustice, and exhausting
labor which constituted her entire adult life, she has retained
the joyous vitality, the effervescent and tempestuous passions
and illusions of a girl. More than this, reduced by the extremi-
ties of suffering in her last days to a life verging on despair,
when her sole sustenance was an agonized longing to see her
son, still she finds the strength and the wisdom to acknowledge
the claims upon him of the mistress who had destroyed his
marriage; still she finds fortitude to accept as her only daughter's husband the man who had slain her firstborn child. Well
might she echo Priam's famous lines:

> I have gone through what no other mortal on earth
>   has gone through;
> I put my lips to the hands of the man who has killed
>   my children (*Iliad*, xxiv, 505-6).

If Russian literature has always been distinguished for
its persevering heroines, none surpasses Ilyinichna Melekhova
since none suffers greater adversity with more equanimity.

There is something regal in Grigory's wife Natalya, which
emerges slowly as she matures. A proper daughter and wife,
she masks her feelings behind a girlish decorum until, under
the pressure of her husband's mocking indifference, passion
bursts forth and she attempts suicide. It is after this that we

begin to witness the flowering of her rich, abundant nature: we watch her discover a mature indulgence of the flesh in order to please her children's father; we watch the growth of her love for her family, a love so potent that it seems almost tangible; finally we see her destroyed by the discovery that, in spite of her adequacy, she is insufficient for Grigory. Realizing in her own chaste way that her mind and character have developed greatly, that she has become a noble woman, wife, and mother, that experience has not contaminated her as it does so many, but left her pure; realizing that all this is not enough for her man, who cannot or will not be satisfied, she first curses him but then relents and dies obsessed with the desire to be cleansed, to be purified of and in her own blood, which her husband had somehow tainted. Her death, like Ilyinichna's and Aksinya's, is a terrible judgment upon Grigory, who is in a sense their executioner.

Aksinya Astakhova's development is limited. Her character seems fully formed by the time that she, as a girl, was raped by her father and then promptly given into the hands of a brutal husband. She is a person made for passion and willing to endure all misfortune in order to fulfill her capacity for it. For this reason she is at times rather obtuse, and Grigory rightly calls her "diseased" with love. The sole motivation in her life is an intuitive quest for emotional satisfaction, and for this the mind is not a relevant organ. What grandeur she has, comes from the incredible depths to which illusion and passion carry her, indeed to which she wilfully follows them. In her, passion is a subterranean conflagration. Her strangely magnetic love for Grigory draws him downward, step by step to new levels of savage, sensual delight and momentary oblivion. Even Listnitsky, whose illicit affair with her was brief, felt a lifelong craving for the heavy, numbing passion in which she wrapped him.

She is, as it were, pure substance, pure matter animated, as the epithets associated with her signify, by a smoking inner fire. Grigory recognizes that, like opium, she blights and poisons those to whom she brings the intoxicating sense of extinction; he knows that her love captivates more than the senses.

So limited in mind, so accustomed to scorn and insults, so frequently driven to live in darkness, following the fierce impulses of her nature, so loyal to the urging of her own love-destiny, she is cut down almost by accident when her blind will has too long countered the equally blind movement of history. The magnificently somber irony of her life reveals itself fully when Grigory buries her on the steppe, for she lies faceup with blank, half-open eyes still searching the sky, though the sky and the sun have turned black to mark her passing. As Natalya is associated with daylight and sunshine, so Aksinya is associated with darkness. One would like to place on her grave Picasso's wartime painting of a candle that sheds black light.

Of the other women in the Melekhov family, Darya is moved by lust rather than passion, though even she is redeemed by an unselfish desire to share her gross pleasures with men. Dunya is all laughter and music. Moved by the same gaiety and innocence that moved her mother, she is the one character in the book properly equipped to participate in the new and better life of the future, since she is utterly selfless and, therefore, utterly free.

The category labeled "adversaries" differs from that used by Soviet critics, who invariably distinguish between protagonists (Reds and their sympathizers) and antagonists (Whites and their sympathizers) and then place the hero in between. While this division is legitimate when applied to the first half of the work, and while it assists greatly in any social or historical interpretation, it distorts what I take to be the book's central meaning in its final form.

The male characters of *The Quiet Don* seem to retire into secondary positions because the hero is so imposing. Unlike Othello, Grigory has no Iago to act as counterpoise; instead he has three women, and the male foils come, not singly, but in groups, as if Grigory's prodigious figure required several men for balance.

This is not to say that the book lacks well-drawn male

characters. The portraits of Grigory's father and brother, his friend Koshevoi, and the comical Prokhor Zykov are impressive; and there is a gallery of fascinating minor figures: for example, the Korshunov men, Bunchuk, Fomin, Listnitsky, and others.

Pantelei is probably the most memorable of all. Erratic and irascible, he makes a sturdy but uneasy patriarch. He typifies at once the headlong strength, the vainglory, and the injustice of the old Cossack order. Lacking the first vestige of refinement, he hurls himself upon life with the ferocity and determination of a sly bull. And as long as his society retains sufficient coherence to supply secure standards of behavior, he succeeds admirably. To his confusion, however, the society collapses. He stands bewildered, scratching his fleas, no longer an obeyed father, no longer the head of his house, no longer brave and clever, no longer anything at all but a pitiful scrap of humanity swirled down the river of defeat and left dead in a backwater. Almost unremembered, Pantelei's death is unique in the work, the sole example of death presented as finality rather than as a necessary prologue to rebirth or revival.

In addition to Pantelei there are other characters who stand for the old order and function together as a gravitational field drawing Grigory toward the warm comforts of a secure past, providing meaning and coherence to his life. Initially his brother, Pyotr, plays a leading role. Older and more stable, he often exasperates both his brother and his wife by failing to share or even understand the contradictory impulses besetting them. Pyotr's strength is his simplicity and single-mindedness, which permit him to concentrate his energies but lead to an early and cruel death.

Of greater importance is Izvarin. Because he is better educated than most Cossacks, he embraces the relatively sophisticated concept of a middle-road between the Whites and Reds, advocating Cossack autonomy. He gave Grigory a lesson in history which he never forgot:

"If the Bolsheviks get the upper hand it will be good for

the workers and bad for the rest. If the monarchy returns, it will be good for the landowners and suchlike
and bad for the rest. We don't want either the one or
the other. We need our own, and first of all we need to
get rid of all our protectors, whether Kornilov, or Keren-
sky, or Lenin. We can get along without them on our own
land. God save us from our friends and we'll manage our
enemies ourselves" (Part v, Chap. 2).

Here is a doctrine which strikes responsive chords. Here
again is a chance for the old freedom, an appeal to the old
pride and exclusiveness. It is the doctrine of the so-called
"Greens": the old order but without landlords, Soviets without
Communists. It is a doctrine doomed from the first because
it was intolerable to both landlords and Communists; hence it
led to the futile brigandage of Fomin's band. Despite the fact
that Grigory refuses to follow Izvarin at once, it is Izvarin's
doctrine to which he, gropingly and without understanding it
clearly, adheres by instinct.

At the opposite pole from Pyotr and Izvarin is a constellation of characters embodying the revolutionary alternative
which at times stirs Grigory's sympathies. The most important
figures are Garanzha, a Ukrainian conscript, whose burning
faith converts Grigory to the Bolshevik cause and sets him on
his pursuit of truth, and Mishka Koshevoi, Grigory's boyhood
friend, tempered hard by humiliating treatment during his
youth and by an implacable viciousness engendered during
the Revolution. He follows the logic of his destiny to such
extremes that his cause becomes as obnoxious to Grigory as
that of Mitka Korshunov on the other side. Indeed, Koshevoi
appears to symbolize everything factitious and fulsome in the
Bolshevik promise—as well as everything worthy and strong.

For many critics, he is the decisive character in the book,
upon whom they feel they must stake their personal integrity.
Soviet critics must approach him cautiously because he becomes a Communist;[14] Western critics must despise him because he shoots helpless old men. The moment it occurs to
Western critics that Koshevoi comes closer to representing

Sholokhov's personal viewpoint than Grigory does, alarms sound violently in their heads and they conclude that Sholokhov's artistry is an accidental virtue in an otherwise brutal Bolshevik. One would think their reading of Western fiction, with all its concern for the "alienated" hero, might have prepared them to understand Koshevoi better.

Excepting Grigory, Koshevoi is the one truly alienated character in the book. The rest are displaced persons, perhaps, but this involves banishment or destruction of the home, not alienation. Koshevoi comes closest to being Grigory's foil, as Sholokhov realized when, during the writing of the last volume, he said that Koshevoi would have to be "advanced from the rear and more attention focussed on him." There were, of course, extraliterary reasons at this time for enhancing Communist heroes in fiction, which may account for Sholokhov's revising the scene when Koshevoi is whipped by the village elders, softening his humiliation slightly. Nonetheless, Sholokhov needed Koshevoi precisely as Grigory's antagonist in the last volume, if he was to continue the symmetrical development of characters.

Mishka, we should remember, is a fatherless boy with an eye as keen as Sholokhov's own. It is he who sees poetry in horses, who wants to make love to all the women in the world, who has the wide-eyed craving for knowledge when Stockman arrives in Tatarsky to repair sewing machines and forge new souls. He is a waif, close to vagabondage, and therefore an outsider who can see emptiness behind Cossack pretensions. Unlike Grigory, he draws conclusions from what he sees, which frees him for action; but initially he shares the sense of alienation that has always characterized the sensitive man caught in a disintegrating social structure which still remains viable so that one cannot quite make out the new world through the cracks in the old. He is the character most like those heroes in the short stories who seem autobiographical. He knows, as Sholokhov did, the humiliation of growing up *in*, but not quite *of*, Cossack society, where his class alone made him almost a peasant, almost a creature with water in his veins instead of blood, as the pedigreed would claim.

There is a passage in Gibbon's *Decline and Fall of the Roman Empire* which details a Christian's predicament in a pagan world and at the same time describes the alienation of every man committed prematurely to faith in a new order:

> . . . It was the first but arduous duty of a Christian to preserve himself pure and undefiled by the practice of idolatry. The religion of the nations was not merely a speculative doctrine professed in the schools or preached in the temples. The innumerable deities and rites of polytheism were closely interwoven with every circumstance of business or pleasure, of public or of private life; and it seemed impossible to escape the observance of them without at the same time renouncing the commerce of mankind and all the offices and amusements of society. The important transactions of peace and war were prepared or concluded by solemn sacrifices in which the magistrate, the senator, and the soldier were obliged to preside or to participate. The public spectacles were an essential part of the cheerful devotion of the pagans, and the gods were supposed to accept as the most grateful offering the games that the prince and people celebrated in honour of their peculiar festivals. The Christian, who with pious horror avoided the abomination of the circus or the theatre, found himself encompassed with infernal snares in every convivial entertainment, as often as his friends, involving the hospitable deities, poured out libations to each other's happiness. When the bride, struggling with well-affected reluctance, was forced in hymeneal pomp over the threshold of her new habitation, or when the sad procession of the dead slowly moved towards the funeral pile, the Christian on these interesting occasions was compelled to desert the persons who were the dearest to him rather than contract the guilt inherent to those impious ceremonies (Chap. xv).

This is Koshevoi's world when he must take the military oath, participate in community life, marry a woman. The very words, let alone the thoughts, taught to him from childhood will now damn him. Nor does he extricate himself completely from traditional patterns. Already a self-appointed scourge of the "White hydra," a man who slaughters prisoners and sets the "crimson cock" burning all across the land, Koshevoi relapses at once into Cossack vanity when he returns home on leave:

> He took a colourful rug from the wall of a merchant's house in Karginskaya and fastened it under his horsecloth. He found a pair of almost new striped *sharovari* in a Cossack's chest, tore up half a dozen women's shawls for three changes of foot-cloths, and slipped a pair of woollen gloves into his pack to put on just before he rode down into Tatarsky.
>
> From time immemorial it had been the custom for a soldier returning home to be dressed in his finest. And Mishka, though a Red Army man, was still in the grip of Cossack tradition, and devoutly made ready to observe the old custom.
>
> His horse was a fine dark sorrel which he had taken from a Cossack whom he had cut down during an attack. The horse with its graceful bearing and speed was something to boast of, but Mishka's saddle was not too good; the leather was scratched and torn, the metal parts were rusty. The bit and snaffles were in like state, and he had to do something to improve their looks. Fortunately he had a happy inspiration. In one village he found a nickel-plated iron bedstead standing outside a merchant's house, and on the four bedposts were polished metal knobs that brilliantly reflected the sun. It was the work of a moment to unscrew them and to fasten them by silken cords, two to the rings of the bit, and two to the bridle-strap across the horse's forehead. The knobs gleamed like the white noonday sun on his horse's head, glittering so unbearably that the animal was dazzled and stumbled as it went. But although its sight suffered and its eyes

watered, Mishka did not remove the knobs (Part vi. Chap. 65).

One must suppose that if Sholokhov placed high hopes in Koshevoi as a lad capable of developing quickly into a shining hero, he was disappointed. Men change slowly, carrying as they do the weight of all their past. Strive as he will for a better life, refractory humanity and the inherent limitations of his own soul drive the zealous reformer one heartbreaking step back for every two paces ahead. Perhaps a wiser man than Koshevoi could have salvaged more members of the Melekhov family than the nephew; but he is a provoked man, taught by experience to scorn peaceful rural life and to suppress his earlier acquiescence to nature's charms. He craves the city. He dedicates his life to building a better world, without realizing that he himself is a flawed instrument. He loves animals more than he loves men—certainly an inauspicious sign in a social engineer.

Sholokhov sees all too clearly what Western commentators are all to reluctant to grant him, that Koshevoi scarcely represents the highest ideal of a Communist or a man. Along with his Bolshevik conscience, Koshevoi has in him something of the popinjay, which Sholokhov makes no attempt to conceal. What must the conversion of this exuberant boy into a relentless judge have cost Sholokhov? How are we to measure the disappointment that lies between Sholokhov's expurgation of Anna Pogudko's hymn to the Communist future (Part v, Chap. 16) and his descriptions of Koshevoi's pathological suspicion and blind insistence on settling old accounts? Stalin might have gloated over these things because, from his point of view, they may be interpreted as vindicating the "hard cold facts of life," which include the temporary ascendancy of brutes like himself. But are we to believe Sholokhov was equally myopic? Like recorders of Icelandic sagas, Sholokhov tells us how it was, not how it ought to have been. This is why Western critics say Sholokhov has no "ideal"—and why he insists he wants only to tell the "truth." But readers should hear bitterness and pity—perhaps even self-pity—in

Sholokhov's voice over the fate of Koshevoi as well as Grigory Melekhov. One surmises, though he cannot prove, that if there is any "self-criticism" in *The Quiet Don*, it is to be found first of all in Koshevoi.

Between Koshevoi and Garanzha stand numerous figures exercising greater or lesser attraction upon Grigory. Although Grigory and Ilya Bunchuk never meet, it is Bunchuk whose position in the story allows him to typify the powerful attraction which revolutionary doctrine has for Grigory. At the moment of their greatest passion, when they watch the women they love die, they are clearly brothers in spirit, though in politics one is a Bolshevik martyr and the other a reluctant White.

What distinguishes all of the prominent male characters is their partisanship. Each has his own ideological and social cause, his own convictions, his own commitments. All represent one or more of the attitudes which men can entertain and live by during a time of revolution. Even Prokhor Zykov, the prankster and buffoon, lives consistently—by laughter if not by faith. What separates them from the hero is that he shares all attitudes but accepts and lives by none.

Grigory Melekhov has been called the *bogatyr* (Russian paladin) of the book, the Hamlet of the steppe, an eternal rebel, a latter-day Don Quixote. He is all of these, though neither so literary nor superhuman as the titles might suggest. If, as Aristotle says, the great action should be advanced by a hero who is good and occupies a mean between saintliness and depravity, then *The Quiet Don* is singularly blessed. Grigory, beginning as an errant and a fractious lad, gains in stature and dignity as he pursues his destiny until he reaches a position seldom rivaled in modern literature for valor and endurance, yet in no quality is he so far beyond the average man that emulation is discouraged.

The stages of his career are instructive. At first Grigory's life is instinctive, almost animal. Physical satisfactions alone answer his inner needs, though a craving for freedom and individuality presently reveal to him his capacity for a tumultuous and erratic emotional life. His suspicion of inequity and injustice in Cossack social life, dramatized by the dichotomy between desire and duty when he is torn between his mistress and his wife, is transformed into conviction under the pressures of military service; and war rips away the social masks, exposing the contradictions between illusion and reality. Introduced to Bolshevism (ironically by a mere peasant), the most radical diagnosis of society and the most radical doctrine for curing social ills, Grigory discovers hope; and his inarticulate longing for freedom and justice is temporarily systematised and given direction. He consciously searches for "truth."

But the pursuit of truth leads him into untried, alien ways. His Bolshevik faith demands that he befriend the Jew, the peasant, the outlander, demands that he transfer his allegiance from a rural to an urban life, demands finally that he betray his own family, his nation and most of the traditions absorbed during childhood. Disillusionment sets in. "No matter how bad the lord is, the lout become a lord is ten times worse" (Part vi, Chap. 20). His wife, his home, his bullocks, the epaulets and medals won with his own life's blood all draw him back toward the old illusory peace and contentment of an instinctive life. Under the pressure of Bolshevik vindictiveness he abdicates from his search for truth, tries to deny the contradictions in Cossack life, and seeks consolation in the idea of Cossack exclusiveness and homogeneity. Just as each man has his own "truth," so the Cossack people have theirs, apart from Russia, apart from humanity.

> "The Reds are fighting so that they can have a better life, but we've already fought for our better life. . . . There's not one truth in this life. The one who wins eats the one who doesn't. And I've been looking for a truth that doesn't exist, wearing my heart out over it, going from one to the other. In the old days, they say, the Tatars tried to grab the Don lands and make us slaves. And now it's Russia. There can be no peace with them! They are foreign to me and to all the Cossacks. The Cossacks will realize it now. We deserted from the front, and now

everybody's like me . . . but it's too late" (Part vi, Chap. 21).

But as Grigory, against his own better judgment, retreats into animal individualism, seeking oblivion in sex, alcohol, and even death, he is periodically overcome by ennui and a sense of purposelessness:

> But each morning, satiated with the amorous fevers of the latest diversion, Grigory thought with sober indifference: "I've lived and experienced everything in my day. I've loved women and girls, I've ridden the steppe, I've rejoiced in fatherhood, I've killed men and faced death myself, and delighted in the blue sky. What new thing can life show me? Nothing! And I can die! It won't be so terrible. I can play at war without risk, like a rich man gambling. My loss won't be great" (Part vi, Chap. 42).

But *Weltschmerz* avails nothing. He must go on, hopelessly trapped between illusion and reality, as we witness in the description of his behavior during the battle of Klimovka. While he is leading a cavalry charge,

> An enormous white cloud billowing in the spring breeze obscured the sun for a minute or two and, overtaking Grigory, a grey shadow slipped with apparent slowness over the rise. He turned his eyes for a moment from the huts of Klimovka to this shadow gliding over the damp brownish earth, and to the bright yellow joyous light fleeing before it. An inexplicable and unconscious desire to overtake the light speeding over the ground took possession of him. He struck his horse and put it into its fastest gallop, and after a few minutes' desperate riding the horse's outstretched head was lit up with a sprinkle of sunlight, and its ruddy coat suddenly gleamed brilliantly golden (Part vi, Chap. 44).

Only through temporary lapses from sanity or dreams does Grigory, until the very end, see himself and his world truly, but he remains heedless. His characteristic vacillations become almost crazed, compulsive. He goes on blindly, driven by passion for a cause and finally by despair, because the cause itself and all the illusions that went into its making are destroyed from the very moment when the Cossacks make their long-awaited contact with the liberating White Army from the south (Part vii, Chap. 5). And Grigory knew this even before it happened. Most of his illusions were stripped away when he killed the sailors and when he learned of his sister-in-law's bloodthirsty slaying of Kotlyarov. Thenceforth he "lived continually in a state of cold numb indifference," believing vainly that the only thing left to him in life was his passion for his mistress. This is the state in which he remains until the Cossack vendee is finally crushed and the insurgent army pushed into the sea. We see it when Grigory buries Sashka, the old retainer at Yagodnoe, beside Aksinya's infant daughter (Part vii, Chap. 6) and again when, under the command of White officers in British uniforms, he "for the first time in his life evaded directly taking part in a battle . . . [because] he realized . . . clearly all the senselessness of what was going on all around him" (Part vii, Chap. 11). We see it last and most dramatically during the White retreat when for a moment Grigory's fate and that of the whole Cossack people are united. In this one brief scene the entire Cossack history of glory, betrayal and despair is revealed to Grigory. Ill with typhus, he has told Prokhor, "Carry me on—until I die. . . ."

> From Prokhor's face he realized that he had been heard and, reassured, he closed his eyes, accepting unconsciousness as a relief, sinking into the thick darkness of oblivion, withdrawing from the tumultuous, noisy world. . . .
>
> All the way to the village of Abinskaya Grigory remembered only one thing: one pitch-dark night he was awakened by the sharp, penetrating cold. Wagons were moving several abreast along the road. . . .
>
> With an effort Grigory pulled the ends of the sheep-

skin around himself and turned over on his back. Across the black sky the wind was driving massive, rolling clouds southward. Very rarely a single star flared for a moment like a yellow spark through a tiny gap in the clouds, then the impenetrable darkness once more enveloped the steppe, the wind whistled mournfully in the telegraph wires, and a fine, beady rain sprinkled down.

A column of cavalry was moving along the right-hand side of the road. Grigory caught the long-familiar rhythmic jingle of tightly braced Cossack equipment, the muffled and rhythmical squelch of innumerable hoofs in the mud. No less than two squadrons had passed but the squelch of hoofs still sounded: a regiment must be riding by at the side of the road. Suddenly, in front, the valiant voice of a solo singer flew up like a bird over the silent steppe:

O, down by the river, brothers, down by Kamyshinka,
On the glorious steppe, the boundless steppe of Saratov. . . .

Many hundreds of voices took up the ancient Cossack song, and high above all danced a tenor accompaniment of astonishing power and beauty. Covering the basses as they died away, the ringing tenor still fluttered somewhere in the darkness, clutching at the heart. But the soloist was already beginning the next verse:

There the Cossacks lived and spent their lives as men of freedom,
All the Don, the Greben, and the Yaik Cossacks. . . .

Inside Grigory something seemed to snap. A sudden spasm of tears shook his body; his throat tightened with sorrow. Choking back his tears, he waited hungrily for the solo singer to begin and, when he did, soundlessly whispered after him words he had known since childhood:

And their ataman was Yermak, son of Timofei,
While their captain was Astashka, son of Lavrenty. . . .

The moment the solo singer struck up the first words
of the song the Cossacks travelling in the wagons ceased
talking, the drivers stopped urging on their horses, and
the whole train of thousands of wagons moved along in
a profound and sensitive silence. Only the clatter of the
wheels and the squelch of hoofs kneading the mud could
be heard as the soloist, carefully enunciating the syllables,
sang the first words of each verse. An ancient song which
had outlived the ages lived and ruled over the sombre
steppe. In artless, simple words it told of the Cossacks'
free ancestors who at one time had fearlessly shattered
the tsarist troops, who had sailed the Don and the Volga
in their light pirate craft, pillaging the tsarist ships,
"squeezing" the merchants, the nobles, and the governors;
the Cossacks who had humbled distant Siberia. And now
the descendants of these free Cossacks, shamefully retreating after being defeated in an inglorious war against
the people of Russia, listened to the mighty song in a
gloomy silence (Part vii, Chaps. 27-28).

Nowhere in Soviet literature does a scene so powerfully
communicate the sense of despair and futility of an old world
crushed by the new. Aristocracy lives on its memories, its
special past; whereas the commonality live on hope and expec-
tation. Here somehow is the last mighty outcry of all that was
venerable, glorious, and primitive. When these singers pass
beyond the Don-side hills, they seem to vanish entirely from
the earth, displaced by a new order which is machine-driven,
efficient. From this time on Grigory seems more and more to
be a remnant of some bygone era accidently left behind and
forgotten.

History has cheated him. His worthy cause is transformed
into a crime, leaving him to face the inevitable punishment
for his actions. He seems prepared to make amends by joining
Budyonny's cavalry and serving loyally and bravely; "he says

he's going to serve until he's atoned for his past sins," Prokhor
reports. But the Reds cannot trust him, and as soon as his
service is no longer essential to the war effort, he is demo-
bilized and sent home to face local authorities who remember
his record all too well. If his contribution to the Red cavalry
is not sufficient atonement, all he can add to it is verbal assurance that he has learned his lesson:

> "I've served my time. I don't want to serve anybody
> any more. I've fought more than enough for my age,
> and I'm absolutely worn out. I'm fed up with everything,
> with the Revolution and with the counter-revolution. Let
> all that—let it all go to hell! I want to live the rest of my
> life with my children, to return to the farm, that's all.
> Believe me . . . I say that from the bottom of my heart!"
> (Part viii, Chap. 6.)

That Grigory is honest here cannot be doubted; that a
fanatical Communist like Koshevoi will refuse to believe him
in view of his past cannot be doubted either. Grigory's fate
is sealed. He must be punished. No matter how pleasant a man
he has become, there must be retribution; hence, the only
thing he wants from life, peace, is forbidden. It is at this time
that he finally sees his position cooly and accurately. He
recognizes that for him the choice between Red and White was
simply impossible, that Korshunov and Koshevoi "are both
tarred with the same brush," that he is therefore totally lost.
He cannot choose to accept punishment; he cannot choose to
expiate crimes which he does not consider crimes at all but
only mistakes which he was justified in making because the
Reds themselves first offered provocation. Thus, he runs away
again and coincidentally falls in with a group of men who
cannot make their peace and must fight, though he realizes that
he and his fellows in Fomin's band of fugitives are little better
than brigands completely cut off even from their own people.
Without the desire to find truth, without hope of achieving
peace, without a cause, he lives once more the old free Cossack life among men who, in true Cossack fashion, prefer

halfwits to Jews. Nothing, however, that Grigory does now
has any meaning. The former numbness and ennui return.
Lying on the sun-hazed steppe, watching the distant, pre-
historic burial mounds, Grigory

> had a strange feeling of resignation and peace as he
> pressed his body to the rough earth. It was a long familiar
> feeling. It always came after he had experienced anxiety,
> and at such times he seemed to see everything around
> him with fresh vision. It was as though his sight and
> hearing had grown keener, and after such a time of agi-
> tation all that previously would have passed unnoticed
> now attracted his attention. With equal interest he
> watched the whistling, slanting flight of a sparrow-hawk
> pursuing some tiny bird, and the deliberate crawl of a
> black beetle which struggled over the distance between
> his two elbows, and the gentle swaying of a blood-red
> tulip rocked by the wind, gleaming with a brilliant virgin
> beauty. The tulip was growing quite close to him, on
> the edge of a crumbled suslik-burrow. He had only to
> stretch out his hand to pluck it; but he lay without moving,
> with silent rapture admiring the flower and the stiff leaves,
> which jealously preserved drops of the morning dew
> within their folds. Then he shifted his gaze and long, un-
> thinkingly watched an eagle hovering above the horizon,
> over a dead city of suslik mounds (Part vii, Chap. 15).

The eagle, ancient symbol of Russia; the dead city of suslik
warrens, new symbol of the Cossack nation: this is Grigory's
world.

Yet, once more an agonized spasm moves him to seek
peace and try to make some sense of his life. He returns for
Aksinya unaware that the world is long since closed to him.
His fatigue fortunately protects him from the savage irony of
his son's life when Aksinya relates the story:

> . . . once Mishatka ran in from the street trembling all
> over. "What's the matter?" I asked him. He burst into

tears, and such bitter tears too! "The other boys won't play with me, they say my daddy's a bandit. Mummy, is it true he's a bandit? What are bandits?" I told him: "Your daddy isn't a bandit at all. He's just—unlucky." But he pestered me with his questions: "Why is he unlucky, and what does 'unlucky' mean?" I simply couldn't explain it to him. It was they who started to call me "Mother," Grisha; you mustn't think I taught them to. But Mikhail [Koshevoi] was quite good to them—quite kind (Part viii, Chap. 17).

The new world, having destroyed Grigory, takes his only son (Koshevoi, not Grigory, will in all probability raise him) and takes finally his woman, the last human being on earth with whom he could dream of going on. Shot by men from a grain-requisitioning detachment, Aksinya dies beneath Grigory's eyes. "And, going numb with horror, he realized that it was all over, that the most terrible thing that could happen in his life had already happened. Now he had nothing to hurry for. Everything was finished." Self-preservation alone sustains him. ". . . He himself still clung convulsively to the earth, as though his broken life was indeed of some value to himself and others. . . . He lost his native wit and his former daring." He lives like an animal, terrified by the least noise in the forest. He returns to the basic crafts, carving spoons and dishes and toy figures from wood or stone. And in the end he performs his "act of submission," throws his weapons into Father Don, and returns to his son: "This was all life had left to him, all that for a little longer gave him kinship with the earth and with the spacious world which lay glittering under the chilly sun."

This is Grigory Melekhov, the man foredoomed to loneliness, the man who tried all life and found it wanting, who foresaw his entire life in dreams from the beginning yet who played it out to the end. His dreams are synopses of terror, bred from psychic insecurity as well as physical assaults against him (Part iv, Chap. 4; Part viii, Chap. 6).

The moment he dozed off he had a dream which he had
dreamed many times before: . . . Over the brown fields,
over high-standing stubble, lines of Red Army men were
moving. The first line extended as far as the eye could
reach. Behind it were six or seven other lines. The men
drew nearer and nearer in the oppressive silence. The
little black figures grew, increased in size, and now he
could see them coming on at a swift, stumbling stride,
on, on, on, coming within firing range, running with
their rifles at the trail, in flappy cloth helmets, with mouths
gaping silently. Grigory was lying in a shallow trench,
convulsively jerking the bolt of his rifle, firing again and
again; under his fire the Red Army men stumbled and
fell headlong; he thrust in a fresh clip of cartridges and,
glancing for a second to either side, saw the Cossacks
leaping out of the neighbouring trenches. They turned and
ran, their faces distorted with fear. He could hear the
terrible beating of his heart; he shouted: "Fire! You
swine! Where are you going? Stop, don't run!" He shouted
at the top of his voice, but his voice was terrifyingly
weak, scarcely audible. He was seized with horror. He,
too, jumped up, and as he stood he fired a last time
at a dark-faced Red Army man who was silently running
straight towards him. He saw he had missed. The soldier
was not young and had a tensely serious, fearless face. He
ran lightly, his feet hardly touching the ground, his brows
knitted, his cap on the back of his head, the edges of
his greatcoat tucked up. For a moment Grigory stared at
the approaching enemy, saw his glittering eyes and pale
cheeks overgrown with a short, curly beard, saw the
broad tops of his boots, the little black eye of the slightly
depressed rifle-barrel, and above it, rising and falling
rhythmically, the point of the dark bayonet. An inde-
scribable terror took possession of him. He tugged at the
bolt of his rifle, but the bolt would not shift, it had
jammed. In despair he beat the bolt against his knee, with
no result. But the Red Army man was now only five paces
away. Grigory turned and fled. Before him all the bare

brown field was sprinkled with fleeing Cossacks. Behind him he heard his pursuer breathing heavily, heard the hollow thud of his boots. But he could not run any faster. He had to make a terrible effort to force his sagging legs to move faster. At last he reached a gloomy, half-ruined graveyard, jumped across the fallen fence, ran between the sunken graves, the crooked crosses and little shrines. Yet one more effort and he would be safe. But now the thunder of feet behind him increased, grew even louder. The pursuer's burning breath scorched his neck, and at that moment he felt himself seized by the tail and skirt of his greatcoat. A muffled cry burst from him, and he awoke (Part vii, Chap. 9).

Like Cain, he and his people wander across their broken paradise, searching for meaning. Expiation is granted only when Grigory understands that all causes are false and that the one truth is existence itself, made meaningful by human sacrifice and suffering, and dignified by the individual man's submission to the inscrutable course of human life. He cannot become a Cossack "aristocrat," he cannot be a farmer, he cannot form a viable family, he cannot join the Party. Physical reality has hounded him through the valley of the shadow, without, at last, even hope for the comforting rod and staff. Not God-given shrift, but man-given amnesty is all that can be expected. This is why *The Quiet Don*, if it is a Communist book at all, is Communist chiefly in its vindication of Lenin's famous conviction that life, and life alone, teaches men. But the lesson is not one that Lenin supposed.

The highest compliment that can be paid Grigory Melekhov, the quality which places him above other twentieth-century literary heroes, is that he is a man, mature, imperfect, and complete. He has little in common with the diseased creatures who populate so much contemporary fiction. Because his own sickness, his own split personality, is presented as a tragic flaw rather than a badge of honor, his vision transcends the pitiful and sophisticated despair of the stereotyped romantic hero in contemporary Western literature. He invites men, as it were, to take up their burdens and follow him since there is neither dignity nor hope in passive complaints against the weight that must be borne. He learned Achilles' lesson.

Concerning language, we may describe Sholokhov's general development as a process of abandoning an early infatuation with obtrusive starkness on the one hand, "ornamental prose" and embellishment on the other—and then perfecting a consciously simple style. The linguistic exuberance of his earliest stories continues into the opening sections of *The Quiet Don*; so that we find, for example, when Listnitsky listened to a soldier singing, it was as if "a string was tautened with the increasing beat of his heart, and the low timbre of the voice plucked the string, setting it vibrating painfully." "The oily puddles between the railway tracks reflected the grey, fleshy sheepskin of the sky." "The sun hung as though set edgeways on the rusty crown of the roof and was about to roll down on one or the other side." As the Soviet critic, Kirpotin, has pointed out:

> All these "monstrous" [*chudovishchnye*] tints of clouds, "orange-blossom" [*apelsinovye*] streams of setting sunbeams, "bacchanalian [*vakhanalnye*] spectrums of color, "malachitean" [malakhitovye] grasses, "drained out whiteness" [*vypitye blednostyu*] of faces, "desolated" [*opustoshyonnye*] eyes, even "crucified" [*raspyatya*] windmills as well as numerous terms foreign to Sholokhov might almost always have substituted for them simple, direct expressions.[15]

As in his early, blunt juxtapositions of white and black, violence and calm, cruelty and kindness, so in his early imagery he often built too baldly, rarely pursuing the subtler implications of his comparisons or striving to make both

members of the comparison function in some overall meta-
phoric or symbolic pattern. The source of Sholokhov's images
is the local scene (farming, fishing, nature in general), and
such a limitation might have been redeemed if he had taken
the trouble to use it with some recognizable design, rather
than abandoning each image as soon as it achieved sufficient
precision to gain a momentary brilliance. ". . . A breeze was
blowing quietly as though fanned from the wings of invisible
passing birds"; "the smoking fire of the Pleiades was burning
out in the sky, the Great Bear lay to one side of the Milky
Way, like an overturned wain with the shaft sticking up."
These images make their random appearance in a single paragraph, but without cumulative effect (Part iv, Chap. 4).

Some of the excessive figures in the early volumes were
removed from later editions; moreover, by the time Sholokhov
began writing the last half of the work he had learned not
only to avoid them but to invent the epic similes which illuminate this section of the work. To be sure, similes with epic
resonance appear in the early volumes; for example, Grigory
Melekhov's "heart had grown hard, dry like a salt-marsh in
drought; as a marsh will not absorb water, so Grigory's heart
would not absorb compassion." Yet, never do we find anything
equal to the celebrated image that appears in Part vi after a
long paragraph describing Grigory's unusual ability to handle
his sabre with either hand that gave him an advantage over
enemy cavalrymen: "As the practice stick, cut expertly slant-
wise from its pole, drops without a tremor, without changing
its position, and falls point downward into the sand beside
the pole from which the Cossack sword has cut it, so the hand-
some Semiglazov fell from his rearing horse and quietly slipped
out of the saddle, his hands clutching at his sabred breast"
(Chap. 37). The effectiveness of such a Tolstoyan image in
context depends precisely upon its formality, which not only
terminates the previous exposition concretely but elevates it.
One is reminded of the famous bee image (Napoleon's emblem) in *War and Peace* (Part xi, Chap. 20). Occasionally
Sholokhov reverses the procedure, placing his image ahead of

exposition, but the effect remains the same, as in his description of Aksinya's love for Grigory:

> In winter the biting winds howl over the steep slopes above the Don, sweeping a white flurry of snow from the bare ridges, piling it into drifts and caking it hard. Glittering like sugar in the sun, blue [*goluboi*] in the twilight, pale violet in the mornings and pink at dawn, that mighty crag of snow hangs over the cliff. And hang it shall, menacing in its silence, until the thaw eats it away underneath, or burdened by its own weight, it is dislodged by a gust of wind. Then, with a muffled roar it will plunge downwards, crushing the stunted thornbushes, breaking the bird-cherry that clings shyly to the slope, dragging in its wake a foaming, skyward-leaping train of powdered snow.
>
> Aksinya's love, that like a snowdrift had been piling up for so many years, needed only one gentle push. And her meeting with Grigory, his tender: "Good morning, Aksinya dear," had been enough. But what of him? Was he not dear to her? Had she not been mindful of him all these years, returning to him every day, every hour in ever-present memories? Whatever she thought of, whatever she was doing, her thoughts were always turning to Grigory. So does the blind horse plod the everlasting circle of the water-wheel (Part vi, Chap. 50).

In the final sections of *The Quiet Don* the formal simile is supplanted by subtly symbolic natural descriptions (for example, the autumn associated with Pantelei's labors—Part vii, Chap. 24), although in the book's very last chapter Sholokhov returned to the epic simile of a steppe fire.

Sholokhov's poetic diction and attention to the distinctions between dialect and formal words in his vocabulary are often impressive. He extends Tolstoy's device in *War and Peace* of distinguishing between Russian *Moskva* (Cyrillic) and French *Moscou* (Roman) or Russian *step* and French *steppes* in the minds of characters. Sholokhov applies it, for example, to the

distinction between three words for "house": *dom* (the general term), *kuren'* (a peculiarly Cossack term), and *khata* (a White Russian and Ukrainian equivalent). "Khata" is derogatory; for example, Koshevoi distinguishes between his own miserable hut (*khata*) and the Korshunov's patriarchal homestead (*kuren'*). *Dom* is a more neutral term used to describe a home without associating it with the old Cossack order. It is not surprising that the Great Russian peasant word for hut, *izba*, is virtually absent.

Sholokhov's unusual sensitivity to smells and colors provides a series of poetic epithets, the most remarkable of which is the word "blue" (*goluboi* as distinct from *sinii*). His use of it is similar to the poet Essenin's. As the critic L. Levin has observed, "for Sholokhov the epithet 'blue' has a special sense with nothing in common with the simple color. 'Blue' . . . means poetic, inspired, beloved, surrounded by distant happy memories, the past which cannot return, or that which is coming in the unknown, misty future."[16]

An additional source for the extraordinary variety in Sholokhov's language is his use of folk idioms. A. A. Gorelov identified fifteen forms of folk expression in *The Quiet Don*, from the obvious songs (about four hundred lines) and sayings (over two hundred) to obscure charms, lamentations, and traditional jokes.[17] The inclusion of these things accounts not only for the air of authenticity in the work but also for the sense of operative preternatural forces and often for the quick shifts in mood and rhythm, for example from a melodious, lyrical passage to one with a militant, strident rhythm; from humor to caustic sarcasm.

Sholokhov resorts frequently to the epistle, the communique, the manifesto, the essay, and once to the diary for forms which vary the normal narrative pattern and tempo of the work. In his descriptions he discontinued his early search for the bizarre, startling phrase, preferring instead the slow accumulation of minutely observed color, sound, and smell.

Unquestionably, his outstanding device is the lyrical or pathetic digression which he probably inherited from Gogol

and improved by charging it with extraordinary passion and couching it in folk language:

> Beloved steppe! The bitter breeze ruffles the manes of mares and stallions. The horses' dry muzzles are salty with the wind and, scenting its saltily bitter breath, they chew their silky lips and neigh as they taste the tang of wind and sun. Beloved steppe under the low-hanging Don heaven! Winding ravines, dry valleys, ruddy banks, expanse of feather-grass woven with the darker traces of horse-hoofs, mounds rising in a wise silence, guarding the buried Cossack glory. . . . Low I bow and as a son I kiss your fresh earth, Cossack steppeland of the Don, soaked with blood that will never rust (Part vi, Chap. 6).

It will be noted that, while certainly moving and dramatic, such an apostrophe is, nonetheless, subjective. Its power is incantatory, not rational. The idiom is purely folkish. Never in the last volume does Sholokhov indulge himself thus. This is why the dirge for bereft wives in Part viii, Chapter 2 surpasses the one in Part v, Chapter 1, however terrifying the latter may seem. Natural descriptions are invariably better integrated, more functional in the narrative of the final volume. For example a steppe eagle sailing "far off in the deep blue heavens . . . winging away from the approaching storm" is made meaningful in terms of Natalya's inner sense of peace (Part vii, Chap. 4); melting spring snow acquires relevance by comparison with the dissolution of Fomin's band (Part viii, Chap. 13).

From the first, the language of Sholokhov's characters is decorous. The intonations, dialects, vocabularies, and often mispronunciations of characters are probably the most important things lost in translation. These (together, of course, with folk songs) are virtually untranslatable,[18] though the English translator provides commendable renditions, for example, when Kopylov reprimands Grigory for his crude behavior and illiterate pronunciation. ". . . And the way you speak! It's horrible! Instead of 'quarters,' you say 'quawters';

instead of 'evacuation,' you say 'evakiation'; for 'apparently' you say 'it looks like as if'; instead of 'artillery'—'antillery.'"

In a recent book on film versions of Sholokhov's work, A. Vlasov and A. Mlodik tell a story which demonstrates Sholokhov's sensitivity to the verbal quality of living speech. When approached with the request to read passages from his work over the radio, he said, "I *could* read, only what would happen? I really must decline, not because I don't want to do it, but because I can't read the dialogues where one has to change his intonation." In other words, he could record with his hand what his mouth could not reproduce.[19] Indeed, he never neglects an opportunity to characterize an individual by his accent (Garanzha's Ukrainian, a Siberian soldier's substitution of the soft "*s*" for "*ts*," the hard "*g*" that Cossacks always hear in Great Russian speech) or vocabulary (the tendency of Bolsheviks to import and misuse high-sounding foreign words or Litsnitsky's predilection for bookish, elegant expressions). Except for the White generals, who sometimes sound as if they were reading their speeches from a newspaper, no two characters in *The Quiet Don* speak exactly the same language; indeed, some of the minor characters are memorable largely because of their highly individual style, for example, old Grishaka and Prokhor Zykov.

The advantage of saturating fiction with regional dialect is obvious enough. It authenticates character and event. There is, however, a major disadvantage: regional vernacular channels the mind along familiar paths and thus curtails it. While it preserves folk wisdom, it also confirms habitual errors. Perhaps this is why "universal" institutions, like the Roman Church, so long preferred Latin—why pure Communist prose translates so readily and sounds equally wooden in all languages. The intense subjectivity of lyrical language (and vernacular *is* lyrical) inhibits all but the greatest writers from reaching universal significance.

In *The Quiet Don* there is a delightful moment when an illiterate Cossack assures Ilya Bunchuk that Comrade Lenin could not conceivably be a Russian but must, rather, be a Cossack because "There's Pugachov; wasn't he a Cossack?

And Stenka Razin? And Yermak Timofeyevich? That's it! There's not a man who has ever raised the poor people against the czar who wasn't a Cossack. And you say he's from Simbirsk Province! I'm ashamed to hear such words, Ilya. . ." (Part iv, Chap. 17). The episode is, in the first place, amusing. It also functions, as Communist critics always remind us, both as a realistic representation of the spontaneous loyalty which Lenin often evoked and also as an exemplum or parable which might endear Lenin to readers—especially Cossacks—not yet converted to his cause.

Yet, this folkish humanization of Lenin diminishes him as an intellectual, as the keen, impersonal theoretician and administrator of revolution. So thorough a cosmopolitan cannot be portrayed fully in folk idiom because it is too rural, too familiar, and too proud. Contrast Tolstoy's description of the Council at Fili in *War and Peace* (Part xi, Chap. 4). A six-year-old peasant girl witnesses the scene, and Tolstoy enables us to observe it partly through her mind and vocabulary; yet, the central figure, Kutuzov, acquires monumental stature at the end. Tolstoy removes little Malasha from the room four short paragraphs before Kutuzov utters those terrible words: the French "shall eat horseflesh yet, like the Turks!" He emerges as more than a folk leader; he becomes Napoleon's peer. It is a curious fact too that when Tolstoy tried to deflate Napoleon's grandeur by viewing him through wounded Andrei's eyes after Austerlitz, he sunds unconvincing (Part iii, Chap. 19). Sholokhov succeeds completely when he discredits the "distinguished personage" who visited wounded Grigory in hospital (Part iii, Chap. 23). His irony is more savage than Tolstoy's in the devastating scene when Czar Alexander I interviews the messenger, Michaud, from Moscow (Part xii, Chap. 3).

What Sholokhov's private conception of Lenin is, we do not know; but the Lenin of *The Quiet Don* (and of the short stories) is a mere folk-hero or perhaps a prototype of Stalin. Certainly it is clear that the model which the novel's major Communist hero, Koshevoi, strives to emulate is not cosmopolitan Lenin, but the practical Soviet nationalist and bureaucrat,

Stalin. Sholokhov's fidelity to regional language dramatizes a mentality which very likely put many first-generation Communist intellectuals on their guard against his art. Many modern social engineers suspect that behind the lyric temper of the regional writer (Faulkner, Giono, or Hamsun) lurks a reactionary, a crypto-fascist.

Not only in dialogue but in the narrative as well, Sholokhov enjoys the advantage of the Russian language itself, which has preserved a wider channel to its primitive past than most modern languages. Russians themselves will express pride that their language, while perhaps not so full of abstractions as English or German, contains many more emotion-laden synonyms for individual objects. Coenesthetic resonances persist. The tangible becomes numinous. There is a magic in Russian that derives, perhaps, from its rural habituation, so that often a figure of speech that equates, for example, an animal with some object comes closer to metamorphosis than metaphor.[20] In addition, Russian retains, at least for literary purposes, some of the solemn cadence of Church Slavonic. Little wonder that Sholokhov's Cossack-Russian, even more rural and traditional, should communicate an epic authenticity as well as a regional flavor.

It was unfortunate when Sholokhov's use of dialect decreased in Part vii of *The Quiet Don* and vanished almost completely from Part viii. He had apparently lost the sheer joy of articulation in a vivid, concrete language; and from this time on, his prose becomes less effective.[21] The ponderous verbosity of the Communist threatened to strangle the artist's racier idiom. His greatest passages are those in which he strikes a balance—asking perennial human questions or describing recurrent human dilemmas in the vibrant dialect that is uniquely his own.

The description of action, characters, and language brings us to the question, What meaning do they impart to the reader? We may note, first of all, that Sholokhov gradually altered the book's meaning over the fourteen-year period of its composition, especially by deleting or rewriting earlier passages. Destroying an old civilization and building a new one according to Communist or any other prescriptions is not, as he first imagined, merely cruel and costly, but always liable to perversion by men dehumanized in the process.

But *The Quiet Don* is not a book about Communism; it is not a treatise, but an epic dramatization of man's quest for meaning and happiness. As we learn from the central action, the search leads from an objective attempt to define "truth" to a subjective and catastrophic attempt to define "self." At precisely those times when the question "Who am I?" displaces "What is right?" the hero's fortune is reversed and his glorious cause gradually degenerates into criminal brigandage. Admonished by the very people whom he sought to defend and forewarned repeatedly through dreams which he cannot heed, Grigory comes at last to the revelation that "truth" is not particular, but universal, that human dignity is reserved for those whom suffering has taught to submit to the exigencies of life.

Man's lot is hard. Having asked the question about man's role, Sholokhov approaches an answer slowly, reluctantly. His question is posed during the ominous pause between the end of the war and the beginning of the Revolution before the Cossacks must, one by one, make their fateful commitments to the future:

> Who can foresee where he will meet his death? Who can guess the end of the human road? Hard it was for the horses as they plodded away from the village. Hard it was for the Cossacks to tear sorrow for their dear ones from their chilled hearts. And as they travelled that road many remembered their homes, and many heavy thoughts were pondered. And maybe tears as salt as blood slipped over the saddle, down from the stirrup to the hoof-gnawed road. And will the gold and azure flowers spring up in this place during spring time? (Part vi, Chap. 13.)

Time eventually answers these questions for men. Ultimately, every man goes to meet death; Grigory is but the tardiest. The gold and azure flowers spring up eternally but have little meaning for men negotiating their destinies. Less simple than a flower's life, a man's is all entangled with concepts of crime and punishment, sin and redemption, action and responsibility. And the end of the human road is precisely human accountability for it. This is why Listnitsky's "Dostoevskian" conclusion ("Everything is lawful to me") not only typifies this intellectual aristocrat's moral and physical mutilation but reveals his bankruptcy as well (Part vi, Chap. 5).

Sholokhov seems vexed with Grigory because he naively expects an easy peace, an easy way out of the historical dilemma and because he tries to evade responsibility for his actions. But nowhere is it suggested that Grigory could have behaved differently. He does only what he can, all that he can. For this he must be held accountable, but to say that he is right or wrong, to defend or condemn him is beside the point. His life, for which he must bear witness and punishment, is its own justification. Being is all.

But "being" is meaningless unless it is translated into human terms. "Being" alone, in art as in science, is "naturalism"; and Sholokhov, while he might have been liable to the charge of naturalism and objectivism and even, therefore, inhumanity in the early parts of *The Quiet Don,* is in the end not liable. "Being" experiences a gradual accretion of human meaning precisely in proportion to the stripping away of human illusions in the last volume of the work. The false illusions of Cossack pride and exclusiveness and individuality fail and vanish so that Grigory's life is absolutely devoid of meaning. The old meanings are visibly delusive, the new alternatives visibly fraudulent. What, then, is left? Endurance and perseverance. More important, submission. A lifetime of endured suffering brings Grigory at last to the sole gesture which has meaning. He learns what his mother and sister somehow knew instinctively. When his rifle and cartridges fall into the Don, all the illusions of individuality and exclusiveness that nourished and perhaps deluded man for five hundred years, all the illusions which sustained an entire society, fall with them. Henceforth there is only one meaning: a man must live out his life fully; he must endure, which means he must ultimately stand and face the wide, cold, glittering world; he must, in short, achieve a consciousness of necessity, which is, I think, equivalent to the tragic vision of life. Not "being," finally, but ripeness is all—the readiness for death.

This at least seems to be what Sholokhov is saying. Red, White, or Green are transitory phenomena. Man's illusions change; man changes imperceptibly, if at all. And man's life is emphatically not meaningless. Unlike Pasternak, or a multitude of Western writers, Sholokhov never insults humanity; he never overemphasizes human degradation and corruption; he never, despite his detachment in the final parts of *The Quiet Don*, becomes so impersonal and inhuman that he fails to distinguish humanity's high place in the order of things. In addition, Sholokhov writes off nothing to fate or blind necessity. There shall be no gods before Man. Sholokhov's world belongs to man, and men must pay for it. Not "original sin," but social sin, prompted by instinct and environment, is the pit into which man falls and from which he must extricate himself.

This is demonstrated indirectly by Sholokhov's handling of important death scenes in which not only beauty and dignity are usually present but love which carries on after death and, even more important, youth, the symbol of revival and the vehicle of perpetuation. (Witness the deaths of Natalya, Darya, and Ilyinichna.) Only when the person who dies represents the irrevocable passing of an entire way of life or an illusion is death portrayed as finality (Pantelei's and, to a lesser extent, Aksinya's), but even in these cases one is not permitted to forget that life goes on, that graves must be dug by the living, that the sun continues to shine for the quick as well as the dead.

Sholokhov demonstrates his humanism directly by overcoming the inclination to celebrate nature for its own sake, which characterizes the early books and makes even such a splendid paragraph as his apostrophe to the steppe seem to be a capitulation to an amoral material world. Equally convincing evidence of his humanism occurs in a passage which I take to be central to the entire Don cycle, a passage which puts the earlier digressions into correct perspective and indicates Sholokhov's recovery of Greek wonder at the world and man's place in it:

> Numbed with memories, Grigory lay down on the grass not far from this tiny, dearly cherished cemetery and gazed long at the majestic expanse of blue sky above him. Somewhere in the heights of that infinite space winds were wandering, and the cold clouds floated in the gleaming sunlight; but on the earth which had just taken Sashka the merry ostler and drunkard to itself life was still seething as furiously as ever. From the steppe that crept in a flood of green to the very edge of the orchard, and in the tangle of wild flax around the borders of the ancient threshing-floor, he could hear the incessant pulsating cry of the quails; susliks were whistling, bumble-bees were humming, the grass rustled under the wind's caresses, the skylarks sang in the spirtting light of the sunset, and, to confirm the grandeur of man's place in nature, from somewhere a long way off down the valley came the persistent angry mutter of a machine-gun (Part vii, Chap. 6).

This is not ironic. Man fights, loves, works. Action, not thought, avows the primal man. Sholokhov celebrates the time of destruction when old forms of life are swept away in preparation for the new, a time when participants in this cruel process suddenly seem "precivilized." We witness an advent in *The Quiet Don*, a "second coming" in the sense that W. B. Yeats used the term. This is why the book, for all its tragic overtones, leaves the impression of affirmation, even optimism. Man's honor and grandeur survive his suffering. This is also why the book runs counter to recent existential and experimental novels in the West that seem equally rudimentary and cruel. It shares some of the ruthlessness that occurs in the fiction of Beckett or Robbe-Grillet when they seek to lay bare elemental man, but *The Quiet Don* carries us to the threshold of civilized life. Decadent Western fiction all too often seems decivilizing by comparison. Thus, Soviet critics eagerly claim that many current French writers, as well as Faulkner or D. H. Lawrence, however brilliant their *artistic* virtuosity, fail to supply the symbolic actions that prepare men to face the future.

One would err by failing to note that *The Quiet Don's* significance is restricted by the fact that none of its characters knows enough about the world to sense the full implication of events. One may contrast it profitably with *The Leopard* by Sholokhov's Italian contemporary Lampedusa. Moreover, the scarcity of cities with their industry and technology inhibits the treatment of urban problems that are crucial in this century of war, revolution, and the loss of individuality. The very lack of these things, however, has advantages; without them Sholokhov can concentrate not only on the original stability of his rural society but precisely upon the process of disintegration during its most climactic moments. It is enough, perhaps, that in the end as the new world closes upon the last of the *bogatyri,* Sholokhov explains that Red Army patrols run Fomin's horsemen to earth by telephoning their movements ahead. Even the last pathetic illusion of Cossack freedom in his steppe fastness now closes.

In summarizing Sholokhov's achievement, it cannot be said that his invention is of the highest order or that he is a major innovator in form and technique. Except for his lyrical and folk-epic qualities, there is almost nothing in *The Quiet Don* that he could not have learned from Tolstoy. Inadequately educated, he had to learn as he worked; and the improvement between his clumsy and imitative first compositions and the final three parts of *The Quiet Don* testifies that he learned much. Clearly his early stories, with their frequent sentimentality, and his two other novels do not rival it. His genius is best seen in his judicious selection of detail and sense of proportion, in the passion which suffuses his work and animates his characters, in his poetic diction and the vigor of his figures and descriptions, and last in his syncretic power, which permits him to contain Dostoevskian contradictions in a single, steady conception that is Tolstoyan but without Tolstoy's mechanistic justifications. In addition, his is the first great portrayal of rural Russian life, from the viewpoint of rural Russia itself rather than the viewpoint of the aristocracy or intelligentsia.

Rarely in contemporary fiction is there an equally insistent vindication of individual right that does not degenerate into madness and egocentrism or founder on paradoxes between the claims of reason and emotion or between the individual and the community. At the same time, nowhere in contemporary fiction is the individual subjected so ruthlessly to the demands and needs of the community, nor are the rights of "the people" more fiercely championed. Sholokhov transcends the contradiction, refuses to commit himself to either side, retains both his sanity and dignity without retreating one step from objective fact or sacrificing one jot of reality to illusion. He evidently learned that, in the words of the poet Calderon, "the greatest crime of man is that he ever was born." Grigory Melekhov's tragic flaw is that he is a living human being.

The sundry gods which have failed so many men in the twentieth century have not, therefore, failed Sholokhov; for his god appears to be Man, who cannot fail except through self-annihilation. What he learned is that when this world's Christs go up to Calvary, they die there, but the people who walk along, impelled by hate or curiosity or love, watch and learn and walk down again. Where other writers' heroes discover either some rationalistic system or some privately or socially sanctioned mysticism, Sholokhov's people walk steadily forward, alone in a meaningless universe, but by their presence and activity inspiring the void with meaning. Not many men have written who can tolerate reality on its own terms with so little assistance from illusion. Perhaps no one, least of all Sholokhov, can tolerate it for long. After *The Quiet Don*, conventional Communist illusions rapidly fill the void in

Sholokhov's work just as the Soviet social order filled the vacuum left in the wake of revolution.

Because almost all Soviet critics pose and answer affirmatively the question of whether *The Quiet Don* is didactic, a further word is necessary. The book *is* tendentious according to the original Marxist prescription, which holds that "a socialist-biased novel fully achieves its purpose . . . if by conscientiously describing the real mutual relations, breaking down conventional illusions about them, it shatters the optimism of the bourgeois world, instills doubt as to the eternal character of the existing order, although the author does not offer any definite solution or does not even line up openly on any particular side."[22] But this is not to say that Sholokhov followed any recipe.

Russian critics are probably correct in asserting that *The Quiet Don* details the collapse of the Cossack illusion (the "third way"), but they are mistaken to claim that the illusion collapses because it is inferior to the Bolshevik alternative or even because it is wrong. It is merely obsolete, an historical anachronism. They fail to see that the unluckiest and unhappiest days in history are those when no "third way" exists: between paganism and Christianity, Catholicism and Protestantism, monarchy and commonwealth, bourgeois and proletarian democracy. For Sholokhov the Revolution involves neither victory nor defeat, only waste—but inevitable and necessary waste because there is no other way out. Every alternative is tried but found wanting. Sholokhov's commitment is to man, who must, after all, go on living. And insofar as Bolshevism identifies with the continuation of life, insofar as it truly is the "wave of the future," Sholokhov is committed to it and his book brings its readers to share his commitment.

Only in this sense is the novel "revolutionary." Koshevoi must stand as Sholokhov's condemnation of the Bolshevik tendency toward doctrinaire fraud that inhibits the future and interferes with the natural proliferation of human life. One must recognize, moreover, that Sholokhov's suspicion of human perfectibility and of the efficacy of human institutions, that his eloquent celebration of man's right to love and to suffer and to salvage from the past every enduring value are profoundly conservative.

As a Cossack champion and as a socialist citizen, Sholokhov inherits, both from tradition and politico-economic theory, an urgent need for individuality. He knows as well as any Russian does the taunting letter that Cossacks of the Dniepr sent to the seventeenth-century Turkish potentate, Mahomet IV, but would have sent to any power on earth that presumed to threaten or even question their autonomy. He knows as well as any Russian does that the land was covered by 1922 with the graves of men and women who believed they were dying for a life better than that under the czarist tyranny, better indeed than that hitherto known on earth, precisely because they expected it to liberate the individual for the first time in history.

At the same time, Sholokhov absorbed from his culture the sense of community (*sobornost*—"congregationality" or ecumenical catholicity) which has for centuries influenced Russian development and attracted perhaps more attention from Western thinkers than any other characteristic of Russia's history. Since Sholokhov has no strong feeling for religious community in any orthodox or conventional sense, his feeling focuses all the more intensely on *social* community so that the worst sin of all is to become cut off from one's people and, by extension, from humanity in general. The ultimate sin is crime against "the people." This is fratricide because it violates the essential brotherhood of all men. The most dramatic scenes of murder and execution in Sholokhov's works are those in which the inhumanity of the acts is emphasized. When a man has offered provocation by breaking his ties with the community, then his executioners are absolved, as when Bunchuk liquidates Kalmykov or when punitive detachments hunt down Fomin's band. But when the man is simply a soldier doing his duty or a creature honestly seeking his destiny along with his fellow men, then no matter what his creed or allegiance, his elimination is a martyrdom and his executioner a criminal. This is true of Whites, Chernetsov or Pyotr Melekhov, for example, no less than a Red hero such as Podtyolkov.

The antinomy between Cossack individualism and social communion is exaggerated by a comparable contradiction within modern socialist doctrine, which insists that liberation of the individual from middle-class domination is of cardinal importance yet relies methodologically upon class and mass movements in which the individual almost loses his identity, becoming an infinitesimal, though somehow integral, atom in the grand process.

In Sholokhov, the combination of these opposed tendencies leads first to an escapist search for security in the natural, simple wisdom of physical nature, then to exasperation and disgust at man's propensity to betray his brothers, to defile all relationships as a result of his need for self-determination and self-definition, and finally to a recognition that human life itself transcends each man's individual fate but invites every man to participate in the larger destiny of mankind by retaining love and enduring all things with dignity. It is this larger meaning that makes conventional Soviet interpretations over the past twenty years specious. To say either that Grigory Melekhov is guilty of committing an "historical error" by not following his own people into acceptance of Soviet government or that he is an "apostate" or "renegade" is to miss the point entirely. As the most recent Soviet critics recognize, he is too Promethean for such treatment.[23]

The wisdom of Sholokhov's (and Communism's) faith in man alone remains a major question. If he were readier or abler to examine or even tolerate a fuller range of man's *intellectual* experience, passing beyond the merely physical, then his vision might encompass more than Tolstoy's or Thomas Mann's. His faith in man might seem more satisfying. But to do this, he would forfeit precisely the epic resonance that makes *The Quiet Don* unique in modern fiction.

Faith in active man, working man, sustained Sholokhov (and Communism) during a brief heroic age. Today the faith has visible inadequacies. It built an ugly, uncomfortable, and oppressive nation that can improve only when the Party learns to accommodate *thinking* man. Wit and grace alone can consolidate the victories of brute strength. Sholokhov seems incapable of accommodation. If Communism evolves in order to accept the full range of man's intellectual experience, it will leave Sholokhov behind just as the Soviet Union left recalcitrant Cossacks. —But then, at last, it will have to face the big question: Is it wise to place faith in man, however comprehensively and grandly we define him? Only when they seek answers to this question will Russians, for the first time since they became Soviet, begin contributing to the great colloquy of Western civilization, as they did a century ago.

Chapter V

A New Beginning and End
Virgin Soil Upturned

The two halves of *Virgin Soil Upturned* were published almost thirty years apart (1932 and 1960).[1] Volume I represents a new departure in subject matter and technique by comparison with *The Quiet Don*, but by the mid-fifties, when he wrote the second volume, Sholokhov's technique had suffered, largely from desuetude but perhaps also because he had undergone harsh treatment at the hands of Stalinites. (We should not forget that Sholokhov—or some editor—mutilated the 1952 "revised" edition of Volume I by making literally thousands of emendations.)[2] A tendency toward verbosity that began in the last part of *The Quiet Don* and in *They Fought for Their Country* now becomes painfully evident. It is as if Sholokhov were victimized by his own verbal magic so that the colorful *skazes* (vernacular tales) of *The Quiet Don* often grow tedious in *Virgin Soil Upturned II*; the old laconic narrative becomes contrived; digressions seldom reach their former brilliance. Most striking is the author's growing need "to set the world straight" instead of simply telling his story. The evangelistic wasp that stung so many Russian writers both before and after 1917 finally reached Sholokhov. Sadly for him, the gospel he chose to evangelize turns out to be simple-minded by comparison with Dostoevsky's or Tolstoy's.

In *Virgin Soil Upturned I*, on the other hand, tempo is breathtaking. It is a novel in perpetual climax, like Dostoevski's *Devils*, though the disturbances that animate it are more physical. One is not surprised when Nagulnov, as pure a Dostoevskian character as one could imagine, has a prophetic dream one night, then exclaims the next morning almost in the words of Dmitri Karamazov: "What a dream I just had! A splendid dream!"

No doubt the epic sweep of *The Quiet Don* re-creates the rhythm of revolution more convincingly than the tumult of *Virgin Soil Upturned I.* The former's scope provides perspectives which make it more impressive as a literary performance and more memorable as an instrument for communicating the lessons of history; yet few Soviet books, I think, so successfully thrust us into the hour-by-hour, day-by-day turmoil of rapid social transformation as *Virgin Soil Upturned I.* This is why many early critics congratulated Sholokhov for having triumphed over his old Cossack infatuation and written a superb "proletarian" book. One critic prematurely claimed that *Virgin Soil Upturned I* was the logical conclusion of *The Quiet Don*—"in truth the fourth volume"—because at last Sholokhov had written a book that served as a weapon calculated to hasten social change.[3]

Long-term policies and the specific decisions of Party functionaries, while they precipitate events and ultimately guide them, seem to vanish like fires lost in an impenetrable roil of smoke. We see only the smoke. At the moment of reading, our vicarious experience matches the characters' "real" experience as we tumble along together, uncomprehending, muscles tensed expecting the unseen blow. Kataev's *Time Forward!* or Gladkov's *Cement* seem tepid by comparison.

As one might predict, *Virgin Soil Upturned I* is better focused as a novel than *The Quiet Don,* just as *Anna Karenina* is better focused than *War and Peace.* Its concentration on the lives of fewer characters confined within a narrower setting heightens impact, though it may diminish significance. Certainly, the connections between characters are more intimate and their collisions more frequent, which leads to greater intensity in the experience we have with the novel and enables us to keep the *dramatis personae* constantly under surveillance. Few individuals wander into the action and then vanish, as happens again and again in the epic. One difficulty, however, is that the novel lacks a hero—or rather, its heroes are dissolved in the Party nucleus, perhaps even in the collective "people" of Gremyachy Log. Concentration on a single action (founding the collective) unifies volume one and conceals a latent vagrancy among the characters which emerges clearly in volume two, making it episodic. Thus, *Virgin Soil Upturned*'s "multiple hero" may make good socialist realism, but it jeopardizes art. Especially in volume two, as in his war novel *The Fought for Their Country*, Sholokhov loses the equilibrium between the distinctive individual and the community. Unconsciously, he dramatizes the problem that agitates all theoreticians of the modern novel: does the deterioration of individuality in modern life signal the death of the novel as a form, since the novel's fate seems, in large part, tied to the history of individualism?

As in *The Quiet Don*, so in *Virgin Soil Upturned I*, the precipitating force arrives on the Cossack scene from beyond the steppe. Nascent conflicts abound locally but remain quiescent until a Party organizer from Moscow and a White agitator with alien ties converge and strike the spark that reignites old Cossack hatreds. As always in Sholokhov's work, the world's great ideologies deny individual men's petitions for peace, even in remote expanses of steppe land. There is no deferment.

Perhaps it is this fact of upheaval in an environment which ought to be insulated and arcadian that exacerbates savagery. We take violence for granted in cities undergoing industrialization, hence the harshest events in Soviet "factory novels" come as no surprise. The novelty of *Virgin Soil Upturned I* is that it foreshadows, especially for Western readers, the unexpected turbulence that experience has now taught us to accept in South America or Asia. Precisely in the "backward" and rural areas revolution shows its ugliest face. Sholokhov witnessed it firsthand—not as an adventuresome, idealistic youth, but as a man whose very life was jeopardized. Involvement may account for the difference between this novel and Zola's *Earth* or Bunin's *Village*, which seem by comparison to be more literary but less authentic.

Not only because it is the best "Five-Year Plan novel" but because it supplies a new kind of literary experience, one is willing to call *Virgin Soil Upturned I* a prototype of "socialist realism." At least it was such books as this that Karl Radek meant to describe when he wrote that "Socialist realism means not only knowing reality as it is, but knowing whither it is moving. . . . A work of art created by a socialist realist is one which shows whither the conflict of contradictions is leading which the artist had seen in life and reflected in his work."[4] *Virgin Soil Upturned I* supplies the symbolic action for achieving a new collective consciousness.

But if Volume I is a striking example of socialist realism, what is Volume II? Unlike *The Quiet Don*, which creates a unified impression despite the fourteen-year period during which Sholokhov composed it, the two volumes of *Virgin Soil Upturned* do not create a unified impression. Soviet critics tell us that the shift in tempo and tone occurred because Volume I records the violent commencement of collectivization, while Volume II methodically works out the consequences of established collectivization. There is some truth to this because, by the time he wrote Volume II, collectivization had become a fixed landmark in the Soviet scene, while Volume I was written, as he said, "in the heat of the moment" during 1930.[5] More important, however, is the change in Sholokhov during the intervening thirty years. The great purges, the Second World War, and Stalin's "mad years" and death rise like a wall between the two volumes and interrupt their continuity.

To be sure, the major characters remain and are recognizable, but inexplicable things have changed them. They seem tired. They talk more and do less. Impetuous Nagulnov, once cured of his Trotskyite Left-deviationism, becomes ineffectual and silly—almost a clown, and Sholokhov links him constantly with Shchukar, the book's official "jester." His impassioned idealism, like that of Anna Pogudko in *The Quiet Don*, has grown hollow. Davydov cures himself of a sensual infatuation with Nagulnov's wife and transfers his affections to Varya Kharlamova, the epitome of rural maidenhood. Resolutions and reconciliations supplant conflict. The only scene in the book

that echoes the relentless violence of Volume I, describes
Ostrovnov's murder of his aged mother by starvation. It occurs
in the second chapter and would seem to be Sholokhov's answer to criticastors who have carped for years about his
"gruesome, excessive naturalism." Otherwise, the book walks
loquaciously along, populated with minor characters, for example, Shaly, Arzhanov, Nesterenko, who come to the fore
with long edifying speeches. It reminds one of Panferov's
Brusski, which Sholokhov condemned as a bad novel thirty
years ago.

The difference between the two volumes of *Virgin Soil
Upturned* may be described in this way: when he wrote
Volume I, Sholokhov was explaining the Party to the people;
when he wrote Volume II, he explained the people to the
Party. In 1930 the Party was volatile, aggressive, more than
willing to unhinge the world with its sledgehammer. History
may prove that collectivization was Communism's last major
innovation—perhaps also its gravest mistake. By 1960 a recalcitrant people had absorbed the blows and begun to remind their
leaders that patience, loyalty, and industry were, after all, the
virtues upon which Soviet success depended, the virtues which
not only enabled Communists to realize their good ideas but
protected them from their own foolhardiness by compensating
for bureaucratic folly and Stalinist brutality.

This is why the two books seem to run almost in opposite
directions. The first instills infectious activity; the second
invites meditation. One says "Do!"; the other, "Think!" *Virgin
Soil Upturned I* is didactic history; *Virgin Soil Upturned II* is a
"wisdom book" and a book of parables. One emphasizes that
aspect of socialist realism that demands the portrayal of reality in its revolutionary development; the other emphasizes
socialist realism's educational preoccupation.

Thus we may say that Sholokhov has followed the traditional pattern of development that characterizes so many
Russian writers: Gogol, Goncharov, Tolstoy, and Gorky all
went this way, though Tolstoy never lost the knack of telling a
tale. Even Turgenev and Dostoevski were afflicted with verbosity toward the end. Of the major writers, only Chekhov

saved himself—though perhaps this was an accident, depending on his refusal to move outside the short story form when he wrote fiction.

The two halves of Sholokhov's novel differ from each other; but we must not forget that both differ from Western novels, whether they are realistic, romantic, or symbolic, because Sholokhov's subject matter is different. In *Virgin Soil Upturned* the characters are not only Cossacks as in *The Quiet Don* but Soviet citizens involved in the creation of a new way of life. Critics who contend that great characters in literature transcend social and temporal limitations are partly mistaken because they forget that King Oedipus or Sir Gawain have very little in common with Robinson Crusoe or Willy Loman, no matter how "eternally human" all four may be. Just as capitalism brought new heroes to the fore, so socialism and Communism have "new men"; and their appearance in literature necessarily brings about qualitative changes. Lillo's *London Merchant* (1731) and Vishnevsky's *Optimistic Tragedy* (1934) may serve as samples representing the two types.

Virgin Soil Upturned is an instructive novel, each volume in its way, because it confronts a crisis at the very root of social life that arose in Soviet Russia during collectivization. This was the Big Revolution. By comparison, 1917 was a textbook case, albeit catastrophic. 1917 was, in a sense, a radical administrative rearrangement. Communists, like their revolutionary forebears for over a century, tore off the aristocrats' epaulets and snatched the bourgeoisie's purses. The ensuing howl was ear-shattering but predictable and anticipated. But in 1927—actually in 1930 when they implemented the policy of liquidating kulaks as a class—Communists put their hands on every man's groceries. Even an aristocrat can go on living without his epaulets; even a businessman can survive without his wallet; but who can live when the ruler walks into the very fields of the land proclaiming that every grain of wheat, every egg, every suckling pig is mine? To be sure, he never says "Mine," always "Ours." But to believe requires that one ignore an immediate constriction of the belly which fears hunger, and that one consciously, rationally acquiesce to an ideal of equity represented by the ruling party.

This is the crux. This is what precipitates the "women's insurrection" in *Virgin Soil Upturned I*, Chapter 31—which echoes a similar event in the French Revolution. This is what provokes Nagulnov's tempestuous indignation at Bannik (Vol. I, Chap. 24) when he declines to bring his grain to the collective. When Nagulnov asks why not, Bannik answers:

"Because it will be safer with me. If I give it to you, there won't even be the empty sacks left in the spring. We're getting learned, too, you can't fool us."

"How can you distrust the Soviets? You mean you don't believe us?"

"Believe you! We've heard enough lies from you and your kind!"

"Who lied to you? What about?" Nagulnov paled visibly and rose slowly from his chair.

Bannik appeared not to notice the effect of his words and went on smiling quietly, showing his strong uneven teeth, but there was resentment and bitter rage in his voice when he said, "You'll gather in our grain, then send it away in ships to foreign countries, won't you? You want to buy them motorcars for your Party members to go joyriding in with their bob-haired women? We know what you want our grain for! That's your equality!"

"You're out of your mind! What are you blathering about?"

. . . Bannik went to the door but the hatred that blazed up in him was so fierce that he could not restrain himself, and as he gripped the doorhandle, he threw over his shoulder: "As soon as I get home I'll throw that grain to the pigs. I'd rather they gobbled it up than you, you spongers!"

"Seed? For the pigs!" Nagulnov reached the door in a bound, pulled out his revolver and struck Bannik on the temple with the butt.

That Bannik was right in spirit, if not the letter, because he sensed the possibility of duplicity which Stalinism soon substantiated is beside the point. The important thing is that without faith in the Party's good will, nothing works. Nagulnov has faith and, hence, cannot tolerate the lack of it in others. The process of rooting out his own previous affection for property and acquiring the new faith was so traumatic that he is subject to epileptic seizures. His is the lucidity of a fanatic, which disqualifies him as a good example of the "new man." Indeed, even the nominal hero of the novel, Davydov, fails. Recent Soviet critics, in their attempt to foster a Sholokhov cult,[6] often overpraise Davydov, forgetting V. Goffenshefer's apt query in 1936 that although Davydov is excellent as an ideal Bolshevik and admirably fitted for his job,

> can you say, with your hand on your heart, that, with all honor to Sholokhov's talent, Davydov is for us the absolute ideal of the new man, the ideal toward which not only . . . the Party worker sent into the country is striving, but also the scholar, the engineer, the educator, etc.? Of course not. The same can be said of Kataev's Margulies, the "professional" ideal of the engineer. . . .[7]

Even Davydov falls short. For one thing, he, like Nagulov, carries with him too many scars from the old world. In Volume II Sholokhov branded Davydov with an "obscene tattoo," excellent symbol of old disgrace which shames its wearer. Only the pure in heart *and* body will be admitted into the Red paradise. Thus, the "new men" of the transitional stage between old and new give their very lives that others may enter the scarlet gate. For Varya Kharlamova's sake, Davydov and Nagulnov must be sacrificed—indeed willingly, perhaps foolishly, sacrifice themselves, realizing that, unclean as they are, they at least make good stepping stones.

This "new man," however imperfect, is as different from the middle-class hero or, more recently, the romantic intellectual hero as they are from the aristocratic hero of antiquity or the Middle Ages. All are men, to be sure, but between them

lie the turned pages of history—the record of illusions about
men that actually determine the men themselves. This is why
Marxist critics such as Lukacs and Fischer argue for the superiority—historically speaking—of socialist realism, though this
confers no automatic success on any individual socialist-realist
work. If one believes in human progress, then he must say that
each age in some way surpasses those before—even when, as
in the Soviet Union after 1917, the general cultural level declined. *Virgin Soil Upturned* purports to speak for a surpassing
generation, though between its two volumes falls a shadow
of doubt—a shadow so dark that Sholokhov's attempt to dispel
it with "bright" episodes of young love, devotion to principle,
and humor often seem counterfeit. To substitute sentimentality
for sense forfeits both authenticity and conviction. It casts
doubt on the very possibility of "new men" and justifies any
critic's disregard for Davydov and other major "heroes."

The crucial character in *Virgin Soil Upturned*, as Soviet critics
note almost without exception, is a man who occupies relatively few pages: Kondrat Khristoforovich Maidannikov. What
makes him attractive is not only that he is an effective instrument for propaganda (this the Communist critic likes) but
that he alone seems to possess a mind complex enough to
warrant analysis. Other characters in the book are firmly
drawn but, to my mind, wholly self-explanatory. One could
follow the lead of Soviet critics and trace the lines of temperament or political conviction that distinguish each member of
the Party nucleus or the counterrevolutionary group. But this
is tedious.

The major Communist figure, Davydov, has been a favorite with Soviet school teachers for over thirty years as exhibit
A of the new Soviet man. He represents all the qualities that
Soviet citizens are supposed to esteem. Or at least he did until
recently when the surge of interest in culture brought about
by prosperity has made urban Russians want to sweat less

profusely than Davydov does and to have better table manners. Many find him intellectually unstimulating. But his moral equipment remains a model for the young, who are often required to catalog his virtues on examinations.

What are the characteristics that have made Davydov one of the great pedagogical instruments in the Soviet Union? First of all, he is rank-and-file proletarian. A sigh of relief blew through Soviet criticism in 1932 when Sholokhov gave readers an alternative to his customary heroes from the land, men as vacillating and unreliable as steppe weather. Here was a character with machine grease on his hands, not mud and manure. His timepiece was the factory whistle, not the rooster. Moreover, he belonged to the aristocracy of the Soviet working class because the Party had conscripted him into the ranks of the twenty-five thousand factory hands who were sent into the country to lead the offensive for collectivization. These men constituted a proletarian Society of Jesus or Home Mission Society whose gospel was Stalin's sermons, and they were as severe with unregenerate Russians as Christian missionaries often are with heathens.

An ordained shepherd of the people, Davydov was obviously designed to combat heresies of every description: he restrains the Communist mystic, admonishes the careerist, and goads the laggard. But this is only his official business. It says nothing of those personal qualities that make him a credible human being. Beyond his official duties and his pure Marxist pedigree, he has interesting virtues and vices that set him apart from the Party heroes of most Five-Year-Plan novels.

His seminal virtue is not doctrinal orthodoxy, but simplicity. Western readers may attach little value to this quality, but for Russians it often seems basic. The highest compliment they can pay a man is to call him "simple" (*prostoi*), probably because simplicity means candor, directness, and honesty. Its antonym is not "complex," but "deceitful" or "dishonest"— precisely the vices that Russians often attribute to Communist Party behavior and procedures.

Davydov is a simple man. He loves life and considers it inseparable from work. "Work equals life" is the simple equa-

tion that explains the man. Indeed, it explains most of the
novel's characters. Davydov adds the proletarian dimension to
an environment already saturated with work. This explains
why the line blurs between working with tools in a factory,
trudging behind a plow, declaiming to collective farmers, or
making love to a woman. All action is labor. Even the mind
toils in thought so that the thinker groans and sweats with
effort.

As always, Sholokhov champions labor with a zeal exceed-
ing Carlyle's. Sholokhov's man is a fierce-handed creature
whose life is physical struggle with environment. He seizes
objects in nature (handfuls of earth, fish, women) even "mental objects" (ideas, dreams) as if he were a titanic potter
forming and firing elemental clay for his own use. With his
prodigious vitality and strength, he seems almost to cancel
death because he is plural rather than singular. One of the
striking qualities of *Virgin Soil Upturned* is that Sholokhov
creates characters with distinctive personalities who at the
same time remain half submerged in the mass-man who
spawned them. Davydov is all twenty-five thousand shock-
workers—and their fathers and children as well. He is selfless,
literally. One feels that the Sholokhovian man, with his raised
fist and his eyes searching the sky, grows fur on his shoulders,
scales round his waist, and bark from there down to his earth
and granite-rooted feet. Doubtless Sholokhov would deplore
the inhumanity of such an image, yet his characters conjure it
up once they lose their Cossack identity and turn exclusively
to scratching the soil. Even urban Davydov degenerates from
machine operator to ploughman, while the Cossack remnant
stoops to outright degeneracy.

Because of his simplicity, Davydov has only the slightest
understanding of the cultural and economic implications of the
events in which he participates. He senses no contradiction
between compliance with Party directives and the exercise of
his own initiative. Part of his appeal to Soviet readers rests on
his independence. He seems to enjoy all the freedom of action
that any responsible citizen could desire. He can do almost
anything he wishes—to make collectivism work. That his will

and intellect limit his wishes is beside the point. Within his *capacity* for action, he can act freely. Thus, he emerges with his integrity intact, and readers respect him.

Having equipped him with a rudimentary faith in Marxism, Sholokhov cannot permit him to raise moral questions about dekulakization or sophisticated economic questions about per capita productivity. These would violate his simplicity and destroy his consistency as a character. To exhibit defects in his character, Sholokhov can only devise flaws that result from an excess of his chief virtue, simplicity. He can be gulled. His love for life makes him vulnerable to seduction by Lukerya Nagulnova, who is a counterfeit symbol of fertility. His love for work enables Ostrovnov to impress him as an energetic and efficient agronomist. But Ostrovnov too is counterfeit. Davydov's love for Communism, which he believes unifies work and life, remains steadfast because he cannot see that, from Stalin's mint, it too may be counterfeit.

As a workman with Marxist convictions, he must be tough, tenacious, and unyielding. As a person who loves life, he must be flexible, adaptable, and accessible to tenderness. Put the two together, and we have not a paradoxical or contradictory man but a credible Communist. Move him into a rural setting, and he liquidates "class enemies" ruthlessly or justifies the starvation of prosperous farmers by the irrelevant argument that capitalism had driven his mother to prostitution (Vol. I, Chap. 8). On the other hand, young people attract him, and the very process of generation fills him with emotion. When he scratched up a wheat shoot, he "experienced a bitter feeling of pity for the millions of seeds buried in the earth, so painfully reaching up towards the sun, and almost certainly doomed to die. The knowledge of his helplessness maddened him" (Vol. I, Chap. 37). As in Sholokhov's earliest stories, the sense of dissolution within a natural process can lead all too easily to loathing for human beings who inhibit it.

The two sides of Davydov's personality are unified, not divided, when his mind steps in between. He uproots noxious kulak weeds and plants healthy Communist seed. It never

occurs to him that tares may accompany his precious grain—
that Stalin's collectivization may be totally mistaken.

Sholokhov does not elaborate the gravest defects of all:
Davydov's rashness and ignorance of farming. To be sure, he
writes parables for Arzhanov and Shaly warning against headlong measures. But he does not explain the implications of
Davydov's death, perhaps because it illustrates too clearly
what happens when love for work and love for life collide.
Davydov hurls himself into the task of liquidating enemies
with an enthusiasm that can be considered suicidal. He loses
his life precisely because of excessive devotion to revolutionary
work.

As for Davydov's ignorance of farming, Sholokhov was in
no position to tell the entire story. No Soviet writer between
1930 and 1960 dared to hint that Communists have never
learned to operate a rural economy. Post-Krushchevian revisions in agricultural policy, the visible failure of collectivization in Eastern European nations, and the extraordinary fact
that after more than thirty years of collectivization the Soviet
Union still imports grain from abroad all testify to Communist
ineptitude. Sholokhov could not say so. He probably did not
believe it in the thirties and, like other Communists, could
discover no viable alternative in the sixties short of total de-
centralization. This is one reason why Volume II of *Virgin Soil
Upturned* seems uncertain by comparison with Volume I.

A dead Davydov remains heroic, a man of integrity and
devotion. A living Davydov could have been no more than
another bungling, collective-farm chairman, like ten thousand
others in Russia. This explains both his inadequacies as a
human being and as spokesman for an ideology. He is a candidate for failure, but death saves him and seems to validate the
worth of his simplicity. His ideology supplies ready answers for
all important questions and, thus, inhibits thought.

This is why he is much less interesting than Maidannikov,
who occupies far fewer pages. Symptomatically, Davydov is
a fair man who arrives on the scene in daylight, whereas
Machiavellian Polovtsiev is dark and comes by night. Both of
them obviate commentary, however prominent their roles in

the novel. Volatile Nagulnov, Maidannikov's sole competitor in complexity, attracts because of his temperament rather than thoughtfulness—unless we wish to consider as "thought" his conclusion that women are the opium of the people.[8]

The villain Ostrovnov has appealed to many Soviet critics because his involuntary pride in large-scale agricultural methods and the achievements of collectivism counters his hatred for the Soviet system. He suffers an intriguing—and human— ambivalence. Thus, he is Maidannikov's foil, lacking only the latter's faith. Unlike Maidannikov, however, Ostrovnov seems a little synthetic, his inner division too neatly black and white, his dreams made to order.

Closely associated with Maidannikov at the novel's calamitous conclusion is Andrei Razmyotnov, the local Party chairman, whom Sholokhov, as Soviet critics justly claim, regards most highly. Like Maidannikov, he is the steadfast, middling man—the mediator, according to Arzhanov's fable, who trots patiently along between galloping Party leaders and the plodding people. Even structurally he functions as a median. He is a widower inhibited from marriage by the memory of his beloved first wife rather than by the indifference of Davydov or the misogamy of Nagulnov. He establishes a temporary pseudomarriage with Marina Poyarkova but separates from her at once when she becomes religious. Before he discovers an appropriate woman at the end of the novel, he plays guardian to a pair of nesting pigeons and in his zeal for conjugal success threatens the community's cat population with extinction. No images could reinforce more strongly his role of defender of the family than the honor he shows his mother (Ostrovnov, by contrast, murders his) or the visits he makes to his wife's untended grave. Then, too, he has a saving innocence. Free from both the fanatical zeal of his Party peers and the intemperate hatred of their enemies, he has to be taught a lesson in class intransigence by Davydov (Vol. I, Chap. 9) and a lesson in the efficacy of brutality to uncooperative peasants by Nagulnov (Vol. I, Chap. 24). Yet, he remains pure in heart, preferring to trust rather than suspect his fellows, so that villainous Ostrovnov consistently dupes him. Like

Maidannikov, therefore, he endures. He pursues his quiet way, resigned to suffering because his faith enables him to accept pain as the result of his own fallibility or the product of revolution's harsh necessity. He, along with Maidannikov, is the guarantor of a brighter future; he buys his people a tractor engine and insists on a good education for Varya.

Maidannikov differs from other main characters because he not only thinks a great deal but changes as a result of his thoughts. While for others the realization that life is complicated comes as a surprise, for him life has for a long time been a "fishnet" that he has struggled to untangle.

Yet, the reader feels dissatisfied with Maidannikov—and with Sholokhov for overlooking or ignoring him. One wants to know more; one needs to know more; indeed, after so many suggestions that there is more to Maidannikov than meets the eye and after so many hints at another world in which he has lived physically and mentally, one is perhaps vexed with the author for leaving too much unsaid. For example, we first meet Maidannikov walking toward a platform to address his fellow peasants who shout:

> "Going to read your speech?" Dyomka Ushakov asked grinning.
> "Take your hat off!"
> "Say it by heart!"
> "The fellow writes his whole life down on paper."
> "Educated, eh!"
> Maidannikov pulled out a greasy notebook and thumbed hurriedly through the scribbled pages (Vol. I, Chap. 9).

Interest is aroused. Where did the greasy notebook come from? How and when did Maidannikov come to use it? What is so amusing about him? But these questions are never answered satisfactorily.

More important, we learn that Maidannikov had been religious in his childhood; he had once fallen "on his knees before the dark icon of the Old Believers and, saying a prayer, dried his eyes as dry as he could so that the angry God should not see a single tear." Yet, we later find that "Kondrat [Maidannikov] had long since ceased to believe in God, and now he believed in the Communist Party." What torments must Kondrat have endured, what a rending must there have been of the "fishnet" which was his life? Of this, however, we learn nothing.

We see him at a time in his life when all conflicts have, on the surface at least, been resolved save one. One strand only of the old fishnet still confounds him. Having picked his way through the mesh of religion which his mother taught, Kondrat has come at last to confront the barrier which seems to bar him from a better life, the barrier that he calls "property" ("I'm sick with a longing for my property") but which we would call the acquisitive instinct, realizing that this is the complex abstraction for which Maidannikov's simpler and more concrete "property" must stand. In fact, "property" comes to mean not only acquisition but a way of life and an attitude toward it.

Reason has carried him this far. Reason and his greasy little notebook ("I write down what I feed on," he says with unconscious ambiguity) have conspired in a deft calculation: working hands plus worked land equals a quantity of grain; subtract seed, food for the hands and livestock, and the state grain-tax; then subtract boots and clothes, paraffin, matches and soap. The remainder is about zero. "And that's taking a good year, when the harvest is all right. But suppose there's no harvest at all? What am I then? A helpless old man!" That he cannot go on this way is eminently reasonable, all objections to the new way of life, to collectivism, notwithstanding. Thus, he tells his opponents, "You don't think enough about your life . . . ," implying that they think too much of their *illusions* about life, that prejudice and custom supplant reason. ". . . You can't see anything but your own cow and your coopy little farm. It may be rotten, but it's my own, you think."

Maidannikov says this, believes this, yet he too is infected with the poison. His ox with its lilac eyes has filled a place in his mind and satisfied some inarticulate longing. Remembering the worry and labor which he had devoted to this animal

from the time of its birth and remembering almost with gratitude the ox's service, the alleviation of poverty which it brought
his family, Maidannikov looked at the ox and burst into tears
the evening before he delivered it to the collective stable. That
night he lay awake and thought: ". . . you must crush that
mean petty feeling of regret for your own property, and not
let it worm its way into your heart."

Before dawn he fell into a doze. Even in sleep he
felt sad and ill at ease. Collective farming did not come
easy to Kondrat. With tears and blood he tore apart the
belly-cord that bound him to his property, his oxen, his
scrap of land . . . (Vol. I, Chap. 10).

The ox goes. Maidannikov joins the collective, saying in
his stilted application, "*I ask you to be allowed into the new
life, as I am in full agreement with it.*" But agreement is not
so simple. The new life has its troubles too. Seven collectivized
chickens die from overcrowding in the inadequate coops, and
Maidannikov wishes there might be at least one cock in each
individual yard to serve instead of a clock. Each man, when
his turn comes to watch over the stables, tries to give his own
stock better hay; "they all take root by their own horses and
never care for anyone else's." Each complains against the
handling of his own stock by the others. "Ha, you want more
than all the rest of us" is heard on every side. Moreover,
Maidannikov feels impelled to leave his hut whenever possible
"to avoid the sight of the terribly deserted yard and to avoid
his wife's afflicted reproachful eyes." His daughter has no
shoes and must spend the winter on the stove.

What is it that drives a man to suffer these things? Why
does Maidannikov remain in the collective when even Diemid
the Silent, a poor peasant, withdraws? These are difficult
questions to answer because during the crucial weeks between
Maidannikov's entry into the collective and sowing time, he
vanishes from the story. This is the hard time when everything
seems to go wrong. Ostrovnov deliberately injures the farm's
cattle; Nagulnov discredits the collective when he high-hand-

edly administers a beating to one of the men for not delivering
the grain quota; fearing their precious seed-grain will be given
to another farm, a group of peasants revolts, breaks open the
granary, and thrashes Davydov unmercifully. During the third
week of March over a hundred individual farm units withdraw
from the collective. But of Maidannikov we hear no word until
he turns up in the fields plowing, as if nothing out of the
ordinary had happened.

We can, however, infer certain things about his motivation.
Heritage is important. His mother was an "Old Believer," and
it is probably fair to ascribe intense conviction and a strong
inclination toward communal life as major characteristics of all
Old Believers, since persecution was their lot for generations.
Faith was their source of energy as community life was their
instrument for resisting an alien world. Life seems to Maidannikov to provide no alternative to the collective farm if he
is to improve his lot. The tallies in his notebook tell him so.
Moreover, he has something of the martyr in him. Suffering
for his new-found faith supplies a kind of pleasure; it sets him
off from, or above, those people in the world who have not
suffered enough and who have, consequently, neither learned
to share his faith nor sympathize with him and sustain him in
his sorrow. He looks jubilantly to the day when, having
achieved his victory and vindicated the collective, he can go
forth expostulating with the wayward laggards:

> Kondrat thinks of the need the country is suffering while
> it carries out the five-year plan, and clenches his fists
> under the sackcloth blankets and with hatred addresses
> his thoughts to the workers in the West who do not sup-
> port the Communists, "You've sold us for good wages
> from your bosses! You've betrayed us, brothers, for an
> easy life! And why is it you still haven't got Soviet power
> in your countries? Why are you lagging behind? If you got
> down to it, you could have had a revolution by now, but
> you keep hanging about and can't get started, and some-
> how you're out of step and don't know where you're going.
> Or can't you see across the frontier how hard it is for us

to build up our country? What poverty we suffer, going
about barefoot and half naked. But we grit our teeth and
work. You'll feel ashamed, brothers, to have had everything done for you! I wish I could make a great tall post
for you all to see, then I'd climb up on top of that post
and I'd tell you a thing or two, that I would!" (Vol. I,
Chap. 19.)

Finally, it is clear that Maidannikov loves productive,
efficient work. "He was in favor of only those who worked
being allowed to eat and walk the earth." And he seems to
believe, though this is not explicit, that large-scale planning
and strict management, which are visible ideals of the collective farm, are essential to productive work. It is rational, like
Maidannikov's meticulous bookkeeping or his exposition of the
techniques of plowing. He has more in common with the efficient kulak, Ostrovnov, than Soviet critics like to admit.

These evidently are the reasons why he remains steadfast.
Unlike Lyubishkin's faith, however, Maidannikov's is not un-
critical. He has little patience with absolute equality or with
cooperation in all endeavors. For example, he is dissatisfied
with "collective plowing" because everything depends on the
speed of the front plow. When it stops, all the others stop
too (Vol. I, Chap. 36).

In Chapter 9 he acknowledges the impossibility of yoking
a strong ox with a weak one, which is what collectivism
threatened to do. Yet, he has no answer to the asperity and
turbulence that characterize personal relationships within the
collective except the refrain: "It's all come from the struggle
we've had to get property." He is even less well prepared to
meet advocates of individualism than Nagulnov, who at least
has his towering righteous rages to fall back on. When a man
jocularly asks, "Will the cocks go on fighting under socialism or
won't they?" Nagulnov explodes into insults and threats that
may abash questioners but never convince them. Under similar
provocation, the best that Maidannikov can do is to advise
those who wish to remain outside the collective not to interfere
with those willing to enter. Only when danger to his ideal takes

a visible form (Atamanchukov's perverse and obviously criminal attempt to disable the bullocks by plowing in the rain)
does he find a resolute and effective defense.

We come to the view, therefore, that while Maidannikov
may have abandoned the old life on reasonable grounds, he
accepts the new largely on faith. Insofar as Maidannikov banks
on the collective as a sound economic investment, he is rational; but his feeling for the collective is clearly based on
more than economics. His criticism of certain experiments
with collectivism in no way indicates that his attachment to
the collective is very reasonable or analytical. He is as prone
to influence by the outward signs and symbols of his ideal as
his mother doubtless was by the iconostasis:

> Nine hundred miles distant from Gremyachy Log, stone-
> bound Moscow also has its night life. Engine whistles call
> out loud and long, motor horns sound like the chords of a
> huge accordion, tramcars clang. And behind the tomb of
> Lenin, behind the Kremlin wall, borne up on a cold blus-
> tering wind, a red flag flutters in the glowing sky. Lighted
> from below by the white glare of electric light, it blazes
> and streams like flowing scarlet blood. Its heavy folds
> droop for a minute and then the strong wind lifts it and
> whirls it about, and again it flutters and flaps, pointing
> now west, now east, blazing with the purple flame of
> rebellion, and summoning to the struggle. . . .
>
> Two years ago Kondrat Maidannikov, who was in
> Moscow for the All-Russian Congress of Soviets, walked
> into Red Square. He looked at Lenin's tomb, at the red
> flag gleaming triumphantly in the sky, and hurriedly
> pulled off his old cavalry cap. His head bare, his home-
> spun farmer's coat flung open, he stood for a long time,
> motionless and silent (Vol. I, Chap. 19).

No longer a farmer with tallies in his notebook, Maidannikov here is a peasant in holy Moscow substituting the Soviet
flag for the sacred relics or saintly mummies of Russian religion. Much of what he was predisposed by his youthful en-

vironment to accept, he has kept, transferring his allegiance between symbols whose substance is essentially similar. The hammer and sickle seem to promise more immediate relief from life's hopelessness than the cross.

But actually, the problems inherent in the society Maidannikov knew as a child have simply been transposed into the society in which he lives as an adult. So little has his struggle with the fishnet of life availed him that when finally he has untangled much of it, in the very center remains a hopeless snarl. Just as earlier his typical Cossack impulse to assert himself had resulted in a reasoned rejection of those things which stood in his way (for example, religion with its emphasis on humility) and in a less-reasoned acceptance of the Communist creed, partly at least because it appeared to be an instrument for further self-assertion against the old life; and just as earlier the rejection of the Old Believers' God must have entailed expulsion from the communal group and must therefore have pained Maidannikov, who clearly longs for identity within the community; so the very pattern of self-assertion and rejection of the group which his life had taken formerly now continues to function under new conditions which have ironically revived features of the old. Insofar as Communism is identified with Maidannikov's personal emancipation, he can worship at its scarlet shrines as if they were a substitute god. However, let it make the slightest claim on him, one that acts as a limitation, that circumscribes his mind, and he resists automatically. Experience and his notebook taught him to resist the old gods; he did and became lonely. Now experience dictates restraint toward the new gods, and again he is lonely.

Maidannikov's emotional attachment to his property, his obsessive "mine" rather than "ours," is not an accidental defect in his character generated solely by the struggle to acquire goods or to improve his family's fortune; it too is part of his heritage. His father was a Don Cossack, a member of that unique and privileged caste which delighted in its delusions of independence, which fostered a raw, competitive individualism, and which served proudly and loyally as the czar's repressive fist. In 1905 when his "father had been serving as a conscript, his company had knouted and sabred the striking weavers of Ivanovo-Voznesensk and had defended the mill-owners' interests." Except for this, we are told nothing about the father. But we do not need to know more. Put simply, he is the violent, virile Cossack.

His wife, Maidannikov's mother, not only disapproves violence but insists that even tears are coercive and offensive in the eyes of God, Who

> ". . . has told the poor to be patient. And now He will get angry that the poor keep crying and crying and He will gather up all their tears and make them into a mist and cast it over the blue seas and hide the sky. And then the ships will lose their way across the water and one of them will strike a hidden rock in the sea and sink. Or God will make the dew of tears. And one night that salty dew will fall on the corn over all the land, near and far, and the bitter salt will burn up the grain and a great hunger and famine will strike the world. So if you are poor you must never cry, or you will cry down trouble on your own head" (Vol. I, Chap. 19).

But the Cossack heritage is almost as strong in Maidannikov as the Christian. On the one side, there are individual achievement, acquisition, pride, property; on the other, abnegation, unselfishness, community. These are the ingredients which Maidannikov must somehow mix together if he is to have any sense of completeness. Simply to disregard some element of his personality in order to effect a comfortable reconciliation with life is hardly suitable for one so honest. And by the end of the first part of *Virgin Soil Upturned*, he is not completely reconciled.

When Nagulnov asks him why he has not joined the Party, he says:

> "No, Comrade Nagulnov, my conscience wouldn't let me join the Party just now. I'd go and fight for Soviet power again and I'll work well in the collective farm, but I can't join the Party."

"But why?" Makar said with a frown.

"Well, you see, though I'm in the collective farm now, I still miss my property." Kondrat's lips trembled and he broke into a rapid whisper, "I'm eating my heart out over my oxen and I'm sorry for them. They don't get the care they should. Akim Beskhlebnov rubbed my horse's neck with the yoke when he had it in a cart, I saw the mark and couldn't eat the whole day afterwards. . . . Fancy putting a great yoke like that on a small horse? And that's why I can't join. If I still haven't turned my back on property, that means my conscience won't let me be in the Party. That's how I look at it" (Vol. I, Chap. 37).

"Mine" still takes precedence over "ours." Only experience can teach him, only when life itself makes clear the collective's superiority, as it must once have made clear the inadequacy of his mother's creed, can Maidannikov overcome his longing for property.

Little wonder, then, that he accepts Nagulnov's verdict: ". . . don't join yet. We'll fight mercilessly against all shortcomings in the collective farm. All the yokes will be made to fit." If your dreams, your subconscious, are not pure, the sacrosanct portals must not be entered; but this impurity will be washed away when the farm succeeds. Maidannikov's problem is how to take, or perhaps justify, the final step.

In *Virgin Soil Upturned II* he takes the step immediately after the amusing scene when Davydov, instead of provoking the women to revolt again by his inflexibility as in Volume I, conciliates them by allowing them to attend Mass. It is one of the great lessons about the need for Communists to have faith in the people, to accede to their demands at times. Only then does Maidannikov join—acting, as his wife says, "like a girl before her wedding."

The story of the meeting (Chapters 22-23) at which Kondrat Maidannikov's application for membership is accepted is one of the funniest and at the same time most incisive in the Sholokhov canon. Enthusiastically endorsed by the Party nucleus, Maidannikov will indubitably be admitted; but suddenly old Shchukar avails himself of his right to object. In his own inimitable style, he asserts first that Maidannikov is no saint, to which Nagulnov retorts, "We're not accepting Kondrat into paradise, but into the Party." Then Shchukar comes to his point:

> "I've read a lot of these here booklets and I know for sure, and I'm ready to argue with anyone about it, that after socialism the next thing to come will be communism, and I tell you that categorically! And that's where I have my doubts, Kondrat my boy. You entered socialism sheddin' tears all over the place, so how are you goin' to enter communism? You'll be wading in tears as sure as God's holy! That's what'll happen to you, and I can see it now! So I ask you, citizens and dear old women, what good will he be to us in the Party, a tear-shedder like him?
> ". . . I can't stand all these serious folk, can't bear 'em, and certainly not in the Party! What bloomin' use are all these gloomy-guts to us? Just to give all good folk the hump, to break and ruin the Party rules with their long faces? . . . I tell you we ought to take cheerful, lively people into the Party like me, but instead they keep on rakin' in all the serious kind. . . . There's Makar [Nagulnov] for instance! Ever since he straightened up as if he'd swallowed a steel rule back in 1918, he's been goin' around as serious and stuck up as a crane in a marsh. You never hear a joke or funny story out of him, he's just a great big chunk of solid gloom dressed up in trousers, that's what he is!" (Vol. II, Chap. 22.)

Uncle Shchukar's language is amusing, but the truth he utters is as old as Communism, indeed as old as revolution itself: the revolutionary, from Savonarola and Cromwell to Robespierre and Paine, is a grim-faced inquisitor whose ultimate success depends on his ability to restore the human balance in himself as soon after the necessary fanaticism of Terror as possible.

Sholokhov's answer to the thin-lips is the same in this

scene as it was in *The Quiet Don* when he made Grigory's young sister the one person both able and deserving to enter the new life. Maidannikov's first defender is his oxen driver, virginal Varya Kharlamova. Significantly, the meeting ends with Davydov's proposal to establish a creche and kindergarten in order to free women for equal participation in building the new life. Thus, old Shchukar's humorous artistry and the apolitical vitality of women become an indispensable counter-balance to the masculine will and reason of Communism. With equilibrium restored, Maidannikov not only enters the Party but becomes the new chairman when Nagulnov and Davydov stupidly throw their lives away.

We may justly complain that Kondrat Maidannikov is inadequately portrayed or perhaps that his potentialities as a fictional character and social symbol are inadequately realized. His importance rests, however, on his active participation, apprehensions notwithstanding, in the life of the brave new world—which turns out to be very brave but not very new. Troubled by what he sees around him and what he feels within, he is at least unobsessed and undiseased, the product of sanity and maturity, not frustration or spite as are so many contemporary figures. He could be a character in Huxley's *Island*, except that his experience is "real," not theoretical. *Virgin Soil Upturned* is one of the finest studies of agricultural collectivism under the Communist system. And Kondrat Maidannikov is the central figure, the common man, the symbol of the mass, honestly searching for a better life but withholding total allegiance until a reciprocity is achieved between the leaders and the led.

———————

If it is true that Sholokhov revised his attitude toward Communism and began to recognize greater complexity in human motivation and behavior by the middle thirties, as is indicated by the textual evolution of *The Quiet Don*, then in the second volume of *Virgin Soil Upturned* the new attitude and the increased perception should be evident. They are. Unfortunately, however, Sholokhov avoided situations which would have forced him to explain both how mistaken and how vicious the Party became during the purges. Instead of carrying his narrative up to 1931 or 1932, as he first said he would, he terminates it in the autumn of 1930, thus avoiding the later periods of collectivization which wrought far worse tribulations upon the people and upon him personally than did the first year. Winter is coming and the end of *Virgin Soil Upturned II* is far from optimistic. It bears out his prediction in 1955:

> The content of the second book is the cruel struggle of two worlds—darkness and light. In essence, this is the last skirmish in the great battle of "who wins?" It will answer the question posed already in the Don tales. In this skirmish even our side was not without victims. But the new wins out, wins the collective system, socialism. One thing I can firmly say—the finale will be dramatic; there will be victims. The times were severe; the struggle led not only to life but to death, and there were no few victims.[9]

The exuberance of the chapters devoted to the collective-farm meeting when Maidannikov and others were inducted into the Party and when even grim-faced Nagulnov beamed smiles on everyone vanishes, replaced not merely by sadness or pessimism but by something worse: the curious pain of the final three chapters depends on the perfunctory dispatch with which Sholokhov rounds off his story. Razmyotnov's wedding in Chapter 27 is a cheerless, utilitarian affair, reminiscent of Koshevoi's with Dunya Melekhova. In Chapter 28, on the Monday of the final calamity an east wind blows. Old Agei drops dead from a stroke; Kuznetsov's wife shrieks through the difficult delivery of a son; the Abramov family announces a shotgun wedding; a former Imperial Army officer turns up to instigate revolt; and Uncle Shchukar's partner, the goat Trofim, falls down a well and drowns. "That was the last incident in a day filled with great and petty events," writes Sholokhov at the end of the chapter, as if he had just added 1 + 1 + 1 + 1. . . .

But this is not quite the end of the story. Nagulnov and Davydov thoughtlessly throw their lives away. Reputed to be shrewd veterans and seasoned Communists, they rashly assault the enemy stronghold like a pair of boys waving cap pistols at a tank. Uncle Shchukar withers beside their graves; the murderers are captured; virginal Varya will continue her education supported by the local Party unit; beautiful Lukerya grows fat but thrives in Shakhti, safe at last from rural righteousness; and the book ends as "the last thunder of the year rolled overhead." Having bade his mangled heroes a personal farewell, Sholokhov dismisses them with *"vot i vsyo"*—"and that is all"—a sentence as crushing in its finality as Thackeray's gesture of slamming the lid on his puppet box at the end of *Vanity Fair*. With that sentence Sholokhov keeps himself in the company of writers who concede little to illusion and bear witness to *waste* as the ruling principle of reality—yet go on scratching the sand or carving ice. "To tell the novelist to stop writing novels," said Sholokhov, "is synonymous with telling the farmer to stop tilling fields." One hand craves the pencil, another the plow handle. The inertia in our very atoms speeds us on, however futile motion may seem, playing our cellular or atomic arithmetic and always contriving new equations. Even art, perhaps man's best way of stealing a little back from time, seems slightly futile, no matter how much passion the mind lavishes on it; and Sholokhov reminds us of this with his perfunctory conclusion. He shares the sense of waste and the sense of life that Tolstoy and Homer knew, so that Achilles' words to Priam in the last book of the *Iliad* might supply a just benediction: "Come then, we also, aged magnificent sir, must remember to eat. . . ."

I called *Virgin Soil Upturned II* a book of parables, and the parable is one of the writer's methods of equation-making. In *Virgin Soil Upturned*, Aesopian fables displace the Homeric similes of *The Quiet Don*. In addition to Naidyonnov's tales and the rooster allegory which began in Volume I, there is Arzhanov's description of his cherry-wood whip handle or his distinction between gallopers, trotters, and those who go step by step—that is, two kinds of Party men and the people. There

is the facetious but ominously pertinent attempt to silence
Shchukar by telling him that, since critics of Party decisions
must be disposed of, he can only choose whether to die by
bullet or ax. That amazing "Fordson tractor of a woman,"
Kupryanovna, walks sermons and laughs tracts on the irre-
pressible life-energy of the people that no dogma can long
contain. Like almost every character in Sholokhov's work, she
is an unreconstructable individualist.

More often than in *The Quiet Don* or *Virgin Soil Upturned I*, folkish language becomes the vehicle of parables that
convert easily into abstractions so that characters and events
lose their particularity. Unfortunately, in Sholokhov's hands,
this leads to fuzziness of conception and wooden moralizing.
For example, the blacksmith, Shaly, becomes too much the
deus ex machina, too much the conventional wiseman quietly
awaiting the right moment to step forward with the right
answers. Sholokhov avoided making him the stock-type old
Bolshevik so familiar in Soviet fiction, but he comes perilously
close. The villains too (at least the erstwhile White Guard
officers) are stock-types, less imitations from reality than ideological fabrications.

As usual, trouble begins at the moment when Sholokhov
consciously abandons things and deeds for ideas and essences.
His conscious transactions with universals remain disastrous,
even when, as in *Virgin Soil Upturned II*, his intention is precisely to discredit what he believes to be bad abstract thought
—for example, the dogmatism of Polyanitsa. One thing Sholokhov cannot do is debate issues; he can only portray them in
action. Although his rooster allegory is sprightly, the parable
of the whip handle goes awkwardly. This aesthetic fact about
Sholokhov's work has an interesting by-product. It refutes
the claim that his books are concocted according to Communist recipes, hence that they distort reality for propaganda's sake. Sholokhov cannot make good fiction this way,
even when he tries. He works his verbal magic most successfully when the words point, not up to ideas, but outward to
reality or back at themselves, as when Uncle Shchukar begins
using "educated words" such as *"agiotage"* (French for "finan-

cial speculation") which he defines as "to live and rejoice in
the wide world" because the second syllable is the Russian
root for "life" (*zhi*) and the rest is sheer sound, all the more
lovely for its ostentatious vowel prefix.

Virgin Soil Upturned remains a rural novel in which even
the most sensitive character, Maidannikov, is blind to any conflicts beyond the immediate collision between the individual
and the community. The world of *Virgin Soil Upturned* is a
world in which children and old men have still to walk en-
chanted alongside the first roaring tractor that will presently
come to the Don. Sholokhov's tractor-hymn in "Light and
Shadow" (1949) reveals that he is a belated adulator of the
machine. Apparently neither Maidannikov nor the author understands that even when Communism makes compromises
with the "scab of property" in order to preserve the middling
peasant's individual identity, greater forces than Communism
or love of property will cancel the bargain. Those forces are
industrialism, technology, and the increase of population. Together, these three transcend all political systems and mock
men's age-long quest for individuality.

Excellent passages notwithstanding, the general tendency of
Sholokhov's work since *The Quiet Don* demonstrates a diminu-
tion of energy which is fatal to the kind of art he cultivated.
The writer whose powers of invention are not of the highest
must expend enormous energy inspiring the base matter of
reality with life. Sholokhov may have described himself when
he said: "Talent, figuratively speaking, is 'God's spark.' Man is
born with it. But with little talent, persistent daily work is
necessary, sleepless nights, constant quests for form. Without
this, even a great talent may remain sterile. It often happens."[10]
When the quest for form fails, everything goes flat. There is
flatness in his unfinished novel about the Second World War;
and his story, "A Man's Fate," for all its humanity, approaches
the supine. Perhaps he has, as one critic predicted, exhausted

the "golden treasure" of youthful impressions. The cultural "thaw" came too late to save him.

So harsh a judgment comes reluctantly because, especially in "A Man's Fate," the burden of endured suffering, the celebration of heroism and the almost desperate affirmation of hope make one unwilling to condemn it for technical reasons. This is particularly true when one of the most learned and astute Soviet scholars, D. D. Blagoi, found in it a "balanced inverted symmetry" which Sholokhov had never excelled: "The boat leaves—the man and boy approach; the boat returns—the man and boy depart."[11] And within this frame we have the story of a man's setting forth into life and war and returning to peace but also nearing his own end—all of it set on a flooded spring day, at once dangerous and prematurely warm, perhaps signifying difficulties which his young companion must confront and overcome.

But no matter how complex and relevant the structure, "A Man's Fate" goes clumsily. It was conceived, apparently, as a polemic against Hemingway's *Old Man and the Sea*, which Sholokhov regards highly,[12] yet condemns because it emphasizes man's isolation.[13] The apparatus squeaks; the allegory is patent and ponderous. Most significantly, Sholokhov's return to the framing device and the first-person-singular narrative of some of his early stories betrays a want of confidence in the supreme epic voice that he perfected as narrator of *The Quiet Don*. No mature writer returns to his youthful experiments with impunity. If he succeeds, he has usually accomplished little; if he fails, the result is doubly grievous. Solzhenitsyn's *One Day in the Life of Ivan Denisovich,* not Sholokhov's "A Man's Fate," presages the future direction of Soviet literature.

Sholokhov became the greatest Soviet prose writer, but he paid—perhaps voluntarily—a high Soviet price for it. Not only his Cossack background but the revolutions of 1917 and 1930 supplied Sholokhov the *life,* the new experience, that is the initial ingredient for all great art. That was society's gift to him. But it was his own personal genius, his *artistic* gift, that transformed life and created actual works of art. Just as he witnessed the consequences of a "great cleavage" in the lives of his people, so he experienced a great cleavage within himself between the chaotic outer world registered by his senses, and an inner world conceived by imagination where order originates. His successful work, like all art, heals the rupture, makes the two worlds reciprocal. But both cleavages were too great; he could not sustain a balanced vision. This is why his life and work since the thirties seem filled with anger and uncertainty. He is a spiritual casualty of the very cleavages in modern life that he celebrated.

Appendix A:

Sholokhov's Career

The remarks about Sholokhov's life in Chapter 1 terminated with the time when he was firmly established as an apprentice story writer in Moscow. Even before his labor was rewarded in the form of published stories, he grew restive in the capital. It seems likely that Sholokhov's dissatisfaction with life in Moscow resulted primarily from his inability or unwillingness to adjust to the "intellectuals" with whom he associated. A large majority of "Octobrists" (many of whom became "On-guardists" and then members of the Russian Association of Proletarian Writers—RAPP) came not from working-class or peasant backgrounds, but the prerevolutionary intelligentsia. Sholokhov, like the American novelist William Faulkner, whose early career is comparable, apparently felt more comfortable among family and friends in his own region. Early photographs of him with a curved pipe propped meditatively between his teeth or in a karakul Cossack hat on his head look affected by comparison with those that show him standing in nondescript civilian clothes *beside* true Cossacks.

We may legitimately assume that he had certain members of the Muscovite intelligentsia in mind when he penned the curious preface to his story, "Azure Steppe," in July, 1926, expressing his exasperation and his impulse to inform Muscovite literati and sheltered urbanites of what he must have believed were the "hard cold facts-of-life":

163

In Moscow on Vozdvizhenka at one of MAPP's [Moscow Association of Proletarian Writers] literary meetings, one may quite unexpectedly learn that steppe feather-grass (and not simply feather-grass but "grey, feather grass") has an aroma all its own. Beyond this, one may hear how Red soldiers on the Don or Kuban steppe died choking themselves on high-sounding words. . . .

In reality feather-grass is a vile white grass. It is harmful and without any odor at all. One cannot herd sheep on it because they perish from the grass-beards which penetrate a sheep's skin. Over-grown with plantain and pigweed, the trenches (one may see them along the cattle paths by every *stanitsa*), silent observers of battles not long past, might tell how hideously and simply people died in them.[1]

These are words of a rural youth and a veteran of civil war, if not those of a worker. From both viewpoints, people who used "high-sounding words" probably seemed contemptible. If feather grass was to retain its charm, Sholokhov had, apparently, to return to the steppe where intellectuals could not sully with words the things of nature.

Another indication of Sholokhov's early distrust of intellectuals can be seen in a letter which he wrote to Mark Kolosov in May 1924:

Judging by your remark, everything is all right in my story "The Beast," apart from the title and ending. I had no chance to revise . . . but I think you can do it yourself (it's not difficult). Entitle the story "Regional Food Commissar Bodyagin" if you wish; cut the end up to the line where I describe the place where Tislenko and Bodyagin lie dead. You didn't understand the story's essence. I wanted to show that a man, having killed his father in the name of the Revolution and having been considered "beastly" (of course—in the eyes of the slobbering intelligentsia), will die in order to save a child. . . . That's what I wanted to show, but perhaps I haven't succeeded.[2]

Evidently Sholokhov's ironic title confused the editors; and the new title, "Food Commissar," has remained with the story ever since.

If these attitudes are at all symptomatic, as seems likely in view of Sholokhov's depiction of intellectuals in *The Quiet Don* and his personal antagonism toward them after the Second World War, then we can see why he never lost the ties with his home during the experiment with big-city life. The endless bickering and maneuvering in literary circles may well have irritated a man who wanted to write fiction, not haggle about aesthetics or politics. Unlike many Soviet writers who found their way to the capital and who plunged enthusiastically into cosmopolitan life, Sholokhov resisted the city. In the winter of 1923-24, he returned home briefly in order to wed Maria Petrovna and then, for their honeymoon, took her back to Moscow. But they remained only until May 24, 1924, Sholokhov's birthday, when they returned to the Don, settling first in Karginskaya, then Bukanovskaya, and finally Veshenskaya. "I wanted," he later said, "to write about the people among whom I was born and whom I knew." To do this, he felt he must remain on native ground. Like William Faulkner, Sholokhov derived his greatest inspiration from the regional muse.

Sholokhov's life was relatively uneventful from the time he returned home. During 1924 and 1925 he wrote most of his short stories, and he began *The Quiet Don* in October 1925, working at it more or less constantly until 1930, when he composed the first volume of *Virgin Soil Upturned*. He first rented a room beneath a blacksmith's shop, where he worked steadily. The neighbors inquired what the "young newcomer was doing, all closed up in there?" And village lads reported with perplexity to the inquisitive: "He sits alone, doesn't say anything, writes something, and smokes all the time."[3] Later, he worked in a room in his father-in-law's home where, according to his wife, he wrote for days and nights. "He would come out only for a few minutes to have a bite to eat. When he finally emerged his eyes would be feverish and he would move like a drunken man."[4]

Willi Bredel, the East German critic, has recorded more intimate details about this period of Sholokhov's life:

> He had to work under severe difficulties. Housing was short; friends and relatives pressed him after his name appeared in the papers and magazines. Material cares were often oppressive. But the worst was, as he said, the mockery and irony which was heaped upon him. Some called him dreamer or "spinner," some laughed at him; and even his father, who had provided the means for him to learn to love art, looked unwillingly on his occupation of literary work and he joked about his "scribblings."
>
> Inattentive to the jokes and despite all difficulties, Sholokhov went his way unerringly. He travelled again to Rostov and Moscow and worked in the archives there; he read much, improved his education, broadened his knowledge, travelled about through the towns of the Don region, collected folk songs, wrote out tales told by old Cossacks, and buried himself in newspapers from the czarist period.[5]

The six years from 1925 through 1930 were by far the most productive of Sholokhov's career. In addition to stories, he completed the first three volumes of *The Quiet Don*, a part of the fourth, and the first volume of *Virgin Soil Upturned*. But by 1930 he was involved in a serious controversy that very nearly ruined him and that, as we see now, did grave damage to the creative impulse which had sustained him up to that time.

In 1927, the first part of *The Quiet Don* was rejected by the editorial board of *Oktyabr* because it was a "chronicle . . . which lacked political pertinence." The rejected manuscript went finally to Serafimovich, an honorary editor, who insisted on publication without the radical abridgement that the board demanded. Publication ensued in 1928. But during that winter Sholokhov's reputation was damaged by a rumor that he had purloined the manuscript of his book from a dead White officer. On March 29, 1929, in *Pravda* Serafimovich, Averbach,

Kirshon, Fadeev, and Stavskii (the most prominent leaders of RAPP) repudiated the charge as calumny, but the slander did not stop.

Then trouble developed in another quarter. In the fall a certain Nikolai Prokofev published an article in a Rostov paper, *Bolshevistskaya smena (Bolshevik Generation)*, charging that Sholokhov was no better than Pilnyak, who was the Party's whipping-boy at the time, because he, like Pasternak thirty years later, had published a noncommittal novel, *Mahogany*, in Berlin before Soviet censors cleared it for publication inside the Soviet Union. Prokofev also charged that Sholokhov "stood aside from politics . . . , took no part at all in the life of society . . . ," and hid behind "the little shutters of his house." Further, he accused him of conniving with kulaks and interceding on their behalf by paying taxes for them and in one case by helping to restore a disenfranchised relative's voting right.

That there may be truth to some of these charges seems likely when we remember that Sholokhov's father-in-law opposed the regime and when we note that, as a writer, he needed isolation if he meant to produce. As it turned out, he had indeed aided his sister-in-law in obtaining the franchise, but only after she had broken all financial ties with her father. Sholokhov's accuser had twisted facts in order to fabricate a case against him.

Sholokhov answered him immediately (October 1929):

> . . . The author of the article "Creators of Pure Literature," N. Prokofev, accuses me of complicity with kulaks and anti-Soviet people, and by way of illustration, cites certain "facts." These accusations are false from start to finish. I consider it my duty to state that I agree fully and wholly with the policy of the Party and the Soviet government on the peasant question. I am firmly convinced that in the period of the reconstruction of the rural economy, pressure on kulaks who have held back grain surpluses is the only correct line. Just on the basis of this alone, I could not be a protector of kulak interests.

I categorically deny this unfounded, false accusation. I demand an investigation of the "facts" recited in N. Prokofev's article. . . .[6]

The following month the governing board of the North Caucasus Association of Proletarian Writers repudiated every charge against Sholokhov, and V. Ivanov, secretary of the regional Communist Party, reprimanded both Prokofev and the editor of *Bolshevistskaya smena.*[7]

Whether these attacks stemmed from personal animosity or doctrinaire Communist distrust of a writer who tried to be objective about Cossacks remains obscure. Prokofev's allegations seem personal, not to say contrived. Sholokhov's difficulties were not, however, confined to the Don area. In April 1929 S. S. Dinamov, editor of *Literaturnaya gazeta,* wrote:

It is hard to stand on the shore and watch quietly the spectacle of class fighting class. . . . Sholokhov finds this shore through dispassionate objectivity. He tries calmly and with equanimity to look at both sides. . . . In Sholokhov's treatment of the enemies of the Revolution their negation does not make itself felt. . . . For him the Whites are enemies, but heroes.[8]

At a meeting of the Second Plenum of RAPP, September 1929, one speaker said: "Reading *The Quiet Don* attentively we find that here is an idealization of the old Cossack life, the grief of the author that this life of the wealthy Cossacks is gone." Another said: "The poorer stratum of Cossacks is so pale that one feels at once with what indifference the author looks upon it . . . while the wealthier Cossacks and the majority of White Guardsmen—officers and generals—appear from the author's point of view crystal clear and true to their own ideals. . . . All this compels us as critics to be on our guard and to be particularly concerned with this novel, under no circumstances speaking of it as related to proletarian art.[9]

With attitudes such as these prevalent among Communist officials, we can see why favorable *literary* evaluations of *The*

Quiet Don failed to prevent discontinuation of serial publication in April 1929. Nor was it resumed until January 1932
when Sholokhov convinced the Party of his personal loyalty
and ideological sanctity. At the same time, the first two
volumes of *The Quiet Don* remained on the market, although
the 1931 edition included a cautionary preface by the critic A.
Selivanovsky that admonished readers to beware of contamina-
tion:

> A well-to-do Cossack family molded and conditioned
> Sholokhov's artistic gift. . . . Sholokhov has not been able
> to understand and feel the new world provided by the
> October Revolution . . . A peasant writer entering the
> path of transformation to a proletarian writer—such des-
> cribes Sholokhov's position for Marxist criticism. . . . It
> would be incorrect to put *The Quiet Don* down to the
> account of proletarian literature. Likewise, it would be
> incorrect to deny the significance of this novel as one of
> the samples of the laborious course *of the transfer of a
> peasant writer to the rails of proletarian ideology*—a course
> still far from completed.[10]

By the fall of 1929, Sholokhov was prepared to take measures to silence his accusers, for on the third of October he
wrote a letter, presumably to Fadeev, in which he announced
his intention to apply for membership in the Communist Party
"after this rubbish" about plagiarism ends. And in January
1930 he met with the Central Committee of the Party, including Stalin.[11] What was said at this meeting beyond the
subject of collectivization, we do not know, though Sholokhov
later claimed he came away filled with ideas. We may logically
suppose that what actually happened was that Party functionaries imposed upon him a penance for unspecified sins and
crimes, requiring him to devote himself more strenuously to
overt social activity (conducting local propaganda, assisting
in the formation of collectives) and second that he write something more directly and immediately serviceable to the Party.
I believe this is true because after January 1930 Sholokhov no

longer locked himself behind "the little shutters of his house."
He went into the villages and fields of the Cossack region
campaigning on behalf of the collective millenium. He cam-
paigned also, it should be noted, for his own novel by reading
portions of the unpublished third volume to public gatherings.

Sholokhov's personal distress at this time can be judged
from a letter he wrote to Serafimovich in April 1930:

> Certainly you already know that they won't publish
> Part vi of *The Quiet Don*. I urgently request that you
> take a little time for me and read it yourself. I'd be in-
> tensely happy to receive even a brief note from you stating
> your views on it. I needn't tell you what meaning a word
> of yours has for me—from an elder and a fellow country-
> man. . . .
>
> I received a number of letters from the lads in Mos-
> cow and from readers in which they inform me of and
> inquire about the rumors that are again abroad to the
> effect that I stole *The Quiet Don* from the critic Golou-
> shev—a friend of L. Andreev.
>
> What am I to do Alexander Serafimovich? I'm sick to
> death of being a "thief." They've slung so much mud at
> me. And now a lucky break for all the slanderers: my third
> volume of *The Quiet Don* won't be printed. This will give
> them . . . a chance to say: "Look, he's silent; he wrote
> while he fed on Goloushev; but then the source dried
> up!"
>
> I'm having a productive time just now, finishing
> Volume III; but such a situation does not advance the
> work. My hand stops, and I feel wretched. What kind
> of ill-will is there toward me that my brother-writers
> should take arms against me for the third time? It all
> comes from literary circles.[12]

This letter is especially interesting because it was written
at the very time when Sholokhov was supposed to be joyously
participating in "social work." I have been told by former
Soviet citizens, who lived in southern Russia at the time,

that Sholokhov finally went to court with a libel suit and received a favorable judgment, which silenced the charges of plagiarism—at least in print.[13] His novel, however, was not published; and in the fall of 1930 he left the Soviet Union (accompanied by a friend who was a reliable Communist, Vasily Kudashev) with the intention of visiting Maxim Gorky in Sorrento, obviously hoping for counsel and assistance. In Berlin he found that a visa was unobtainable from Mussolini's government and returned home, where he wrote the bulk of *Virgin Soil Upturned*. At the end of the year he became a formal candidate for membership in the Communist Party.[14]

In May of 1931 he had his manuscript of *The Quiet Don*, Part vi, sent to Gorky, who responded favorably, considering it "better made and more remarkable" than the earlier volumes. Then on June 6 he wrote his famous letter to Gorky—famous because it records candidly some of the harsher facts about the Revolution in southern Russia which official historians tend to suppress. Sholokhov begins with a request that Gorky read the manuscript; then he documents his presentation of events in the novel with quotations from L. S. Degtyarev's book on propaganda work in the Red Army during the Revolution and from official proclamations issued by the Party during the Cossack uprising:

> . . . Certain "orthodox leaders" of RAPP, having read the manuscript, accused me of trying to justify the Cossack uprising in 1919, when I cited facts about the mistreatment of Upper Don Cossacks. Is this so? Without exaggerating the true colors, I described the grim reality that preceded the uprising.
>
> The most powerful men economically in the *stanitsas* and *khutors*—merchants, clergy, millers—got off by paying the monetary contribution and it was the Cossacks, frequently those from the lower social strata, who were shot. And naturally the policy practiced by certain representatives of Soviet power and advanced sometimes even by known enemies, was interpreted as a wish to annihilate not classes but all Cossacks.

But, Aleksei Maksimovich, I had to show the negative sides of the policy of de-Cossackization and mistreatment for middling-peasant Cossacks, because without this I couldn't show the reasons for the uprising at all. And so they not only don't rebel, but then fleas don't bite either!

In Part vi I cite a number of Soviet "zealots" (the chap from the district who came to collect confiscated clothing; the man from Lugansk who was somewhat offended by the Whites; the 9th Army Commissar, Malkin, who actually existed and did the things I tell about through the mouth of the Old Believer carter; and a member of Malkin's board—who was also an authentic type who agitated for socialism in such an original way) in order to contrast them with Koshevoi, Stockman, Ivan Alexeevich [Kotlyarov] and others, to show that not all were such "distorters" perverting the idea of Soviet power.

Certain of my colleagues, having read Part vi but not understanding that my description is historically correct, have conceived a prejudice against the entire section. They are protesting against my "artistic fictionalizing" of things actually taken from life. This prejudice is evidenced by their notations in the manuscript's margins, notations which are frankly ridiculous at times. When an advance Red unit enters Tatarsky, I have the following sentence: "The riders (Red Army men) bounced and wobbled terribly in their dragoon saddles." Beside this sentence stands a note that cries out: "Who?! Red Army men bounced terribly? Is it possible to say this about Red Army men?! Really it's counter revolutionary!"

. . . They place before me as an indispensable condition of publication the exclusion of a number of sections very dear to me (the lyrical pieces and others). It is amusing that ten men propose to throw out ten different sections; and if one were to listen to them all, three-fourths of the work would have to be discarded. . . .[15]

With the intercession of Gorky, the active support of Serafimovich, who visited Sholokhov in Veshenskaya during

the summer of 1931, and Sholokhov's own continuing effort to
fulfill his social "responsibilities" (he gave a series of lectures
on Chekhov, Leo Tolstoy, and Mayakovsky), he managed to
gain full membership in the Party in November 1932. Serialization of *The Quiet Don* and *Virgin Soil Upturned* com-
menced in *Oktyabr* (January-October 1932) and *Novyi mir*
(*New World*) (January-September 1932).

At the end of the final installment of *The Quiet Don* an
announcement appeared: "The fourth volume will be published in 1933." This was not to happen. Lest Sholokhov
fancied that Party membership guaranteed any literary im-
munities, the journal version's expurgations from *The Quiet
Don* must have disabused him. Portions of the climactic
chapter that described Koshevoi's repudiation of Grigory were
removed (Chap. 20); portrayal of the family lamentations
over the deaths of Miron Korshunov (Chap. 23) and Pyotr
Melekhov (Chap. 33) were omitted, and restored only in the
first separate volume edition which was not printed until ten
months later, after a good deal of negotiation, in August 1933.
As for *Virgin Soil Upturned*, the editors at first refused to print
several passages, including the famous description of dekulakization, which was restored, according to Sholokhov, only because of the direct and personal intervention of Stalin. Even
the original title, *With Blood and Sweat*, was rejected; and
Sholokhov turned for advice to his comrades on the regional
committee who suggested several titles including *Virgin Soil
Upturned*, which was taken from the text itself.

But at least the books were printed, and Sholokhov had
apparently obtained Party support. To be sure, he was called
a "confused middling peasant" and a "representative of the
kolkhoz peasantry seeking ties with the proletariat" by one
critic as late as June 1933;[16] but the general response was favorable. Sholokhov's troubles, however, were far from over. By
the winter of 1932-33 the struggle over collectivization in
southern Russia had become savage. "Wreckers" and "harmful elements" of all kinds, both inside the Party and out, were
collaborating with kulaks. They succeeded in introducing virtual chaos throughout the northern Caucasus and Azov-Black

Sea regions. Officials, ostensibly authorized by the Party, confiscated grain which had been given in payment to peasants for their work; they expelled thousands of peasants from the collectives; they arrested collective farmers as well as many of the twenty-five thousand loyal workingmen who had come from the cities in 1930 to help form the collectives. In the area of Veshenskaya alone, over three thousand collective farmers were jailed.

In January 1933, Sholokhov wrote the secretary of the local Party unit, Pyotr Kuzmich Lugovoi, who was apparently arrested or expelled himself:

> Events in Veshenskaya took on a monstrous character. They arrested the best people as enemies of the Party. It is now alleged that you had disorganized the collectives, rustled livestock, planted illegally; and I knew and kept silent. All this is so absurd and monstrous that I can't find words to describe it. A more grievous and more serious charge could not be levelled. With all ferocity and relentlessness we must struggle in order to remove this unmerited, black stain.
>
> About three hundred people are already expelled from the Party. This before the purge! And tomorrow the commission arrives. The region is heading for catastrophe. What the spring will be like I can't imagine even in one of my writer's fantasies. . . . Recent events have somewhat stupefied me. I await your letter. Do you really agree that we did counterrevolutionary work? . . . What shall we do? It's impossible to live with such a stigma.[17]

What Sholokhov did was to write letters to the Central Committee of the Party requesting an investigation of the local leadership. Premier Khrushchev in 1963 revealed two letters that Sholokhov addressed to Stalin. In one (April 16, 1933) he details examples of the "irregular methods" used in procuring grain from peasants, then adds:

> These are not individual instances of excesses, this

is the "method," legalized on a district scale, for grain procurements. . . . If all I have described merits the attention of the Central Committee, then send genuine Communists to Veshenskaya District who will have courage enough to expose, irrespective of persons, those who are to blame for the fatal undermining of the region's collective farm economy, who will really investigate and expose not only those who have used the loathsome "methods" of torture, beatings and outrages against the collective farmers but also those who inspired them.[18]

Two things are important about these revelations. First, they testify to Sholokhov's courage, if not success, in opposing a draconian bureaucracy. Stalin not only disregarded his recommendations but implied that he really did not understand what he was talking about, since peasants ("esteemed grain growers" Stalin called them) were a bad, disloyal lot anyway. Second, Sholokhov's remarks indicate how difficult conditions had become in his area, especially when he requested that the government send food—this to an area viewed normally as an exceptionally fertile "bread basket" of Russia.[19] Sholokhov's literary work, as one might expect, had to be put off at this period, although he did revise Part vi of *The Quiet Don* and collaborate with A. Viner on a stage version of *Virgin Soil Upturned*. It turned out so badly that Sholokhov spoke of writing an original play, instead of condensing the novel.[20]

By July 29, 1934, when a formal investigating commission finally reviewed Sholokhov's credentials, verified his loyalty, and confirmed his Party membership, the literary and political storms had somewhat abated. That spring the first two volumes of *The Quiet Don* had been enthusiastically reviewed in the United States and England, and the novel was being translated into every major language. The stage version of *Virgin Soil Upturned* was enjoying favorable reviews in Moscow, and the book itself was having an extraordinary impact as an educational tool all across the Soviet Union.[21] Sholokhov was becoming a celebrity.

Despite his claim that he was busy with the second

volume of *Virgin Soil Upturned* and the last volume of *The Quiet Don*, what he actually published after 1932 was journalism. It is, indeed, from this time on that the dichotomy between journalistic communication and art becomes most marked. Sholokhov was personally confronting the very issue that had been agitating many Soviet literary theoreticians for years. The extremist positions were, on the one hand, that literature would simply be supplanted by journalism ("newspapers will be the poems of the future") because, under Communism, life and art would be indistinguishable, and, on the other hand, that because literature *is* form and structure, having only indirect connection with chaotic daily life, it would continue to occupy an important place in society. In the saner middle-ground, writers recognized that literature, for the present, was inextricably caught between the demands of form, the demands of communication, and (for Communists at least) the demands of propaganda. Many hoped to see a reconciliation or synthesis of these contradictory claims with the establishment of the national Writers Union and the institution of "socialist realism" as the canonic but latitudinarian form of literature. Sholokhov himself may have thought optimism was justified when spokesmen for the Organization Committee (October 29-November 3, 1932) adopted a conciliatory tone toward both *The Quiet Don* and *Virgin Soil Upturned* as well as toward controversial works by other authors. In fact, however, the demands of propaganda took precedence and the dilemma was resolved by coercion, not synthesis.

The division in Sholokhov's mind can be seen by comparing statements he made in March and October 1934. During the spring he became involved in the controversy that raged round the novelist Panferov's advocacy of collective endeavors in writing, which transformed literature not only into journalism but into bad journalism. Sholokhov so strongly opposed bad craftsmanship that he condemned his friend Serafimovich, who had tried to justify Panferov. Sholokhov took Gorky's side by insisting on higher norms for literary production and on the integrity of language:

It is time to speak of literature in a genuine courageous
language and to call things by their names. We must have
truly new words created by the Revolution, innovations
in our literary form; we must have new books portraying
the greatest of epochs in human history. But we—writers
—will only be able to create works deserving of this epoch
when we learn to introduce new words into literature
and to write books not *ala* Panferov but, on the contrary,
so that ninety-five words are excellent and the other five
good. . . . When our critics break off their liberal lisping
and their patronizing, paternal attitude towards a writer
("though he's snotty, he's mine"); when criticism becomes genuinely revolutionary, merciless, strict, and able
to keep its eyes open in the face of truth—then the
factionalists will stop crying at literary crossroads, ex-
tolling "their" writers and blaming all those who believe
differently. Only under these conditions will we carry out
those many widely proclaimed promises which we made
to Soviet society. Otherwise we remain "honest blab-
berers," but still creators of mediocre works.[22]

Sholokhov sent the article in which these remarks appear
to Gorky on March 4, 1934, with a note: "I send you this
article for examination. If it needs correction, correct it. But
don't, please, send it on to the Organizing Committee of the
Writers Union [which was then preparing for the first All-
Union Congress of Soviet writers]. They'll make mincemeat of
it, so you won't be able to tell head from tail. . . ."

In the fall, speaking to factory workers in Rostov, Sholokhov described his literary problems in a different way:

I wrote *Virgin Soil Upturned* . . . in the heat of the
moment, in 1930, when the memories of events were still
fresh. And when, under these fresh impressions I began to
write and wrote straight through to the end of the first
book, I then confronted a dilemma: already at the very
moment, what I had written was not fundamental, would
not rouse the reader. . . . You write how kolkhozes were

created, but up springs the question of work-days. . . .
Events outgrow and sweep over [*perekhlestyvayut*] people; this is the difficulty of our problem.[23]

Perhaps Sholokhov was guilty of confusing his novel with
a tract or newspaper. Yet his concern for the artistic use of
language and his many remarks about the need for punctilious
attention to every detail in art make it clear that he knew
the difference between journalism and art.

However serious the contradictions were between the
demands of art and the demands of the Party, and however
much they impaired the literary quality of Sholokhov's subsequent work, Sholokhov and the Party were evidently reconciled to each other in July 1934; and the rewards to Sholokhov
were immediate and tangible. He was allowed to take part
—albeit an inconspicuous part—in the First All-Union Writers
Congress; he built a new house—a bright blue one—with an
impressive second-story "birdhouse" (*skvoreshnitsa*, as he
called it) for his study; he was permitted to go abroad in
December and January 1934-35 to visit Scandanavia, England,
and France; and he was, from this time on, elected repeatedly
to various local, regional, and national governmental posts.

His private "birdhouse" seems to have been a vindication
of his right to isolation—but he paid a public price for it.
In return for his blessings, he began to do little voluntary
services for the Party such as composing brief memorials for
Barbusse and Nikolai Ostrovsky—whom he knew only slightly
—or insisting frequently in speeches and articles on the importance of social and Party work in addition to creative writing. To be sure, he finished *The Quiet Don* during the next
five years, but one wonders if he was only speaking literally
when he joked about his study: "You can't stay in it in the
summer—too hot; nor in the winter—too cold.[24]

The treatment of Sholokhov dramatizes most effectively
the Communist Party's suspicion of subjective creativity as a
potential source of heresy. Retreat into privacy by a "dependable" and "responsible" person can be tolerated, even encouraged; but for anyone else, as the life of Boris Pasternak

testifies, a retreat into the creative shell is dangerous. Sholokhov, with his intensely lyrical temperament, had to undergo public discipline that, I think, damaged his art. He was perhaps paying for his privacy when, in 1937, he compared the Soviet writers' lives with those of their peers in the West:

> Capitalism domesticates mercenarily inclined writers; it corrupts even honest writers. . . . The bourgeois writer is put in such circumstances that qualities of individualism are cultivated in him, pushing into the background the social significance of literary art. He is the antithesis of the Soviet writer.[25]

As for "domestication," Sholokhov would seem to be a pot calling the kettle black. It is all too easy, however, to reach the conclusion that any writer who becomes "dependable" has by definition "sold out" to the authorities and forsaken both his own integrity and the cause of art. This easy conclusion finds acceptance almost automatically among a majority of Western critics who yearn to assert that the only good writers in the Soviet Union are those persecuted or martyred by the Party, and that every "reliable" writer is or will be a hack and a toady. That this is not true of Sholokhov at this time may be inferred from remarks he made to one of his biographers, Isai Lezhnev, just after he had completed *The Quiet Don*. Realizing that Party critics would attack him for the tragic finale and ambiguous ending, he said, "I let the manuscript go to the journal without consulting them. I didn't see a different ending; I couldn't write it differently. The book took a long enough time to finish. So I resolved: let them read it already in print—and then let them rail!"

It will be remembered that the sixth part was virtually completed as early as 1929 and that Sholokhov anticipated completing the fourth and final volume, first by 1931, then 1933. He was wrong. We know that editors returned his manuscripts for revision more than once. Part vii (the first half of the fourth volume) appeared in consecutive numbers of *Novyi mir* from November 1937 through March 1938 although many chapters had appeared in various publications in 1935 and 1936. Sholokhov told an interviewer, I. Eksler, in December 1937, that the final part (viii) was finished. The delay in publication for more than two years was caused, according to one unsubstantiated story, by Stalin's insistence that the hero become a Communist. In any case, Part viii was serialized in 1940, and the first single-volume edition of the whole novel appeared in 1941. The obvious question is, why did Sholokhov require so much time to complete the fourth (and in many ways the easiest) volume? And why did he not complete the second volume of *Virgin Soil Upturned* in 1931 as promised?

These questions are not easily answered, but one thing is obvious: instead of writing, he talked—to students, to groups of workers and peasants. Unlike many writers, he did not even keep a notebook. "If I make notes," he said in 1940, "it's very rarely. You write down a felicitous image or metaphor, but the rest somehow you hold in your head." He entertained guests beyond numbering, often simple citizens, who visited his house overlooking the Don as they might visit some shrine. In exchange for their advice on how *The Quiet Don* should end, he conducted them to see the local showpiece, a huge 350-year-old oak tree, and he fed them the traditional strawberry jam. He granted interviews with journalists and various literary dignitaries. Finally, he became an editor and advised young writers. For example, he told Ivan Rokachev to "study your native language more thoroughly; read more—first of all the Russian classics." To another beginner, V. A. Garanzhin, he wrote:

> "The Young Elder" is, actually, not a story. Rather, it's an *ocherk*,[26] its character close to the common newspaper type of *ocherk*, which is similar to a bad photograph. You'll agree that for characterizing the elder, it is insufficient to keep mentioning his "white fluffy beard," and it is equally insufficient for the description of his experiences to use the ornate and studied phrase: "Can it be that I'm already imprisoned by the decrepitude etc. of old age?" All this bespeaks the poverty of your descrip-

tive methods, your ignorance in portraying the outer and
inner features of a man, the primitivism in which you
(expressing it in your style) find yourself imprisoned.

Dialogue is almost wholly absent from your story-
ocherk. This kills a story, deprives it of the living sound
of words. You mishandle language: you're not thrifty
enough with language; and then, where a couple of
phrases would reveal the movement or attitude of a
character, you spend ten phrases on description. These are
customary inadequacies of all beginners. The surest
method of freeing oneself of them is to study attentively
and thoughtfully the best models—the works of former
and present-day writers. . . . For example, Hemingway,
O. Henry. They're first-rate, masters of the short story.[27]

While we know what Sholokhov did during this first
period of literary silence, we do not know exactly why he did
it. It is conceivable that, having lived along the front lines
of the "internal offensive" which the Communist Party waged
during the first Five-Year Plan and collectivization, Sholokhov
saw clearly why purges were inevitable and how they worked.
If this is true, then we can guess that he foresaw the advantages of silence and inobtrusiveness. Invariably it was the
obtrusive man, the flag-waver who was sooner or later compromised and swept into exile. Only the hypocrites, who could
change flags deftly, and the possums survived, although no
one, even the innocent, enjoyed impunity. Already in the first
volume of *Virgin Soil Upturned*, Sholokhov recognized scape-
goating as a feature of the Communist system. After narrowly
avoiding the role of scapegoat himself in 1931 and 1932, he
stopped exposing himself and survived the bloody purge years
far from Moscow. It is only fair to add, however, that he, like
Pasternak, apparently refused to sign petitions echoing Vishin-
sky's famous "Shoot the mad dogs!" slogan during the purge
trials. Moreover, he risked his life as will as his reputation
when, in 1937 and 1938, he was instrumental in reinstating the
Party chairman of his area, Pyotr Lugovoi, and other local
Communist leaders who had been unjustly convicted. Another

comrade, Pyotr Krasyukov, spent sixteen months in prison before Sholokhov arranged for his release.[28] What bargains
Sholokhov struck with Stalin at this time we may never know.

If we may conclude that a combination of official resistance with his own honesty and caution explains the slow appearance of Sholokhov's work after 1932, we have still not
explained why the Party permitted publication of *The Quiet
Don* in any form. The tragic conclusion was so unexpected
that a veritable critical explosion occurred over the book.
Perhaps feeling themselves compromised by their early affection for Grigory Melekhov, some critics now labeled him an
inhuman degenerate. V. Yermilov went so far as to insist that
formerly "tragic" Grigory becomes a "comic individual" in
Part viii. Another critic found Grigory wholly untypical of
the Cossacks—a freak, a "terrible exception," who need not,
therefore, worry anyone unduly.[29] Sanity for once prevailed,
however, and the majority of commentators recognized that,
ambiguities and defects notwithstanding, Sholokhov's book
stood first in the Soviet canon, far outdistancing in quality its
comparable predecessors, for example, Veresaev's *Deadlock,*
Virta's *Alone,* or A. Tolstoy's *Road to Calvary.*

But since high literary quality by no means guarantees
publication of a work in a society where the supreme criterion
is ideological relevance, we must assume that Party officials
sanctioned the last part of *The Quiet Don.* The hand of Stalin
would seem to have been apparent here as the hand of
Khrushchev was in the publication of Solzhenitsyn's *One Day
in the Life of Ivan Denisovich* in 1962. But the question remains, why? Khrushchev evidently wanted a spectacular testi-
monial to the injustice and inhumanity of postwar Stalinism.
What did Stalin want?

An emigré propagandist, P. N. Donskov, suggested that
the publication of *The Quiet Don* together with the playing of
Cossack songs over the Soviet radio, the reinstitution of
Cossack detachments in the Soviet Army, and the establishment of Cossack museums in Novocherkassk and Azov, were
all part of a calculated strategem to enlist the sympathies of
the Cossacks for Communism prior to World War II. Donskov

adds that the strategem failed miserably with the Cossacks, who knew from experience that when it suited them, the Communists would again trample them into the mud.[30] As a matter of fact, however, while many Cossacks defected to the Nazis in World War II, others made distinguished military records. Both Germans and Russians seemed inclined to mollify the Cossack—if we may judge by their preservation of historical monuments in Starocherkassk and Novocherkassk.

That the Party attempted to pacify Cossack antagonism in the thirties is likely. But pacification was not only a bribe; it was a reward for loyalty as well. Sholokhov himself had labored industriously and deserved the Party's gratitude. This does not tell us, however, how we are to interpret the appearance of *The Quiet Don*. The last part could not in the least mobilize public opinion behind some Party program, as *Virgin Soil Upturned* did; nor did it signal any revision in the official interpretation of the Revolution. Two possibilties seem intelligible. The publication of a book without an optimistic ending may be taken as a conciliatory sign that in matters literary a wider latitude could be indulged by writers. There were indications shortly before the war that an increase in tolerance might occur as a palliative to the rigors of the recent purge years, although as late as 1939 Sholokhov saw the long-awaited film version of *Virgin Soil Upturned* transform the novel into the most vapid, inane propaganda—at the censor's behest.[31] Second, it is important to note that *The Quiet Don* is not an inflammatory, revolutionary document. Its *donnée* is not the need for insurrection, but the necessity of submission to the harshest of all truths that the Revolution taught, namely the truth of historical inevitability. Like all classical literature, it acknowledges man's position under the black shadow of time—and it acknowledges this position without the wails or the boasts of the Romantic. There is a time for tyranny just as there is a time for freedom. Stalin had no doubts that his was the harsher time. And Sholokhov (like Machiavelli) dramatized the worst of it.

Some of the revisions that Sholokhov introduced into the

text of *The Quiet Don* during the thirties bear this out.[32] In addition to correcting faulty grammar, strained figures of speech, excessively naturalistic descriptions, and factual errors of dates and troop deployments in the First World War, Sholokhov added or deleted passages, altering the book's meaning. Thus, an episode involving Trotsky vanishes from Part vi, Chapter 57, as does a lengthy footnote which Sholokhov had written to combat the "official" Bolshevik interpretation of the Cossack anti-Communist uprising in 1919.[33]

The major reduction is of scenes describing the relationship between the Jewess, Anna Pogudko, and the Communist, Ilya Bunchuk. Anna loses much of her warmth and vitality while Bunchuk becomes more nearly a Party automaton, deprived of his tenderness and good-natured helpfulness. Reducing Anna's role deprives the book of her memorable soliloquy on the future (Part v, Chap. 16), a passage which remains in the English translation and continues to inspire readers.[34]

Soviet critics without exception suggest that the expurgation of passages from this love story show realism triumphing over naive romanticism in Sholokhov's conception of character. But we may also suggest that Sholokhov, having turned his major Communist character, Koshevoi, into a Stalinist in the last parts of the novel, simply harmonized early parts by stripping them of their glowing idealism. In a world where Stalinist mediocrity and brutality called the tune, what place was there for memories of a dead girl's bright prophecy of the joys of Soviet life?

Sholokhov often speaks as if he were a freer agent than he was in fact. Although his prolonged "silence" shows resistance to official pressure, the revisions of style and content in new editions of earlier volumes reveal submission to ideological as well as literary discipline. But to conclude that this injured his talent and nothing more oversimplifies the situation. One can also conclude that for a man so headstrong and an artist so uncontrolled as Sholokhov was, almost *any* discipline can have beneficent as well as adverse effects. The curtailment of his lyrical and "romantic" excesses in language and sentiment damaged certain passages in *The Quiet Don,* but it also secured for the book a "classical" detachment that accentuated its epic qualities.

For Sholokhov, as for many Soviet writers, the Second World War provided an escape from the oppressive atmosphere of the purge years. Mutual suspicion and recrimination retreated before a wave of patriotism and national solidarity. Like most of his colleagues, Sholokhov became a war correspondent and wrote news releases as well as stories. However, he was not satisfied with the work. He came to detest the common practice of editorial rewriting of material sent in by reporters. He explained, for example, that the custom of making notes of stories told by wounded soldiers in hospitals and then allowing editors to "draw them out" was a disservice. "That's the way to depersonalize and emasculate [*vykholashchivat*] living speech! If they had printed, word for word if possible, what was noted down, without slyly subtlizing it—here would have been precious material. But printing it revised makes nothing —neither an original soldier's tale nor an original literary work."

Sholokhov's objections were, however, more basic than this complaint indicates. They originated, as he told Isai Lezhnev in 1949, in his own temperament as well as his experience as a writer over the previous two decades:

> I became a writer in the first half of the twenties. Like a majority of the people of my age in literature, I began with newspaper work. But I quickly felt that I would not find myself as a feuilletonist. I did not succeed at newspaper work then or now. I sensed this acutely at the time of the Second World War when I had to work for a paper. My character is such that I cannot write rapidly. In no sense am I a newspaperman. I lack the bold

phrase, the operative skill so necessary for itinerant journalistic work.

Let me illustrate with an instance from my experience during war time. I worked then as a correspondent for *Red Star.* . . . Once I was given the task of describing the funeral of an heroic officer who had been killed. I wanted to write lyrically, with great feeling; but what I came up with was not an *ocherk*, and so what I'd written was not printed. There I saw that you wouldn't make a journalist of me. The material of reality presents itself to me in a different light from that which it must have for a newspaper essay: It is a necessity with me to depict things in the broadest context—to write so that the narrative will evoke thought in the reader.[35]

Sholokhov's own more successful wartime narratives are leisurely pieces, often told through the mouth of a soldier so that the idiom is as important as the action. They remain interesting long after many simple battle stories have been forgotten. Nonetheless, their tendentious purpose (to instill hatred of the Fascists) demands concentration rather than spaciousness; and this, one feels, impedes Sholokhov's customary reliance on abundant detail. Only in "The Science of Hatred" did he achieve sufficient concentration to inspire the degree of loathing for German Nazis that he evidently intended. "A Man's Fate," written ten years after the war, illustrates his habitual manner.

On the basis of his own remarks, one might assume that with the restoration of peace, Sholokhov would have time "to depict things in the broadest context." And it may be that freedom from the abnormal conditions prevailing during both the purge and war years could have inspired a new period of intense productivity. But this was not to happen. The Communist Party harnessed literature in a tighter straitjacket after 1946 than the one used during the thirties. To be sure, one might claim that Sholokhov's personal suffering during the war harmed his creativity. His mother perished almost before his eyes when his home was bombed moments after he had removed his wife and children. His library and most of his manuscripts were destroyed. He sustained a serious head injury in a plane crash. But in the harsh school of Soviet life people became inured to suffering more extreme than this. Sholokhov had seen all the damage that violence can do to men by the time he was a teenager. Moreover, the first chapters of his war novel, *The Fought For Their Country*, were an auspicious beginning, albeit somewhat prolix. For the first time he was writing about Russians rather than Cossacks; and the book threatens to become merely another war novel.

That he would have surpassed his epic, *The Quiet Don*, is dubious; that he could have produced competent works seems likely, had not Stalin's "mad years" intervened. The privacy essential to all creative art was once again anathematized. All the energies of every person were mobilized for the gargantuan task of rebuilding the country; and it was believed that any indulgence of subjective feeling would vitiate the total effort. All that was needed were songs that celebrated the glories of production in the rhythms of labor. And one must agree that Soviet recovery after the war was impressive, rivaling that of England, without American financial assistance. In addition, one must recognize that a nation which thrice in thirty years pulled itself up by its own bootstraps in the face of an indifferent or antagonistic world at a terrible cost of human suffering and sacrifice will be a nation inordinately proud of its achievements and inordinately impatient with individuals who break ranks or wish to celebrate their personal inconveniences and hardships. Every artistic expression that became too personal would be sacrificed. Buildings and bread came first, and writers were expected to help make them.

Instead of writing fiction, Sholokhov again retreated into expository prose—often into the most garish and propagandistic journalism. A wiser government than Stalin's might have used him (and his talented colleagues as well) more effectively; but force, not wisdom, was the guiding genius in Stalin's last endeavors. Sholokhov's repeated expressions of dislike for journalism make it obvious that many of his essays are not to be taken seriously, though we probably cannot know which

of them are honest statements of opinion and which are dutiful
or obligatory responses supporting Party policies and pro-
grams. I would not wish, for example, to hold Sholokhov
fully responsible for the saccharine epitaph he penned for
Stalin,[36] for the personal calumnies he leveled at President
Harry Truman or for the fulsome New Year's greetings to the
nation that he published annually during the early fifties. Their
intemperance inclines one to imagine that Sholokhov intended
to parody rather than to enhance an offensive custom. They
did, nonetheless, serve a function: critics who reproached him
for indifference after the war could not say that he maintained
an absolute silence or that he spent all his time on fishing
trips. His friend and editor, Yury Lukin, even published an
essay in his defense, praising him precisely for writing journalism which fulfilled the needs of the time.[37] We may conclude
that his enthusiasm for "the people" and his blatant jingoism
are probably the most sincere elements in this material, because the strains of populism and old Russian chauvinism
ring throughout his work. Reluctantly, we may also suggest
that he contracted the ugliest of all Soviet afflictions: cynicism.

The excess of irrationality to which aberrant Stalinism
led writers—even writers as circumspect as Sholokhov—became evident during the infamous "pseudonym controversy"
of 1951.[38] The affair began with an article by the young novelist, Bubennov, who first explained why the question on pseudonyms was posed at all:

> It is not only because this is a literary tradition which, like
> many others, has out-lived its time. It sometimes even
> does serious harm under Soviet conditions. Frequently
> behind pseudonyms people hide who look at the matter
> of literature in an anti-social way and do not want others
> to know their real names. It is no secret that for certain
> near-literary types and hack writers pseudonyms serve
> as a means of disguise and help them practice all possible
> abuses and machinations in the press. It is no secret that
> pseudonyms are very readily used by cosmopolites in
> literature.

The mention of "cosmopolites" at this time (February 1951) bears the obvious implication of Jews, who, as a matter of fact, do frequently change their names in the Soviet Union, especially if they are writers. Konstantin Simonov, adding his correct name parenthetically (Kirill Mikhailovich), replied to Bubennov, pointing out several first-rate Russian writers who worked under pseudonyms but whom Bubennov did not mention: Boris Polevoi, Pogodin, Boris Galin, Maltsev, Yashin, Aibek, the Tur brothers, and others. Simonov regretted that anyone should even have to justify using a pseudonym: "Indeed, should anyone now seek justification, surely it should be Bubennov himself. . . . It is to be regretted that such a tendency toward conceitedness and 'flashiness' should reveal itself in a young and talented writer."

The matter should have been closed, when suddenly Sholokhov entered the lists in an article entitled "With Visor Lowered." He applied the phrase to Simonov though it suited him far better. Said Sholokhov:

> . . . the pseudo-literary speculators and "beetles" who with facility change their pseudonyms five times a year and in the event of failure with the same striking facility exchange the profession of a man of letters for the profession of furrier or watch-maker—these people are doing literature great harm, perverting our healthy young people who, in a broad flood, are pouring into the mainstream of our mighty Soviet literature.

(Parenthetically, it is amusing to note that at the Writers' Congress four years later, Sholokhov saw the "mainstream of Soviet literature" as a "muddy stream.") Then Sholokhov turns a baleful eye on Simonov: "One is honestly amazed at the incomprehensible vehemence manifested by Simonov in arguing with Bubennov and the unfounded conclusions reached by Simonov in his furious defense. . . ." Simonov, as a matter of fact, was not vehement at all. Regarding Simonov's sentence, "It is to be regretted . . . ," Sholokhov retorts: "What a condescendingly scornful and patronizing pat on the back!

It would be interesting to know when and from whom Simonov got his passport to veneration and immortality."

Two things seem clear: to Sholokhov the use of pseudonyms was not of paramount importance; what he wanted was to insult Simonov in particular and Jews generally (though Simonov is not Jewish). His remark about "furrier or watchmaker" is unmistakably anti-Semitic. In answering him, Simonov makes the following points: a pseudonym is the writer's own personal business. Sholokhov wants to know "whom Simonov is defending?" The answer is any writer whom Bubennov accuses of "hiding from society" just because he changes his name; the connection both in Bubennov and Sholokhov of pseudonyms with hack writers and "beetles" is false and an insult to our literature. The whole problem, concluded Simonov, was "trumped up in search for cheap sensationalism" in the first place. It has no meaning for the "broad masses."

Thus ended one of the most astonishing quarrels among Soviet writers. What did it mean? More important, why did it ever make the papers, since it was surely undignified and perhaps, as Simonov said, of no interest to the "broad masses" (except, of course, for some rare gossip)? There is more than one diagnosis which accounts for all the meager evidence. For one thing, Party conservatives obviously welcomed Sholokhov's endorsement of their anticosmopolitan policy, though his intemperance may have seemed excessive. For another, Sholokhov may have had some special interest in Bubennov, a Cossack writer just beginning his career. Sholokhov may have imagined he was defending a countryman against defamation as he was himself defended by Serafimovich years before. On the other hand, Sholokhov may well have resented Simonov's sudden rise to fame after the war, especially when Sholokhov could not help but realize that he was a greater writer and yet received less and less attention. His name was less often mentioned. His novels were supplanted in school curricula by his wartime propaganda pieces, while Simonov's work was eulogized constantly. At this time he was accused of using vulgar language and Cossack provincialisms to excess, but, of course, Simonov wrote pure Russian. As to Jews, tradition among the Cossacks can account for some anti-Semitic bias. It will be remembered that in the pogroms at the beginning of this century, the Cossack record was most unsavory. But why did Sholokhov devote one of the most moving stories in *The Quiet Don* to the love between the Communist Bunchuk and the Jewess Anna Pogudko, a story which he evidently wrote very early—about 1926? And why did he write sympathetically of the Jew who was expelled from Fomin's band, an incident probably written after 1936? It may be that his vitiation of the Bunchuk-Pogudko episodes in revised editions of his book signals growing anti-Semitism. We know too little about Sholokhov's personal ideas and prejudices to propose any trustworthy generalization about reasons for his conduct in the pseudonym squabble. There is some evidence which would warrant speculation that Sholokhov (perhaps quite irrationally) was simply using anticosmopolitanism as a weapon with which to avenge himself on critics (in this case Simonov) who had been ignoring him deliberately for several years.

The one certainty is that at this period Sholokhov behaved like an infuriated bull. Perhaps he had good reason. All he could write, or at least all that publishers would print, was journalistic trivia. And it would seem that even this was not enough to satisfy Stalin's cultural watchdogs. Certain influential men in literary politics evidently resolved that if Sholokhov did not propose to write new fiction, he could at least rewrite the old, harmonizing it with the linguistic and ideological dogmas of the moment. Thus, in 1953 revised editions of both *The Quiet Don* and *Virgin Soil Upturned* appeared, allegedly with Sholokhov's sanction, which were nothing less than bowdlerizations.[39] The distinctive Sholokhovian idiom was partially vitiated. Diction and syntax, the very *words* which, as he has said again and again, are precious to him, were adulterated. More appropriate cenotaphs for Stalin could not be devised.

Not only was the language altered, lengthy passages were added or deleted to make Whites less human and Communists more appealing. It is as if Sholokhov's most stupid and dogmatic critics of the late twenties suddenly revived and compelled him to emend everything under their supervision.

Stalin's death signaled a suspension of the practice of drastic rewriting, and Sholokhov's novels (as well as those of many other Soviet writers) were restored almost to their original form in 1956, in an edition of his complete works that bore for the first time the phrase "revised by the author," perhaps indicating that Sholokhov was personally satisfied with it.

One feature of this edition that partakes about equally of justice and the sinister irony that often attaches to Soviet affairs is the fate of Sholokhov's reference to Stalin. Originally Stalin occupied only a footnote, but in 1953 this was transmogrified into six glowing paragraphs of text. Now Stalin's name has vanished, as Bronstein's (Trotsky's) did in 1935. The six paragraphs have shrunk to one, and only Budyonny's name survives.

The peculiar exigencies of Communist control over publishing make it clear why, during his visit to the United States in 1960, Sholokhov assured newsmen that censorship was no problem for him. At the same time, there is a story, recorded by Jürgen Rühle, that at the Second Writers' Congress, "when someone asked, when will your next work finally appear, Sholokhov shouted into the questioner's face, 'That rests with you!' "[40]

With the rise to power of Premier Khrushchev, Sholokhov began to publish fiction once more—first, the long story, "A Man's Fate" (1956), and then the second volume of *Virgin Soil Upturned* (1960), for both of which he received Lenin Prizes. His early stories were republished for the first time since 1931. He traveled frequently to Western Europe and accompanied Premier Khrushchev on his visit to the United States. His fiftieth birthday in 1955 occasioned a national celebration. In 1957, making a clear bid for the Nobel Prize, he traveled and lectured in Sweden, Norway, and Denmark; but the trip was not productive. As in 1946, his candidature failed, the award going instead to Boris Pasternak. In view of the Swedish Academy's alleged prejudice against Russians, it seemed likely that Sholokhov, if he meant to win the Nobel Prize, would have to produce another work of outstanding merit. Presumably he tried to do this with the second part of *Virgin Soil Upturned* and the continuation of his novel on the Second World War. His struggle for high quality was revealed by a critic who saw five, even seven variants of pages from *Virgin Soil Upturned*. Time, however, and the endless demands upon him for public service were enervating. Indeed he may simply have lost patience with the Swedish Academy, because in 1963 at a celebration of the hundredth anniversay of Serafimovich's birth, he reminded his audience that Bunin received a Nobel Prize, but Gorky and Serafimovich did not. "As you see, in the international arena as well, valuations are motivated by class interest. And even in this light, in the light of valuations, there is a false ring to the assertions of bourgeois theoreticians that art is by its very nature above classes. . . ."[41]

Had the Swedish Academy waited for another memorable work, it might have waited in vain; for the years, as Sholokhov has acknowledged, have left their mark. When a newspaper man inquired why he rose at four in the morning to write and reminded him of the line in *The Quiet Don* about "the sweet sleep of morning," he retorted: "That was youth . . . but now the sweet sleep is replaced by old unrest."[42] Nor is his home truly a sanctuary for him. The house itself, a Victorian, balustraded edifice with great porches, was built after the war less as a home than as the museum it will eventually become. Annually since 1945 he spends considerable time hunting and fishing in Kazakhstan, with which he became familiar when his family was evacuated to Darinsk during the war. He wrote parts of *Virgin Soil Upturned II* in a small house in Uralsk and in a tent near Lake Chelkar.[43] But his output remains meager and will probably never again approximate that of his golden years between 1925 and 1930—hence the irony of his becoming a "Hero of Labor" only in 1967. A belated, if not anticlimactic, justice in the Nobel Prize came at last in 1965.

In her book *Voices in the Snow*, Olga Andreyev Carlisle tells one of the most revealing stories about Sholokhov that we have—revealing because it helps explain the inevitable but

strangely futile compulsion for vengeance which is an obsessive theme in his work. After interviewing him in 1960, Mrs.
Carlisle wrote:

> Sholokhov is a man kept awake at night by haunting
> war recollections; he is tortured by visions of blood and
> destruction. The last time I saw him he told me of a
> terror-filled nightmare he had had the night before, of a
> duel with a German soldier. Sholokhov was trying to kill
> the German soldier, who continually escaped him. He
> tried to shoot him but bullets would not touch the Ger-
> man. He tried to blow him up but the hand grenade
> wouldn't explode. Finally, striking out with a rusty razor
> blade, he found that the German's neck was made of
> rubber, not to be severed no matter how great Sholokhov's
> effort; soon the razor blade was breaking in his hand.[44]

This is exactly the kind of nightmare that repeatedly
haunts Sholokhov's literary heroes, though sometimes they
dream of being chased instead of chasing others.

His role in Russian letters has become curious. Of the two
major camps that emerged in the fifties after Stalin's death, he
had affinities with both, allegiance to neither. The "liberal"
faction, represented, for example, by Ehrenburg and Yevtu-
shenko, which demanded more emphasis on aesthetic and less
on utilitarian aspects of art, failed to attract his public support;
yet his attacks on the old guard dogmatists were no less
obstreperous and damaging than Ehrenburg's. It was Sholokhov, after all, who demanded more autonomy for literature at
the Second Writers' Congress in December 1954:

> During the civil war the workers and peasants said,
> "Soviet power is in our hands." With complete justice we
> should now say: "Soviet literature is in our hands." And
> the fewer timid newspaper and magazine editors like
> Ryurikov there are, the more urgently needed literary
> articles of audacity and principle there will be. . . .
> *Literaturnaya Gazeta* must be a leader, standing outside

all groups or groupings, a thing for whom only one queen [*dama serdtse*] exists—great Soviet literature as a whole and not certain of her servants, be they Simonov or Fadeev, Ehrenburg or Sholokhov.[45]

And it was Sholokhov who told Czech writers in 1958 that Fadeev had once said to him: "If anyone should ask me what socialist realism is, I should have to answer that the devil alone knows." Then Sholokhov proceeded to define the term himself:

It is possible that Fadeev oversimplified the matter as a joke. My answer would be that socialist realism is that which is written for the Soviet government in simple, comprehensible, artistic language. . . . I remember that Marxist theoreticians first declared my books to be products of a kulak writer and later called me a counter-revolutionary author, but in recent years they have asserted that I have been a Socialist Realist all my life.[46]

On the other hand, Sholokhov attacked both Pasternak and Solzhenitsyn, two writers whose integrity, if anything, exceeds his own,[47] and he invariably supports the general thesis that the Party alone can lead and teach the artist. At the twenty-third Party Congress in 1966, he vilified writers (obviously Daniel, Sinyavsky, and Tarsis, though he did not name them) who had published works abroad criticizing intellectual restriction in the Soviet Union.[48] The intemperance of his remarks, while it perhaps warmed the hearts of Party reactionaries, hardly endeared him to those who hope that civilized debate will permanently supplant Stalinist barbarism in Soviet life. His behavior at the twenty-third Congress and the Fourth Writers' Congress in 1967, together with the affluent private life he enjoys, has gained for him the scorn of many Soviet intellectuals. Some fear that he has drunk away his talent and now advocates the most conservative literary positions as a way of defending his fading reputation. In the letters signed by ninety-five Soviet writers denouncing the Sinyavsky-Daniel trials, Lidia Chukovskaya's indictment of

Sholokhov contained the most caustic remarks, including a charge that he had condemned himself to literary sterility.[49]

Although he identifies himself emphatically with the Establishment, the position which he visualizes for himself within it is, to say the least, eccentric. In *Virgin Soil Upturned II,* there is a parable which I believe Sholokhov may have intended to be interpreted as a confession. Old Shchukar, the village booby, learns from an acquaintance that actors, even since the Revolution, are beaten by the populace and the police whenever they fail to satisfy. He had thought of becoming an artist of this kind himself because he believed nothing was easier than amusing people, but now he decides against it:

> I've always been bullied ever since I was a little 'un! Geese and bulls, and dogs, and I don't know what else, they've all had a go at me. . . .But to get myself killed as an actor in my old age or have some bodily part of me twisted the wrong way round—no, thank you very kindly! . . .The actors can look after themselves. They're a tough lot o' young devils, I reckon. All this beatin' up they go through only makes 'em fatter. But I'm gettin' on in years (Chap. 22).

A moment later his wife comes to fetch him home; and as he toddles off, a neighbor thinks to himself: "God forbid, but if the old man dies, the village will be a dull place without him."

Perhaps Sholokhov would prefer Gorky's old role of detached sage. Unfortunately, he lacks Gorky's range of interest, though he has imitated him by interceding for imprisoned writers[50] and insisting that no mere critic should have the right to clip a young writer's wings. The Soviet press accorded him unqualified acclaim for his Nobel Prize, but this failed to match the public jubilation on his fiftieth birthday ten years before— perhaps a sign of changing taste as well as different leadership in the Soviet Union. At worst he could become a typical reactionary, ill-tempered and full of platitudes or violent tales about the good-old-days when sturdy Red lads liquidated

White villains. If this happens, he may find himself abandoned by the Party, because the Party has begun to change in response to the demands of a new Soviet generation that has less and less in common with Sholokhov.

This, of course, is only Sholokhov's public image. The private side remains largely concealed. How are we to evaluate what we know in order to reach some qualitative estimate of the man? We have at least two generalized pictures of him to reconcile: on the one hand, there is a hard, violent Sholokhov, an intemperate man whose tongue can be as cruel as the Cossack knout and whose vindictiveness toward enemies is predatory. This is perhaps best illustrated by comparing his major fiction with his incidental journalism. Objectivity and compassion characterize the first; sentimental affection or unbridled rage the last. Sholokhov often mars his public utterances with remarks—sometimes about colleagues and fellow Russians, sometimes about foreigners, especially Americans—so rancorous and disagreeable as to become disgusting. In a land where vituperation is all too familiar, Sholokhov's denunciation of Fadeev at the Second Writers' Congress, his attack on Simonov during the pseudonym controversy, his repudiation of Beria, and his condemnation of President Truman (which included a slur against the character of Truman's mother) are most savage of all. In these instances he indulged a language and tone never hinted at in the Don cycle even when he described the most heinous acts of the most despicable people.

On the other hand, there is a respectable Sholokhov, the counselor of youth, the judicious representative of a large constituency, the epic bard of the Cossacks, the father of four children, the solicitous friend. This Sholokhov refrained, like Boris Pasternak, from adding his name to the list of authors who endorsed the liquidation of purge victims in 1937. Loathing rules one Sholokhov; tenderness inspires the other.

The principle of continuity that unites these extremes must, I think, be sought in both the man and his environment. The West German critic, Jürgen Rühle, has devised an attractive interpretation of both:

In the Russian democratic movement of the past century there are two different streams working side by side, one intellectual and one plebian. The intellectual began with the Decembrists. The officers' conspiracy of 1825 grew into the liberal intelligentsia around Herzen, Belinksy and Chernyshevsky, into the anarchists and Narodniki, even into the politicians of the Provisional Government of 1917, indeed even into the Old Guard Bolsheviks who perished in Stalin's *chistka*. On the other hand, there is the revolutionary movement, stemming directly from the people, which begins with the great peasant uprisings of the seventeenth and eighteenth centuries under the leadership of Don Cossacks Stepan Razin, Pugachyov and Bulavin, and leads finally to the unrest of 1905, the revolution of 1917, and the post-revolutionary insurrections. There has never been a union of the two streams: the one stood as far as possible from the people; the other lacked a formulated social conception.

. . . It is significant that Sholokhov's father was a *raznochinets*, a member of the old revolutionary intelligentsia, while his mother was an illiterate Cossack peasant. In him both streams come together. Thus he was able, though of Bolshevik political conviction, to create the figure of Grigory Melekhov whose revolutionary ideas so well express the elemental life-interests and longings of the *Volkmassen* and also the principles of humanitarian democracy. It is no accident that the Bolshevik commissar calls him "an enemy tomorrow." Grigory's attitude leads in a direct line to the uprisings and revolutions after Stalin's death.[51]

One is reluctant to decline such an admirable and convincing scheme for explaining Sholokhov. We must, however, qualify it, first because of its intention to deprive Soviet Communism under Stalin of all historical legitimacy. That this is a convenient propagandistic device by which we can identify Stalinism either with old Russian autocracy or new Western authoritarianism seems obvious. But it is much too neat. It disregards the fact that, historically, Russian tyrants not only oppressed the people but initiated virtually every civilizing reform. Stalin is no exception, no matter how destructive and perverted he became. Moreover, if we try to imagine a successful seizure of power by either the liberal nineteenth-century philosopher Chernyshevsky or revolutionary Pugachyov, we are hard put to assert that they would have been kindlier taskmasters than Stalin.

Also Rühle stretches a point when he implies that Cossacks of the seventeenth and eighteenth centuries had much in common with the Cossacks whom Sholokhov knew in the twentieth. The social forms of life remained; but the spirit animating them was long since dead, as I have shown. Sholokhov conclusively exposed Yakov Fomin's dreams of becoming a true popular leader, a latter-day Pugachyov, as illusory, precisely because times have changed.

Finally, Rühle shares the predicament of most Western critics of Sholokhov: he assumes that Sholokhov's Bolshevik allegiance was a mistake, hence that he could not understand his own literary hero, Grigory Melekhov—who was really a premature "freedom fighter," not an enemy of the people, as Sholokhov describes him. This kind of reasoning leads directly to the conclusion that Sholokhov ridiculously idolizes the young Communist, Koshevoi, who is really a prig and a bore, and that his success as a writer can be accounted for only by some strange process through which true art and humanism triumph over misconceived dogma.

To understand Sholokhov, we must, I think, dig a little deeper than Rühle does. One can legitimately speculate that the driving force behind the man is a passion to justify himself for nonconformity. He was, after all, an only child with awkward parentage—both in the immediate family and in the community. An illegitimate son and an unacceptable Cossack, he had every reason to rebel. Bolshevism may well have seemed the ideal weapon with which to pay back a world that bequeathed a humiliating heritage, as it did, for example, to Mishka Koshevoi.

Passion rather than compassion may be the driving force

behind the writer as well. It would explain Sholokhov's lapses into sentimentality; for passion, unexamined by reason, threatens to become sentimental as soon as it grows reflective; that is, as soon as it is not translated into action. In *The Quiet Don* and perhaps the first volume of *Virgin Soil Upturned* Sholokhov's subject matter provided unlimited action which he animated with commensurate passion. In his earliest stories, however, the subject matter was too fragmentary, while in his later work the authorial attitude grows too meditative. Sentimentality results. It mars "The Shame Child" (1925) as it does the section in *Virgin Soil Upturned II* devoted to Davydov's love for Varya Kharlamova, which Sholokhov himself said he most enjoyed writing.[52] It expresses itself in an unseemly manner when Sholokhov begins telling stories about himself intended to exhibit his compassion: one day he shot a wolf, but when he approached the dead animal, he discovered it was a female still nursing pups. He turned away at once, conscience-stricken.[53] It is possible to grant him the compliment he desired for tenderness. It is also possible to say: "maudlin confessions mitigate nothing," and to remind Sholokhov that animal infatuations of this kind are characteristic of Mishka Koshevoi, who is not an altogether attractive man.

What is important about his sentimentality is that it may explain more than the occasional saccharine passage in Sholokhov's fiction. His vehement affection for his nation and his unrestrained anger at enemies, real or imagined, equally express an unexamined passion that cannot be translated into action. Perhaps the unctuous words he penned to honor Stalin no less than his diatribes against Simonov or Daniel and Sinyavsky represent the same inability or unwillingness to analyze rationally the ideas that these men represented. It can be suggested that what was true for the Cossacks is true for Sholokhov: emotional intemperance conceals uncertainty and insecurity. This may explain why he is reputedly so hospitable when in familiar surroundings but often so rude elsewhere. At the Fourth Writers' Congress, he characterized himself as a "sentimental brigand."

We shall probably have to wait until his death for anything like a complete picture of Sholokhov's private life, though we do know at least what he thinks of his own professional performance. In the late fifties, he explained that "it is especially necessary for the writer to translate the activities of man's soul. It was this captivating quality [*ocharovanie*] of man that I wanted to describe in Grigory Melekhov, but I didn't succeed completely. Perhaps I can in the novel about those who fight for their country."[54] On another occasion he said, "I have corrected the whole novel [*The Quiet Don*] many times, but rereading it sometimes, I think now I would write much of it differently."[55] Today "differently" could only mean "worse," but the fame that his youthful genius finally won has evidently blinded him to the sources of his power as well as the damage done by too many years of social service for the Party. If he is the writer who has succeeded best in living up to Communism's ideal of blending private with public activities, then we must conclude that his example does not make the ideal very appealing, unless, of course, we believe that Bolshevism initiated a new era of human life in which the artist is less precious than the social engineer.

Like his heroes, Sholokhov seems unable to function outside his physical and spiritual environment. Cossack dissolution within the Russian federation parallels, perhaps causes, the evaporation of his literary power. Pure Cossacks caused the vendee in 1918-22; the survivors participated in collectivization like men with their legs broken; the remnant who fought for or against Germany in 1941-45 were mere playactors in a forgotten tragedy. Sholokhov's life—indeed, the very texture of his language—follows this evolution, so that time's passage generates abstractness. In like manner, any spatial shift outside the Don Cossack area brings vagueness in descriptions. Thus, we find in Sholokhov's works an attenuation of reality that is proportionate to temporal or spatial movement. Sholokhov's development from *The Quiet Don* to *They Fought for Their Country* records this tendency.

In a sense Sholokhov's fate and Grigory Melekhov's are identical—except that Sholokhov could not terminate his own life on the last page of a novel, and his attempt to find a way out of his dilemmas along the lines of Mishka Koshovoi ultimately failed. Without a profession or a clan or a future, Grigory simply vanished; whereas Sholokhov had to struggle on, vacillating between periods of resistance to a tyrannical state and alcoholic acquiescence to it. Living where he did, Sholokhov was not only insulated from non-Communist ideas but subjected constantly to the threats and blandishments of the Party. The specter of imprisonment and the promise of pecuniary reward tempted better educated men than he, for example, Alexei Tolstoy, Leonov, and Fedin. Of major writers, Pasternak alone resisted to the end without resorting to exile, like Pilnyak, or to suicide, like Mayakovsky and Fadeev. Sholokhov's relationship with Communism was symbiotic—if not altogether healthy for his art. They share the same impulse to glorify "mankind" just as they share a purely aesthetic disinterestedness about the fate of individuals. This is perhaps why they can be sentimentally humanitarian one moment but adamantly cruel the next. During the time when Sholokhov achieved equilibrium between the two, his artistic impulse balanced his Communist allegiance and he composed his one masterpiece, *The Quiet Don.* It is an ambiguous document, called anti-Soviet by both a conservative West German critic and by the Chinese Communist press,[56] but publicized by Soviet critics as a prototype of socialist realism.

The difficulties he overcame no less than the form his art took made Sholokhov the best example of the virtues and limitations of Soviet literature as a whole during its first fifty years—from epic heroism to drudgery. As Soviet literature enters its second half-century, uncertain but hopeful, Sholokhov's *Quiet Don* should become, not a beacon perhaps, but a lonely landmark like the kurgans of his native steppe, marking the path of human suffering and survival. The man himself will no doubt go on, like Lenin, scorning urban intellectuals who want "pure democracy" yet encouraging young writers to serve the Party and the people with their art.

Appendix B:

The Quiet Don in English

Translated by "Stephen Garry" (H. C. Stevens) and published originally by Putnam and Company in England, then reprinted without alteration in the United States by Alfred A. Knopf, the novel first appeared in two volumes issued in 1934 (*And Quiet Flows the Don*) and 1940-41 (*The Don Flows Home to the Sea*).[1] Apparently as an economy measure, Volume I was reset in reduced type by Knopf when Volume II appeared to make a matched set. This accounts for minor discrepancies between current American and English editions. Reprints of both have been frequent, including a popular paperback edition by the New American Library.

A new edition in English has been made available by the Foreign Language Publishing House in the Soviet Union: *And Quiet Flows the Don* (Moscow, n.d. [1960]), translated by "Stephen Garry" but revised and completed by Robert Daglish. Revision is so extensive that the edition amounts almost to a new translation. This is a four volume edition which follows closely the 1956 Russian edition revised by Sholokhov himself; hence, it will probably remain definitive in English, though it gives no variant readings to illustrate the numerous changes made in the Russian text over the past twenty-five years. As could be expected, it not only includes many passages omitted from the British/American editions, it also omits several significant paragraphs. There are other flaws. For example, in Volume III (p. 381) a character named Umrikhin is credited with teaching Grigory Melekhov the "Baklanov" sabre stroke; yet, in Volume I (pp. 525-27) it was Uryupin who taught him.

The title of the Soviet English edition, the title of each volume of the British/American editions, and the title printed on the boxed, two-volume American edition (*The Silent Don*) are all fanciful or inaccurate, as V. V. Gura cleverly pointed out: "*The Quiet Don* [*Tikhii Don*—some would prefer *Gentle Don*] was first published in English at the beginning of 1934 under the name *And Quiet Flows the Don* [*I spokoino protekaet Don*]."[2] The word "silent," which was attached to the deluxe American edition, is equivalent to neither "*tikhii*" nor "*spokoinyi.*"

Since most readers in England and the United States use the abridged British/American version, my remarks concern that edition only. It is a flawed edition because Putnam's editor, evidently with the approval of Sholokhov's agents in Moscow, insisted on omitting approximately 25 percent of the Russian text. Mr. Stevens, the translator, then had to alter the sequence of the narrative and sometimes introduce new chapter, section, and paragraph divisions in order to maintain continuity. A few additional discrepancies occur because the typescript from which Mr. Stevens translated seems to have differed slightly from the one used for the first published version in the Soviet journal, *Oktyabr*.

In no case, I believe, were politics or ideology of central concern. Aesthetic or monetary considerations alone governed emendation, the aim being to make the novel less expensive and to improve it by rejecting superfluous descriptions and characters. The novel was long; Sholokhov was perhaps not sufficiently selective; paper and binding were costly; British and American readers would possibly be impatient with unfamiliar Russian events and difficult names. Whatever the justifications by publishers, however, Sholokhov expressed his personal dissatisfaction with the abridgement and insisted that "the inaccuracies, which S. Garry allowed, absolutely must be corrected because they often distort the sense."[3]

As a publishing venture, *The Quiet Don* posed serious risks, not only because it was so long but because, in 1931 when a typescript became available in England, it was only half finished and also because its frequent references to living persons (Russian émigrés, British and French military personnel) might expose a publisher to libel suits. We must, therefore, remain grateful not only to Mr. Stevens but to Mr. John Huntington of Putnam Company for undertaking to publish *The Quiet Don* at all.

What have been deleted are: (1) sections and entire chapters presenting historical documents and military information; (2) exposures of White Guard generals as opportunists and of the bankruptcy of counterrevolutionary ideas; (3) names and activities of Allied officers during the intervention; (4) the complete story of Yevgeny Listnitsky's participation in the Civil War with the Whites; (5) the unsavory details of Yelizaveta Mokhova's life and her merchant-father's helplessness; (6) elements of Lenin's teachings and influence; (7) reference to Stalin; and (8) a great deal of racy dialogue and many folk songs. While it may be true that the novel is overburdened with documents, troop dispositions, and actual participants in the Revolution, all of which could be discarded without harming the whole work, it is certainly not true that the elimination of Listnitsky's and Liza Mokhova's stories is harmless. Nor is the abridgement of dialogue exactly beneficial despite the difficulty of rendering colloquial Cossack speech into satisfactory English.

We object strenuously when we find that Soviet editors have deleted passages from *The Quiet Don;* however, our English version is far less complete than any Soviet edition. And this fact suggests a serious problem: how can English and Russsian students come to terms in their critical estimates of the novel when they are reading different versions? For example, how can the person who has read only the translation understand a Soviet critic's persistent emphasis on Grigory Melekhov's "crime against his people?" One might say the Soviet critic is perversely propagandistic, for in the translation Grigory seems merely to have chosen (or to have been predisposed toward) one of two equally unsatisfactory courses of action. The English reader, however, has been spared some of

Sholokhov's damnatory documentation of the White's behavior.
And the English reader has not traced the parallel, contrasting
careers of Listnitsky and Grigory Melekhov, of Liza Mokhova
and Aksinya Astakhova or Natalya Melekhova. Thus, the total
impact of the novel is somewhat different; various emphases
and effects which Sholokhov included are distorted. This is not
to say that in the original version Grigory was offered more
attractive opportunities to take the revolutionary path. The
difference is that in the original a reader is somewhat more
conscious of the unfavorable features of the reactionary cause
which Grigory finally served.

Listnitsky is a landowner and monarchist. Liza is the
degenerate daughter of an emerging Russian capitalist. And
Sholokhov avails himself more than once of the opportunity to
place these individuals beside his major characters for comparison. Consider, for example, the letter (omitted from p. 232,
Vol. I)[4] and telegram (p. 263) exchanged by Listnitsky and
his father:

Father, I have applied for a transfer from the
Ataman's Regiment to the regular army. I received my
appointment today, and am leaving for the front to report
to the commander of the Second Corps. You will probably
be surprised at my decision, but I want to explain my
reasons. I am sick of my surroundings. Parades, escorts,
sentry duty—all this palace service sets my teeth on edge.
I am fed up with it. I want live work and—if you wish—
heroic deeds. I suppose it's my Listnitsky blood that is
beginning to tell, the honourable blood of those who ever
since the War of 1812 have added laurels to the glory of
Russian arms. I am leaving for the front. Please give me
your blessing.

Last week I saw the Emperor before he left for
headquarters. I worship the man. I was standing guard
inside the palace, he smiled as he passed me and said in
English to Rodzyanko, who was with him: "My glorious
Guard. I'll beat Wilhelm's hand with it." I worship him
like a schoolgirl. I am not ashamed to confess it, although

I am over twenty-eight now. I am terribly upset by the palace gossip, besmirching the Emperor's glorious name. I don't believe it, I can't believe it. The other day I nearly shot Captain Gromov for uttering disrespectful words about Her Imperial Majesty in my presence. It was vile, and I told him that only people who had the blood of serfs flowing in their veins could stoop to such filthy slander. The incident took place before several other officers. I was beside myself, I drew my revolver and was about to waste a bullet on the cad, but my comrades disarmed me. My life becomes more miserable with each day spent in this cesspool. In the guards' regiments—among the officers, in particular—there is no genuine patriotism, and—one is terrified to utter it—there is even no love for the dynasty. This isn't the nobility, it's the rabble. This is really the explanation of my break with the regiment. I cannot associate with people I don't respect.

Well, that's about all. Please forgive my incoherence, I am in a hurry, I must pack my things and leave. Keep well, Papa. I shall write you a long letter from the front. Your Yevgeny (Part iii, Chap. 14).

I am very glad, my dear boy, that you have received your baptism of fire. The nobleman's place is out there, not in the palace. You are much too honest and clever to be able to cringe with a peaceful conscience. Nobody in our family has ever done that. For that reason, your grandfather lost favour and died in Yagodnoe, neither hoping for nor awaiting grace from the Emperor. Take care of yourself, Yevgeny, and get well. Remember, you are all I have in the world. Your aunt sends her love. She is well. As for myself, I have nothing to write. You know how I live. How can things at the front be as they are? Is it possible that we have no people with common sense? I don't believe the newspaper reports. They are all lies, as I know from past years. Is it possible, Yevgeny, that we shall lose the campaign? I am impatiently awaiting you at home (Part iii, Chap. 22).

With these in mind, the reader can hardly help but recall and compare the letters passed between Grigory Melekhov and his father.

The reduction of Listnitsky's importance in the novel results in other significant omissions. Thus, at the end of the first paragraph (Vol. I, p. 246), Listnitsky's general tells him:

"I know you will find it difficult to work in your old surroundings, Captain. . . . Aren't you the son of General Listnitsky? . . . For my part I can tell you that we value your kind of officer. Even among the officers, the majority are double-dealers nowadays. There is nothing easier than to change one's faith, and even to serve two faiths at the same time," the chief of staff concluded bitterly (Part iv, Chap. 10).

On the following page at the end of the first paragraph, Listnitsky is checking quarters:

But here an unpleasant incident occurred. As he grasped the door-knob, he saw a drawing, scratched on the wall with some sharp instrument, of a dog's head and a broom.[5] Evidently some of the workers who had repaired the building knew for whom it was intended.

"What's this?" asked Listnitsky, his eyebrows twitching.

The city representative glanced at the drawing out of his sharp mouse-like eyes, and gasped. The blood rushed to his head so violently that even his stiff collar looked pink.

"I beg your pardon, Captain, a vile hand. . . ."

"I hope that this emblem was drawn without your knowledge."

"Why, what do you think? How else could it have been done? It's a Bolshevik trick, performed by some scoundrel."

"The artist didn't hit the mark—the Cossacks don't know enough Russian history. But it doesn't follow from this that we can encourage such an attitude towards us. . . ."

The representative tried to scratch out the drawing with his firm polished nail, smearing his expensive English coat with the white dust as he rose on tiptoe trying to reach the drawing. Listnitsky was polishing his pince-nez and smiling, but a bitter feeling gnawed within him.

"So this is how they greet us, this is the other side of the medal. But does all Russia really regard us as *Oprichniki?*" (Part iv, Chap. 10.)

Here the omission of Listnitsky's story results in the omission of both an historically significant factor of the Revolution and an aesthetically significant factor in defining that purposelessness and lack of principle which often seems to characterize the Whites' behavior in the novel. Of equal significance are the several omitted paragraphs, scattered throughout *The Quiet Don*, which record Listnitsky's memories of Aksinya Astakhova and the lasting attraction she seems to have for him.

The elimination of Liza Mokhova's story deprives the English translation of an entire chapter: the diary of a dead Cossack which should occur in Volume I (p. 223). It is important for several reasons. First, its diary form provides an example of Sholokhov's ability to vary effectively his technique; second, it furnishes an interesting contrast between a middle-class Cossack woman gone to the city for an education and the peasant-class Cossack woman left on the farm. Liza belongs in a love triangle between Mitka Korshunov and the diarist Timofei just as Grigory Melekhov is caught between Natalya and Aksinya. Third, the diary has been attacked in the Soviet Union for its "unsavory and excessive psychological details"; and English readers, accustomed to the works of D. H. Lawrence, may be interested to see what kind of "unsavoriness" for a time provoked the indignation of Soviet moral legislators. Unfortunately the chapter is too long to reproduce here. It is simply the record, kept by a young student, of his affair with Liza and later his participation in the war. The diarist portrays Liza as "a devilish beauty . . . proud of her own figure," for whom nothing exists but the "cult of self-admiration." Her craving for and acceptance of men contrasts quite significantly with the behavior of the novel's other Cossack women, many of whom also indulge the sexual impulse with a certain generosity, yet never relinquish their dignity. In addition, the diary portrays its own writer with keenness and sensitivity so that by the end what Sholokhov has done is to create a new, independent character who acts as a miniature kaleidoscope through which we survey a small segment of Russian society: the young, pseudointellectuals. Though perhaps not integrated sufficiently within the general pattern of the novel, the passage is still perceptively written. At the end, Sholokhov says that many readers had a good smile over this "strange, intimate life and its earthy passions."

Just as the reduction of Listnitsky's position resulted in the loss of other important elements, so here the reduction of Liza's importance results in the loss of an interesting reflection by her father. It will be remembered that, while only a minor character, he is the novel's sole hereditary Russian merchant. As such, he gains prominence in present-day Soviet criticism with its inevitable emphasis on class origin and class psychology. The following deleted passage is, therefore, meaningful. In Volume I (p. 333, after the first paragraph) a letter arrives from Liza asking for money. Old Mokhov cries, thinking: "She's a stranger to me . . . and I to her. She only remembers she's my daughter when she wants money. The dirty little hussy, with her lovers. . . . Yet—as a baby, she had such fair hair, and she was all my own. . . . God!" (Part iv, Chap. 7.)

In reducing the size of the English translation, the editor did not stop with the expulsion of entire chapters but deleted even single sentences and phrases. Thus, at the end of Chapter 4 (Vol. I, p. 52), which explains Grigory's feud with Stepan Astakhov, two sentences are cut: "From this day the bad feeling grew. It was settled on a field in East Prussia two years later." On page 117, at the break, two sentences are dropped from the description of Stockman's early agitation work (later they were omitted from Russian editions as well): "He laid the cocoon of discontent. And who could know that within four years the larva of the strong, vital foetus would break out of the decrepit wall." On page 132, line 11, this clause describing Yagodnoe, Listnitsky's estate, is omitted: ". . . his land—4,000 desyatins—got by his great-grandfather for service in the 1812 Fatherland War, was situated in Saratov province." On page 314, line 17, after the break, a German soldier shouts insults at the Russians: "Comrades! We've shot up you blue-coats often enough. And we'll thrash this outfit too . . . or, as we say, pick ourselves some crows. So hang on. Don't shoot for a while." After the second paragraph on page 384, Bunchuk remembers a friend, a Petersburg worker killed in the war, whose twelve-year-old daughter, now alone, greeted him with bitter tears of loneliness. This passage is important as motivation for Bunchuk's behavior. In Volume II, page 207, the chapter should end with: "Prokhor quickly saddled the horses. Leading them to water, he asked, 'Shall we go home? to Tatarsky?' Grigory silently got up from the water and silently nodded his head." On page 209, the last sentence should read: "The half-company of Tatarsky infantry, *which had deserted from the front,* marched over the sandy dunes. . . ." The italicized phrase was omitted. Finally, in one considerable passage (Volume I, page 209 at the break to page 216 at the break) the English translation substitutes the name "Mrikhin" for "Astakhov" throughout. What happened here, apparently, is that Mr. Stevens translated from a typescript that antedated the one from which type was set for the first Soviet edition. Probably Sholokhov himself made the change (though we do not know his reasons) since Mrikhin was his prewar tutor. It is worth noting that the typescript of the last half of the novel from which Mr. Stevens translated contained several references to Trotsky that never appeared in printed Russian texts.

Of the total number of pages omitted from the English edition, the majority deal with military affairs and White officers. Thus, such names as Kornilov, Lukomsky, Dukhonin, Romanovsky, Krasnov, Denikin, and Kaledin, which figure rather prominently in the original, almost vanish from the translation; if they occur at all, they are often deprived of the

brief character sketches or characterizing statements which
Sholokhov fashioned for them. For example, in Volume I,
page 362, the first paragraph after the break is reduced from
five paragraphs of Russian text. White generals plus Victor
Chernov and Savinkov (Socialist Revolutionaries) are mentioned; Lukomsky and Kornilov discuss the military and political situation and plan the rising. On page 361, line 22,
Kornilov's insult to the delegates of the Soviet continues at
some length. The second paragraph of Kornilov's manifesto
(p. 368) is omitted:

> In these truly terrible minutes in the life of our father-
> land, when the approaches to both capitals are practically
> laid bare to the victorious advance of our triumphant
> enemy, the Provisional Government, forgetting the para-
> mount question of the independence of the country, is
> frightening the people with the imaginary peril of counter-
> revolution, which it is furthering by its own inability to
> govern, its own weakness, its own vacillation.

Entire chapters are omitted from pages 376 and 395 con-
taining Kornilov's letters to Romanovsky and Dukhonin; the
second of these reproduces Dukhonin's marginalia on a letter
showing his army's weaknesses and Bolshevik sympathy. Another chapter is omitted from page 474, which, in addition to
displaying the Whites' hopeless military position, presents the
excellent scene of Kaledin's suicide. Sholokhov reports it "externally," being unable or unwilling to attempt a portrayal of
Kaledin's mental processes, hence, to motivate the deed credi-
bly. The suicide is not witnessed; a tense adjutant rushes from
the room with the announcement. This incident, of course, had
considerable significance during the Revolution. In addition,
Sholokhov's critics like to compare his version with Alexei
Tolstoy's in *Road to Calvary*.

In Volume II, page 24, a chapter is omitted which contains
the meeting between Krasnov and Denikin at which military
coordination is discussed, but conflicting purposes prevent
agreement. Krasnov writes to the German Emperor with the

proposition that German and Cossack troops join hands to liberate the Don homeland as they did in 1807-13, "when Don regiments were found in the ranks of Wallenstein's army, fighting for the liberation of Germany." Krasnov's representative, Cheryachukin, travels with the German High Command and "observes the tremendous operation of Krupp's heavy artillery in routing Anglo-French troops." Another chapter is omitted from page 68 describing the arrival of English and French officers (Sholokhov supplies their names and ranks) in southern Russia "to get acquainted with the situation on the Don and plan a further struggle with the Bolsheviks." Krasnov gives a banquet in honor of the Allied mission and reads a bombastic speech:

> The delegates of "beautiful France" had already acquired a merry twinkle in their eyes from the good measure of champagne they had drunk, but they listened to Krasnov's speech with attention. After a lavish description of the calamities the Russian people had endured under "the oppression of the savage Bolsheviks," Krasnov ended on a note of high pathos. . . .
>
> [Later] Before the interpreter could pronounce the final sentence [of Captain Bond's response], the walls of the banqueting hall shook with three resounding cheers. Toasts were proclaimed to a flourish of trumpets. The assembly drank to the prosperity of "beautiful France" and "mighty Britain," and to victory over the Bolsheviks. . . . The representatives of the allied missions were expected to talk and Captain Bond did not keep his hosts waiting:
>
> "I propose a toast to the great country of Russia and I should like to hear in this hall your beautiful old anthem. We shall not pay attention to the words, I should just like to hear the music. . . ."
>
> The interpreter translated the request.
>
> Krasnov turned to the guests, his face pale with emotion, and shouted in a breaking voice:
>
> "May Russia be great, united and indivisible, hurrah!"

The band struck up majestically with "God save the Tsar." Everyone stood up emptying their glasses. Tears poured down the cheeks of a grey-haired archbishop. "How beautiful it is!" exclaimed Captain Bond, by now slightly tipsy. One of the distinguished guests was so overcome by emotion that in the simplicity of his soul he burst into tears, pushing his beard into a napkin lavishly smeared with caviar . . . (Part vi, Chap. 11).

Three pages of Russian text are omitted from Volume II, page 265. They present information on shipments of planes, tanks, munitions, and instructors from the Allies, and also Communist Party decisions on the disposition of troops. Of utmost importance here is the footnote which Sholokhov included in the first edition of this volume (it was omitted from Russian editions by 1935) on the nature and extent of the Don Cossack rising in 1919:

It is characteristic that an authentic measurement of the Upper-Don revolt has not been presented by our historians who are working out a reconstructed history of the Civil War at the present time. Thus, in the very considerable and valuable work of N. Kakurin (*How the Revolution Was Fought*, Gosizdat, Vol. I, 1925, the Upper-Don revolt is described as follows: [Kakurin's account is long and very detailed, presenting facts, figures, and interpretation. Then Sholokhov writes:] In reality, there were not 15,000 rebels but 30,000-35,000 whose armament in April and May comprised not "a few machine-guns" but 25 "cannons" (including 2 mortars), about 100 machine-guns, and rifles for almost every soldier. Moreover, the last part, devoted to the character of the Upper-Don revolt, is essentially inexact: it (the revolt) was not, as Comrade Kakurin writes, put down in May on the right bank of the Don. The right-bank territory was in truth emptied of rebels by the Red expedition; but the armed, revolting troops and the entire population crossed to the left side of the Don. Beyond the Don along a 200 verst line were trenches in which the rebels sat and defended themselves for two weeks, until their union with the major forces of the Don Army. (M.S.)

Sholokhov's active opposition to inaccurate history is extremely interesting at a time (1933) when distortion was gradually becoming an essential feature of "official" interpretation of Soviet history.

Of the several documents omitted from the English edition, one of the most valuable is "Uprising in the Rear" which should appear in Volume II, page 269. It is an early, official Soviet response to the Cossack defection. Grigory read it from a newspaper clipping picked off a dead "commissar":

UPRISING IN THE REAR

The uprising of part of the Don Cossackry has now lasted several weeks. Inspired by the agents of Denikin—the counter-revolutionary officers—it has found support among the Cossack kulaks, and the kulaks have dragged a considerable number of middle Cossacks after them. It is quite possible that in some cases the Cossacks suffered injustices at the hands of individual representatives of Soviet power. This has been cleverly used by Denikin's agents to fan the flames of rebellion. The White Guard hangers-on in the insurgent area pretend to support the power of the Soviets in order to win the confidence of the middle Cossacks. In this way counter-revolutionary scheming, kulak interests and the ignorance of the Cossack masses have combined together in a senseless and criminal revolt in the rear of our armies on the Southern Front. A rebellion in the rear of an army is the same as a sore on the labourer's shoulder. To fight well, to defend the Soviet land and crush Denikin's landlord gangs, one must have a reliable, peaceful and friendly worker-peasant rear. It is therefore a task of the utmost importance to purge the Don of rebellion and the rebels.

The Central Soviet Government has given orders for this task to be accomplished in the shortest possible time.

Splendid reinforcements have arrived and are still arriving
to assist the expeditionary forces that are fighting this
treacherous counter-revolutionary revolt. The best Party
organizers are being sent to deal with this urgent task.
The revolt must be ended. Our Red Army men must
make themselves clearly aware that the rebels of the
Veshenskaya, Yelanskaya and Bukanovskaya districts are
the direct accomplices of the White Guard generals
Denikin and Kolchak. The longer the uprising is allowed
to continue, the more losses there will be on both sides.
Bloodshed can be reduced by only one means: by delivering a swift, severe and crushing blow.
The revolt must be ended. The sore on our shoulder
must be opened and cauterized with a hot iron. Then the
Southern Front will have its hands free to strike a mortal
blow at the enemy (Part vi, Chap. 58).

Lenin's position in the novel is altered by four omissions.
First, in Volume I, page 284, the passage read by Bunchuk
should begin with these words of Lenin:

The socialist movement cannot be victorious within the
old framework of a native country. It will create new,
higher forms of human social life, when the rightful needs
and the progressive aspirations of the toiling masses of
every nationality shall have first of all been satisfied in
international unity and the destruction of present-day
national partitions (Part iv, Chap. 1).[6]

Second, on page 425, line 15, this sentence concerning Bunchuk
and his feeling of love for Anna Pogudko is omitted:

He knew it [the feeling] well; he had experienced its prick
at all important turns in his life: at the first moment of an
attack when the emotions still were not dulled; or hearing
the slightly burred speech of Lenin, and feeling, like a
prism, how the leader and genius' wisdom burned him; or
loving the intangibly beautiful thread of a life in danger

of extinction, yet deciding upon the dangerous path. He
now felt this feeling again as he stared at the swarthily
rosy cheeks of this girl . . . (Part v, Chap. 5).[7]

The third omission occurs in Volume II, page 67, where, at the
end of the first paragraph, the officer continues:

> "In the old days, in Napoleon's time even, there was
> some pleasure in war. Two armies came together, had a
> knock at each other and parted. No fronts, no sitting in
> trenches. But just try and understand what's going on
> now—the devil himself couldn't do it! The historians may
> have told lies about other wars, but it's nothing to what
> they'll say about this one. It's not war, it's a confounded
> boring mess. No colour! Just mud and utter confusion.
> You know what I'd tell the men at the top? 'Here you are,
> Mr. Lenin,' I'd say, 'here's a sergeant-major for you, get
> him to teach you how to handle a gun. And you, Mr.
> Krasnov, you ought to know how to already.' And then
> let them fight it out like David and Goliath; and the one
> who came out on top got the government. The people
> don't care who rules them (Part vi, Chap. 10).

Finally, in Volume II, page 510, in an omitted chapter on the
routing of the Whites, there is Stalin's letter to Lenin (contained in a footnote) on the military situation. In the text of
the novel itself, Sholokhov wrote: "From the moment when
comrade Stalin reached the Southern Front and when the plan
which he presented (the drive across the Donbass and not
across the Don region) began to take shape—the situation on
the Southern Front was sharply altered." This is the passage
which (in Russian) was expanded in the 1953 edition but
omitted entirely after Stalin's death.

The omissions presented here, though far from complete,
are perhaps the most important ones. That they must be considered in any adequate evaluation of *The Quiet Don* seems
clear enough. Even if it were true that our translation is in
fact a *better* work of art than the original, having been freed

of superfluous elements, this is still no justification. Only critical confusion can result from unacknowledged alterations of a work of art, especially a work of art which has provoked such widely differing estimates, both in the Soviet Union and in the West. In conclusion, however, gratitude should be expressed to the publisher for making the present version available, despite its omissions. The translation is flexible enough to communicate both the narrative's frequent lyrical moods and the rough vigor of Sholokhov's style. And the central narrative, dealing with Grigory's fate, communicates the same dramatic sense of tragedy in the English version as in the Russian. The fact should also be noted that the English version became more complete as it progressed. It is the first volume which suffers most from abridgement.

Notes

Preface

1. P.Gavrilenko, *S Sholokhovym na okhote* (Alma Ata, 1965),
   p. 13.
2. "Western Writing on Soviet Literature," *Survey*, No. 50
   (January 1964), pp. 137-45.
3. L. Yakimenko, *Tvorchestvo Sholokhova* (Moscow, 1964),
   p. 830.
4. *Pravda* (December 11, 1965), p. 4; tr. in *The Current Digest
   of the Soviet Press,* XVII (Jaunary 5, 1966), 29.
5. *Razgovor v serdtsakh* (Moscow, 1930), p. 232.
6. *Ward 7,* tr. Katya Brown (London, 1965), p. 45.

Chapter I

1. V. Goffenshefer, *"Tikhii Don* zakonchen," *Literaturnyi kritik*
   (February 1940), p. 95.
2. William P. Cresson, *The Cossacks, Their History and Country* (New York, 1919), pp. 185-86.
3. *Adventures in Czarist Russia,* tr. A. E. Murch (New York,
   1960), pp. 66-68.
4. F. von Stein, "Die russischen Kosakenheere, Nach dem
   Werke des Obersten Choroschchin und andern Quellen,"
   Petermanns Mitteilungen, No. 71 (Gotha, 1883), pp. 9, 16.
5. Cresson, pp. 150-51. An equally striking story of Cossack
   traditionalism is their refusal to move from Old to New
   Cherkassk in 1805 despite the annual floods that inundated
   the old city on its island-stronghold. A. Savelev, *Tryokh-*

sotletie Voiska Donskavo, 1570-1870 (St. Petersburg, 1870), pp. 110-11.

6. von Stein, p. 15.

7. I. Lezhnev, *Mikhail Sholokhov* (Moscow, 1948), p. 75. Add to this the fact that Cossacks increased five-fold in the century before World War I, with virtually no increase in land area (N. Yanchevskii, "Krakh kazachestva, kak sistemy kolonialnoi politiki," *Na podyome* (Rostov n/D, June 1930), p. 114). In some ways the situation was analogous to that in the United States today where one finds numerous citizens with a frontier mentality living in a coolie environment. The atmosphere grows flammable. Violence toward any convenient scapegoat becomes inevitable.

8. von Stein, p. 25; A. P. Shchapov, *Russkii raskol staroobryadstv* (Kazan, 1859), p. 8; Arthur Stanley, *Lectures on the History of the Eastern Church* (New York, 1862), p. 515.

9. Cresson, pp. 218-19. Cossacks of the older generation have never forgiven the Reds for desecrating Voznesensky Cathedral. They used it as a stable and confiscated the gold during the Revolution. In addition, they pulled down Yermak's statue; but it was soon restored and stands proudly by the church to this day.

10. A. I. Gozulov, *Narodnoe khozyaistvo Dona do i posle Oktyabrya* (Rostov n/D, 1947), p. 22.

11. "I began with a description of Kornilovism, with the beginning of Volume II of *The Quiet Don,* and I wrote quite a bit. Then I saw it was impossible to begin with this and laid aside the manuscript. I set out anew and began with the old Cossack order, with the pre-war years; I wrote the three parts of the novel which comprise Volume I. . . . And when the first volume was finished and I had to continue writing on Petrograd and Kornilovism, I returned to the earlier manuscript and used it as Volume II. It was a shame to throw away the work already finished." A letter to I. Lezhnev, *Mikhail Sholokhov* (pamphlet), (Moscow, 1941), pp. 28-29.

Sholokhov apparently first mentioned the order of composition in 1932 (Yakimenko, *Tvorchestvo M. A. Sholokhova,* p. 89) and explained it further to a journalist in

1937 (*Izvestiya* (December 31), p. 3). It was on the second occasion that he expressed his personal dissatisfaction with the "historical chronicle" as a literary form because it "bridled" (*vznuzdyvat*) the imagination.

12. Most of the biographical material on Sholokhov's life is taken from I. Lezhnev, *Put Sholokhova* (Moscow, 1958) and V. V. Gura's *Zhizn i tvorchestvo M. A. Sholokhova* (Moscow, 1960), except where noted. Lezhnev's book is the best so far for biographical information, despite the fact that it is chiefly a critical work. Of almost equal value is the "chronicle" in F. A. Abramov and V. V. Gura, *M. A. Sholokhov, Seminarii* (Leningrad, 1958), pp. 130-76. This book was revised and expanded in 1962.

13. Lezhnev, p. 21.

14. *Ibid.*, p. 24.

15. A. Palshkov, "Molodoi Sholokhov," *Don* (August 1964), p. 161.

16. *Ibid.*, p. 162.

17. N. Kravchenko, "Sholokhov i folklor," *Literaturnyi kritik* (May-June 1940), p. 213.

18. I. Lezhnev, "Molodoi Sholokhov," *Izbranie stati* (Moscow, 1960), pp. 38, 41.

19. L. Yakimenko, "*Tikhii Don*" *Sholokhova* (Moscow, 1958), p. 16.

Chapter II

1. Sholokhov made this statement in an interview with K. Priima in 1955; quoted in L. Yakimenko, "*Tikhii Don*" *M. Sholokhova*, p. 29.

2. Cf. Herman Ermolaev, *Soviet Literary Theories, 1917-1934* (Berkeley, 1963), pp. 31-32.

3. *Tales from the Don*, tr. H. C. Stevens (London, 1961).

4. Yakimenko, pp. 38-40. The story is partly translated in V. Gura's "Words of Eternal Vitality," *Studies in Soviet Literature*, I (Fall 1965), 17-19.

5. M. Soifer catalogues variant readings of several stories in *Masterstvo Sholokhova* (Tashkent, 1961), pp. 99-125, as does Gura, *Zhizn i tvorchestvo...*, pp. 8-13.

6. Babel may well have recognized this in one of his last interviews (September 28, 1937) when he compared Sholo-

khov's method to Tolstoy's and conceded that he used neither. It is worth noting that he esteemed Sholokhov highly as a genuine artist who lacked "Tolstoy's magnitude because when Tolstoy's nobleman departs and says, 'Cabby—to Tver—for 20 kopeks!' it bears the character of a world-shaking event tucked into a world-wide harmony." To be sure, Babel had not read the fourth volume of *The Quiet Don.* "O tvorchestvom puti pisatelya," *Nash sovremennik,* No. 4 (April 1964), p. 98. Cf. Jirí F. Franek, "Über die Poetik Scholochows—Ihr Gegensatz und ihre Übereinstimmung mit den modernistischen Strömungen," in *Michail Scholochow, Werk und Wirkung,* ed. E. Hexelschneider and N. Sillat (Leipzig, 1966), p. 51.

7. In Russian the title of this story is "Nakhalyonok," literally, an impudent brat. Mr. Stevens' translation, "The Shame-Child," is more descriptive. Cf. "The Brat," tr. Assya Humesky and D. H. Stewart, *The Dalhousie Review,* XLI (Autumn 1961), 324-46.

8. Lezhnev, *Put Sholokhova,* p. 64.

Chapter III

1. A. Kalinin, "Vstrechi," *Mikhail Sholokhov Sbornik* (Rostov, 1940), pp. 152-53.

2. M. A. Sholokhov, *Sbornik statei* (1956), p. 265. Had this introduction been published, English reviewers might have avoided erring a second time. When the second half of *The Quiet Don* appeared in translation, *The Times Literary Supplement* (October 5, 1940) complimented Sholokhov for showing "something of the primitive chaos and cruelty of Russian history as a whole. . . ."

3. For example, see Lezhnev's *Put Sholokhova,* pp. 92-94 and Soifer's *Masterstvo Sholokhova,* pp. 161-66 and 176-85. To minimize Sholokhov's concern for "photographic" realism would be erroneous. After the first part of *Virgin Soil Upturned* appeared, he said: "When a writer errs even in a small thing, he calls forth the reader's mistrust: 'This means,' thinks the reader, 'he may also lie in big things.'" (L. Yakimenko, *O "Podnyatoi tseline" M. Sholokhova* (Moscow, 1960), p. 11.) In 1934 he boasted that ". . . although I was not in the war [World War I], not a single

veteran has found fault or error in my work" (N. Maslin, *Roman Sholokhova*, pp. 36-37). And in 1937 he took exception to S. G. Korolkov's brilliant illustrations for *The Quiet Don* (1935-37). Granting their obvious merits, he nonetheless quoted a letter he had received from a Cossack: "You portrayed a Cossack on horseback. . . . Why [in the illustration] is he astride a Cossack saddle with no connecting strap [*skoshevka*] between the stirrups?" (I. Eksler, "V gostyakh u Sholokhova," *Izvestiya* (December 31, 1937), p. 3.) It is worth noting that Korolkov's illustrations, despite such trivial errors, are by far the most dramatic and revealing done to date. Because he became an émigré during the Second World War, his work is no longer printed in Soviet editions; and Sholokhov has come to prefer a far less interesting artist, O. G. Vereisky.

4. I. Eksler, "V gostyakh u Sholokhova," p. 3.

5. V. G. Vasilev analyzes some of Sholokhov's sources in *O "Tikhom Done" M. Sholokhova*, pp. 42-58. Of many memoirs that the English reader may consult, the most recent and in many ways the most interesting is Gregory T. Tschebotarioff's *Russia, My Native Land* (New York, 1964). Not only was he an eyewitness of many events recorded by Sholokhov, he also has read the same materials available to Sholokhov. Thus, Tschebotarioff confirms (pp. 160, 210-11) Sholokhov's portrayal of the Communist Podtyolkov, while Party critics have complained for years that he is inadequately drawn.

6. Sholokhov's remark on the order of composition appears above in note 11 of Chapter I. For the sequence of "Parts" in Russian, see note 4 of Appendix B.

7. It is important to note that Mishka Koshevoi but not Grigory Melekhov appears already in *Donshchina*, the first section that Sholokhov wrote. M. D. Sidorenko, "Zhizn i tvorchestvo M. A. Sholokhov," Mimeographed pamphlet (Rostov n/D, N.D. [1964?]), p. 7.

8. D. S. Mirsky, "M. Sholokhov," *Literaturnaya gazeta* (July 24, 1934), p. 3.

9. I. Lezhnev, "Za chistotu yazyka," *Zvezda* (June 1953), pp. 161-62. In linguistic composition, the speech in Sholokhov's area was originally a mixture of Russian dialects

(Tambov, Voronezh, and Orlovsk) with a heavy overlay of Ukrainian acquired during the 18th and early 19th centuries. It was this Ukrainian element (over 600 words in the first volume of *The Quiet Don* alone) that Russian readers could not understand. "Smol," "Kazachestvo v khudozhestvennoi literature," *Na podyome* (Rostov n/D, April 1929), pp. 73-74.

10. I. Eksler, "V gostyakh u Sholokhova," p. 3.
11. M. Soifer, *Masterstvo Sholokhova*, p. 67.
12. Nina Gourfinkel, *Gorky*, tr. A. Feshback (New York, 1960), pp. 97, 175.
13. "Iz temy o *Tikhom Done*," *Literaturnyi sovremennik* (May 1941), p. 134. A similar but more extensive comparison may be found in I. Lezhnev, "Traditsiya i novatorstvo M. A. Sholokhova," *Izbrannye Stati*, pp. 78-154.
14. "Sholokhov and Tolstoy," *The Russian Review*, XVI (April 1957), 27.
15. M. Soifer, *Masterstvo Sholokhova*, p. 39.
16. Quoted in Claude Mauriac, *The New Literature*, tr. S. I. Stone (New York, 1959), p. 218.
17. A. Khvatov, "Obraz Grigoriya Melekhova i kontseptsiya romana *Tikhii Don*," *Russkaya literatura* (February 1965), pp. 7-8.
18. *Pravda* (December 11, 1965), p. 4; tr. in *The Current Digest of the Soviet Press*, XVII (January 5, 1966), 28.

Chapter IV

1. *Epic and Romance* (London, 1931), p. 60.
2. *Ibid.*, p. 7. This point is crucial in explaining to recent Soviet critics the error of making Grigory Melekhov a mere peasant. We simply obviate conventional class distinctions (Marxist or other) when we see Cossack society *accurately*—though, to be sure, we must admit that conventional class distinctions were not only latent but rapidly developing. If we do not see Cossack society as a special historical case, if we insist on forcing it into conventional political and economic patterns, then we must accede to the dogmatic criticism of Yanchevskii in 1930 (See footnote 14, Appendix A).

To my mind, one of the ironies in Soviet criticism is

the recrudescence of Yanchevskian determinism in 1965, rendered palatable by a great dose of post-Stalinist toleration and kindly optimism. Yanchevskii reproved Sholokhov for making Cossacks a special people outside the happy revolutionary path to Communist bliss. A. Khvatov (p. 17) and V. Petelin (*Gumanizm Sholokhova,* p. 307) praise Sholokhov precisely because he keeps the door to Communist bliss open by not killing Grigory, thus showing that all people, however special, however grave their sins, can find their way to salvation. Grigory becomes a good Russian peasant after all. The idea of tragedy cannot be tolerated. These two critics, representing perhaps the newest phase of Sholokhov criticism, rely on a remark Sholokhov made in Sofia in 1951:

> People of Grigory Melekhov's type followed a very tortuous path to Soviet power. Some broke decisively away from Soviet power. But the majority accommodated; they took part in the construction and strengthening of our state, participated in the Second World War, entering the ranks of the Red Army (Petelin, p. 298).

This enables Petelin to say that "in *The Quiet Don* there are no tragic flaws, no punishment that would serve as just retribution, nor even the chastising hands of M. Sholokhov. There is nothing of this in the novel. Melekhov was not killed. He remains alive. In this is the humanism of the Revolution and its artist" (p. 307).

In addition, Petelin makes a strong case for "chance," so that he can claim that Grigory is essentially a good-hearted soul afflicted by bad luck (not tragic destiny): for example, he would have turned himself in to the authorities had he not *by accident* run into Fomin. But this makes Grigory no better than the usual pathetic twentieth-century hero—a man born into a world he never made and, hence, not responsible for his own behavior.

L. Yakimenko attacked this interpretation in "Krylatyi realizm," *Znamya* (April 1965), pp. 208-10.

3. Tr. T. E. Hulme (New York, 1915), p. 246. At least one Soviet critic has expressed dissatisfaction with my emphasis on purely literary issues that result from taking *The Quiet Don* seriously as a folk epic: A. Brukhanskii, "M. A.

Sholokhov v zarubezhnoi kritike," *Russkaya Literatura*
(February 1965), pp. 239-42. But a German critic has
advanced an allied claim: Harri Jünger, "Michail Scholochow und die Roman-Epopöe des sozialistischen Realis-
mus," in *Michail Scholochow, Werk und Wirkung* (Leipzig, 1966), pp. 91-2.

4. *American Humor* (New York, 1931), p. 157.
5. *A Preface to Paradise Lost* (London, 1960), p. 39.
6. *Romantic Poets and Epic Tradition* (Madison, Wisconsin,
   1965), p. 14
7. M. Kokta, *Publitsistika Mikhaila Sholokhova* (Kiev, 1960),
   p. 21.
8. *Ibid.*, p. 67.
9. L. Levin, "Iz temy o *Tikhom Done*," p. 143. The passage in
   question has caused no end of argument. V. V. Gura
   suggested a psychological interpretation by claiming that
   Grigory was indeed indifferent and joyless after his crime
   (*Zhizn i tvorchestvo M. A. Sholokhova*, p. 20), but V.
   Petelin insists that he is indifferent only to the White
   cause, since he presently hurries home to save Koshevoi
   and Kotlyarov (*Gumanism Sholokhova*, pp. 281-82). V. G.
   Vasilev discovers only "a philosophical summation of
   Grigory's life, full of contradiction and error" (*O "Tikhom
   Done" M. Sholokhova*, p. 177).
10. "*Tikhii Don* M. Sholokhova," *Pafos budushchevo* (Mos-
    cow, 1963), p. 199.
11. Sholokhov's description of his first draft appears in Note 11
    of Chapter I.
12. *Epic and Romance*, pp. 16, 185-86.
13. Sholokhov has explained that the position of Cossack
    women was different from that of peasant women. "Within
    the family, the Cossack woman was the husband's equal.
    She directed the household. Thus to speak of a *domostroi*-
    tradition among Cossacks is inaccurate. One can speak of
    historical survivals among Cossacks in their attitude to-
    ward women: in the early days a Cossack who no longer
    loved his wife, took her to the square and said "No love."
    And some other Cossack took her without asking her con-
    sent. . . . But the Cossack woman had more rights within
    the family than the Russian peasant woman; she was more

independent. She was prepared for the equality that Soviet rule gave women." V. G. Vasilev, *O "Tikhom Done" M. Sholokhova*, pp. 6-7. One of Sholokhov's funniest short stories confirms this view: "On Kolchok, Nettles and Other Things" (1926).

14. A sample of the dispute over Koshevoi may be found in B. S. Emelyanov, "O *Tikhom Done* i evo kritikakh," *Literaturnyi kritik* (November-December 1940), pp. 198-99. In recent times it is possible for critics to express anger at Koshevoi; thus, A. Khvatov refers to his "political immaturity and cruel methods of struggle." "Obraz Grigoriya Melekhova i kontseptsiya romana *Tikhovo Dona*," p. 31.

15. "*Tikhii Don* M. Sholokhova," *Pafos budushchevo*, pp. 175-76.

16. "Iz temy o *Tikhom Done*," p. 133.

17. "*Tikhii Don* M. Sholokhova i russkoe narodnoe poeticheskoe tvorchestvo," *Mikhail Sholokhov, Sbornik statei* (1956), p. 15.

18. For an excellent study of the problems in translating Sholokhov, see P. Tabakhyan, "*Tikhii Don*" *M. Sholokhova i voprosy perevoda* (Rostov n/D, 1961). His model language is German, but the issues remain constant, especially regarding syntax and rhythm of folksongs and levels of usage in dialect.

19. *Geroi Sholokhova na ekrane* (Moscow, 1963), p. 15. It is reported, however, that his reading from *Virgin Soil Upturned II* was very successful. V. Grishaev, *Nash Sholokhov* (Moscow, 1964), pp. 24-26. Unfortunately, I have not heard records of his reading.

20. Cf. Sidney Monas, "Boian and Iaroslavna: Some Lyrical Assumptions in Russian Literature," in *The Craft and Context of Translation*, ed. Arrowsmith and Shattuck (Austin: University of Texas, 1961), pp. 108, 117-19.

21. Soviet critics often excuse this lapse by saying that "the cultural level of the people" rose between 1914 and 1922; hence, the use of vulgarism and dialect declined. E.g. V. G. Vasilev, *O "Tikhom Done" M. Sholokhova*, p. 190. This explanation is only slightly more ridiculous than the claim that dialect decreases in Part viii because the Cossack "masses" are less in evidence.

22. Engels' letter to Minna Kautsky, November 26, 1885, in

Karl Marx and Frederick Engels, *Literature and Art* (New York, 1947), p. 45.

23. V. G. Vasilev tries to reconcile the two positions by saying that error leads to crime. (*O "Tikhom Done" M. Sholokhova*, p. 17.) See also N. Maslin, *Roman Sholokhova* (Moscow, 1963), pp. 181-84. Most factitious of all was the tendency to resolve all difficulties that Grigory Melekhov's fate poses by the expedient claim that "the people," not Grigory, are the "collective heroes" of the book. This "theory" was apparently first advanced in early reviews of the first volumes, but it did not become widely accepted until L. Yakimenko endorsed it in "O sovetskoi epopee," *Zvezda* (August 1956), p. 147, and *"Tikhii Don" M. Sholokhova* (Moscow, 1958), pp. 231, 498ff. A. F. Britikov finally disposed of the entire theory as nonsense (*Masterstvo Mikhaila Sholokhova* (Moscow, 1964), pp. 10-12) and was supported by V. Litvinov in emphatic and ironic terms (*Tragediya Grigoriya Melekhova ("Tikhii Don" M. Sholokhova*) (Moscow, 1965), pp. 29-34). The compromise position appears in V. Petelin's *Gumanism Sholokhova*, pp. 126-32, 141-44: "the people" are the heroes, but they are perfectly drawn individual characters who coalesce to constitute the mass.

Chapter V

1. *Podnyataya tselina*, Volume I, was published in England with a correctly translated title, *Virgin Soil Upturned*, tr. "Stephen Garry" (London, 1935) and reprinted in the United States by Alfred Knopf under the title *Seeds of Tomorrow*. Volume II was published in England and the United States with the title *Harvest on the Don*, tr. H. C. Stevens (London and New York, 1960). There is also a two volume Soviet edition in English published by the Foreign Languages Publishing House, translated by R. Daglish, undated. The two translations are equally reliable. While Mr. Stevens' is more enjoyable to read, Mr. Daglish's studied coarseness is perhaps a fraction closer to Sholokhov's Russian.

The Daglish text, however, preserves certain alterations of the Russian bowdlerization in 1952. For example, in Volume I, Chapter 19, he has: ". . . great Moscow, city of our fathers, lives even at night" instead of the simpler ". . . stone-bound Moscow." In Chapter 30, he omits the second of two questions asked by an irate peasant: "What are we going to plow with? What they make kids with?" From the second-to-the-last paragraph of Chapter 34, he omits the following two sentences from Nagulnov's statement: "The earth's like a mare; when she's in heat you must hurry to put the stallion to her, for she won't look at him when her time is past. And so the earth is with man." Agafon's description in Chapter 39 of "dogs' weddings" among the young people is deleted. Finally, Davydov's fall with Lushka Nagulnova at the end of Chapter 39 is somewhat muted. Except for the first example, Sholokhov apparently endorses these omissions from the Russian text.

Because Mr. Stevens ("Stephen Garry") was the pioneer translator of both of Sholokhov's major novels, English readers owe him an enormous debt of gratitude. Anyone who has tried to translate Sholokhov's prose recognizes the problems Stevens faced and must acknowledge his success.

It is worth noting that Sholokhov explicitly repudiated the claim by Harrison E. Salisbury (*New York Times* [September 1, 1959], pp. 1, 6) that the novel ended with Davydov's arrest on false charges and subsequent suicide in prison. See "O malenkom malchike Garri i bolshom mistere Solsberi," *Pravda* (March 1, 1960), p. 3. Soviet critics have compared Salisbury's prematurely announced conclusion of the novel to the ending of a translated version of Volume I published in Paris during the thirties which simply stopped with the women's insurrection and the beating of Party leaders. See L. Yakimenko, *O "Podnyatoi tseline" M. Sholokhova* (Moscow, 1960), p. 130.

Nonetheless, P. Mezentsev's impassioned defense of the epilogue chapter of *Virgin Soil Upturned II* makes one surmise that there was indeed a question in the minds of many Russians about the authenticity of the conclusion. A. Polikanov and P. Mezentsev, *Narodnaya kniga ("Podnyataya tselina" M. A. Sholokhova)* (Moscow, 1961), pp. 33ff.

2. I. Lezhnev made a thorough analysis of the bowdlerized edition in "Za chistotu yazyka," *Zvezda* (June 1953), pp. 156-70.

3. I. Makarev, *K proshlamy net vozvrata*, p. 18.

4. *Problems of Soviet Literature*, ed. H. G. Scott (New York, 1935), p. 157.

5. Sholokhov warned in 1935 that the second volume of *Virgin Soil Upturned* would be "more prosaic" than the first. "Dir," "Razgovor s Sholokhovym," *Izvestiya* (March 10), p. 3.

6. Perhaps the most noxious example of this is P. Lebedenko's "Na Sholokhovskoi zemli," *Don* (May 1964) pp. 116-22. The essay contains such remarks as: "It is impossible not to love Sholokhov"; and the author attributes to Mr. Roger Lubbock, a representative from Putnam's publishing house in London who visited Sholokhov, the statement that "I've traveled much and met many people. Among them families of American millionaires and Italian peasants. But Sholokhov's family left on me the best impression of all. It's a remarkably happy family" (p. 121).

   See also the section "Sholokhov—teacher and friend" in I. Sozonova, "M. Sholokhov za rubezhom," in *Tvorchestvo M. A. Sholokhov*, ed. P. I. Pavlovskii (Moscow, 1964), pp. 279-84. Of course, no cultist excess should surprise us after the Armenian composer Dzhivan Ter-Tatevosyan wrote a symphony entitled *On Reading "A Man's Fate" by M. Sholokhov!*

7. "Sorevnovanie s deistvitelnostyu," *O sovetskoi literature*, ed. M. Rosental (Moscow, 1936), p. 23.

8. Of passing interest is the sudden appearance in Soviet criticism of attempts to make Nagulnov an admirable man, partly because he opposed Stalin. See the last chapter of A. V. Kalinin's *Veshenskoi leto* and V. Petelin's *Gumanism Sholokhova*, pp. 426-27, 461. Kalinin was called to task for his exuberance by L. Yakimenko, "Krylatyi realizm," *Znamya* (April 1965), pp. 210-12.

   Criticism has come a long way since the mid-thirties when Sholokhov's treatment of Nagulnov provoked one Stalinist hack to say that he was much too attractive as a man and that his reinstatement by an intolerably lenient Regional Party Committee utterly falsified reality. I. I.

Chekhovskii, O *"Podnyatoi tseline"* M. *Sholokhova,* pp. 26-27.

9. L. Yakimenko, O *"Podnyatoi tseline"* M. *Sholokhova,* p. 131.
10. P. Gavrilenko, S *Sholokhovym na okhote,* p. 75.
11. *Poeziya deistvitelnosti, O svoeobrazii i mirovom znachenii russkovo realizma XIX veka* (Moscow, 1961), pp. 157, 159. Karlheinz Kasper amplified Blagoi's thesis in "Die Position des Autors und Scholochows Erzählung *Ein Menschenschicksal,"* in *Michail Scholochow, Werk und Wirkung* (Leipzig, 1966), pp. 127-30.
12. Gavrilenko, p. 43.
13. A. V. Kalinin, *Veshenskoe leto,* p. 70.

Appendix A

1. Printed in the appendix to *Sobranie sochinenii,* I (Moscow, 1956), 348.
2. Abramov and Gura, M. A. *Sholokhov, Seminarii* (1962), pp. 168-69.
3. Lezhnev, "Molodoi Sholokhov," p. 46.
4. I. Arolichev, "Novelist of the Don Cossacks," *Information Bulletin Embassy of the USSR* (September 27, 1945), p. 8.
5. *Sieben Dichter* (Schwerin, 1950), p. 116.
6. Abramov and Gura, p. 175.
7. "Protiv klevety na proletarskovo pisatelya," *Na podyome* (November 1929), pp. 99-100.
8. *"Tikhii Don* Sholokhova," *Krasnaya nov* (April 1929), pp. 217-18. This article was reprinted in the critical anthology *Mikhail Sholokhov,* ed. E. F. Nikitina (Moscow, 1931), pp. 5-30.
9. V. Goffenshefer, *Mikhail Sholokhov* (Moscow, 1940), pp. 13-14.
10. "Predislovie," *Tikhii Don,* I (Moscow, 1931), 11, 13.
11. Reference to this event in Abramov and Gura (1958), p. 142, was eliminated from the revised edition in 1962, p. 176.
12. Abramov and Gura, p. 176.
13. As recently as the spring of 1966 one could find people in the Soviet Union who still did not believe that Sholokhov wrote *The Quiet Don.*
14. At exactly the same time the most savage attack of all

appeared in a Rostov literary journal, N. Yanchevskii's "Reaktsionnaya romantika," *Na podyome* (December 1930), pp. 129-54. Poor timing minimized its effect. Sholokhov had already persuaded leaders of writers associations in Moscow and his own region that he was reliable; hence, the editors of *Na podyome* printed several refutations of Yanchevskii's position along with his essay.

Yanchevskii, an historian of the M. N. Pokrovskii-school, was an economic determinist who had never discovered that men's illusions and even delusions are just as important in motivating behavior as class background or modes of production. Thus, his attempted exposé of a writer whose genius was precisely for the portrayal of Cossack illusions turned out to be beside the point— despite the fact that he had published seven lengthy essays on Don Cossack history during 1930 aimed at substantiating his views about Sholokhov. The most dramatic example of his capacity for irrelevance is his "proof" that Sholokhov distorted reality by focussing on two well-to-do families (Korshunovs and Melekhovs) when in reality the poor and middling peasants comprised a majority of families in Veshenskaya (p. 132):

Number of Cattle	Number of Owners in Veshenskaya
0-1	1303
2-3	2082
4-5	1611
6-more	791

Yanchevskii's general thesis was that, from the beginning, Cossacks were at best a republic of slave-traders made up originally, not of freedom-seeking runaway serfs from Muscovy, but of Russian gentry seeking new markets for exploitation. The average "Cossack" was merely a mercenary soldier who "served in the Cossacks" just as he might "serve in the army" ("Razrushenie odnoi legendy," *Na podyome* (January 1930), pp. 140, 144). Yermak Timofeev belongs, therefore, to the same "international pleiad of pirates" as Raleigh, Drake and Cavendish. And Czar Mikhail Fyodorovich becomes the "first merchant" of Muscovite monopoly capitalism. (*Ibid.* (February 1930), pp. 125-26.) Thus, the idea that Cossacks were in any sense revolutionary individualists, as Bakunin and Plekhanov imagined ("Evolyutsiya Donskovo kazachestva k XVIII veku," *Na podyome* (April 1930), p. 143), is totally incorrect—indeed, it is a nineteenth century invention of Cossack apologists. Even the notion that Cossacks are somehow a "special" people is fraudulent because the modern Cossack has no lineal connection with the sixteenth to seventeenth-century warriors of Czar Mikhail's time. The Cossack was merely an erstwhile peasant or bargehauler—with delusions of grandeur fostered by the czarist government, the gentry and later the kulaks ("Evolyutsiya naseleniya Dona v XVIII veka," *Na podyome* (June 1930), pp. 134-36).

Against this background, Yanchevskii accuses Sholokhov of writing the Cossack "swan song." He is no better than General Pyotr Krasnov, who published a history in 1909 called *Pictures of the Bygone Quiet Don* in which he denied that any true Cossack, including Bulavin and Razin, ever rebelled against the czar—against boyars perhaps, but never against their precious monarch. Then Yanchevskii arraigns Sholokhov for trying to prove "that Cossacks are a special nationality with a special historical past which does not correspond to the proletarian way of development, that among Cossacks preconditions for the class struggle do not exist, and that the Cossack who deviates from the Cossack path will find destruction if he does not return to the Cossack bosom" (p. 131). So completely does Yanchevskii misconstrue Sholokhov's intentions that he complains about the ruralization of Cossack life, ignoring capitalism, labor, etc. "The Don was not 'quiet'." (!) Then come six accusations: (1) Sholokhov misrepresents local Cossack life by emphasizing well-to-do families who are numerically a minority in the population (p. 132); (2) his idylls of nature and idealized landscapes are pure examples of gentry-thinking, as is the "cult of antiquity" seen in Sholokhov's preservation of old songs (p. 133); (3) even mentioning Cossack "rights" to the land reveals a kulak mentality, just as mentioning "typical" Cossack men and women is an unspeakable example of fraudulent nationalism; (4) his Communist figure (Stockman) preaches only hate, not love for the future; moreover, he is not entirely Russian but German (p. 140)—indeed Bolsheviks are always alien to Cossacks, never natives (pp. 143-44); (5) he deliberately ignores the facts about the Cossack uprising in 1919 in order to make it seem spontaneous, while "we know" it was instigated by the gentry and kulaks with major German support (p. 146); and (6) he is no better than Izvarin, his "favorite hero" (p. 148), as we see when he recounts Podtyolkov's death in almost journalistic language and then describes White officers with "grovelling deference" (p. 147).

Four essays were appended to Yanchevskii's, condemning him; but in only one did the critic actually defend Sholokhov (M. Nikulin, "M. Sholokhov kak gumanist," pp. 180-82). The other three critics (N. Sidorenko, "Za chto propagandiruet *Tikhii Don*?", pp. 155-59; L. Shemshelevich, "Chevo ne ponyal Yanchevskii," pp. 159-66; and D. Maznin, "Ob idee *Tikhovo Dona* i levom zagibe t. Yanchevskovo," pp. 166-80) all adopted a patronizing attitude toward Sholokhov. Sidorenko said he is not proletarian but well-to-do Cossack, which may explain the unacceptable passive, contemplative elements in the book. Shemshelevich believed that Sholokhov, while he is sympathetic toward Bolsheviks, hence not guilty of "Perevalist humanism" (i.e. disinterestedness which is contemptible in Communist eyes), is a petty-bourgeois intellectual in his attitude toward war. Give Grigory Melekhov some education, and he *is* Sholokhov. Thus, Sholokhov is a fellow traveler; he is wrong but Yanchevskii is more wrong for exaggerating Sholokhov's flaws. Maznin's point (developed more fully in "Kakovo ideya—*Tikhovo Dona*?," *RAPP* (January-February 1931), pp. 158-67) was that Sholokhov is a peasant writer and petty bourgeois fellow traveler; hence, he makes errors. At the same time, he, no less than Tolstoy, can reflect reality with partial accuracy. He expresses the mood and ideas of Cossacks in the time of the proletarian revolution just as Tolstoy did of peasants in the time of the bourgeoisification of Russia. Both suffer from an all-forgiving, hypocritical objectivism, which is, to Maznin, the "foulest" (*gnusneishii*) kind of humanism.

It is obvious that these critics were attempting to follow mainline-Stalinism which opposed Left-deviationist Yanchevskii as well as Right-wing Sholokhov. Two years later when Stalin, having liquidated the Left, turned on the Right, Sholokhov had published *Virgin Soil Upturned*, which is safely centrist.

At the end of the debate in *Na podyome*, the editors promised a continuation in subsequent issues, but only one article appeared (A. Malekser, "O *Tikhom Done*," (January-February 1931), pp. 260-64) and defended Sholokhov. Poor Mr. Yanchevskii, in a frantic effort to defend his general position, published the first three parts of a serial essay on economic villainy among rich Cossacks. Then the series stopped, and we hear of Yanchevskii only as a writer of some meager "Literary Parodies" (*Na podyome* (December 1932), pp. 126-28). Indeed, the journal itself was damaged by being mobilized for collectivization in 1932 under a new editor, N. Stalskii—and then destroyed by L. Shauman, who became editor in the spring of 1932 and began publishing anthems commemorating the "wise" Central Committee of the Communist Party and "great leader" Stalin. Only ten numbers appeared from 1933 to the discontinuation in 1935.

15. Lezhnev, *Put Sholokhova*, pp. 228-31.
16. F. Ginsburg, "*Tikhii Don* M. Sholokhova," *Znamya* (June 1933), p. 131. Most critics became ecstatic over *Virgin Soil Upturned* as proof that Sholokhov had abandoned his "middle-peasant" objectivity. I. Makarev (*K proshlomy net vozvrata* (Moscow, 1934), pp. 17-18) was so certain of the change that he predicted a socialist vindication in the last volume of *The Quiet Don* and suggested that *Virgin Soil Upturned* was the logical conclusion of *The Quiet Don*, "in truth the fourth volume"! But in 1936, at the beginning of the purge period, even *Virgin Soil Upturned* was found to have errors. Nagulnov and Ostrovnov are not adequately unmasked and the women in the novel are poorly drawn. I. I. Chekhovskii, *O "Podnyatoi tseline"* M. Sholokhova (Kursk, 1936), pp. 26-31.
17. Abramov and Gura, p. 180.
18. Khrushchev's disclosures appeared in *Pravda* (March 10, 1963). See *Khrushchev and the Arts, The Politics of Soviet*

Culture, 1962-1964, ed. P. Johnson and L. Labedz (Cambridge, 1965), pp. 160-62.

19. Abramov and Gura (1958), p. 147. This letter is not mentioned in the second edition of the book, p. 181.

20. K. Muratova, *Mikhail Sholokhov, Kratkii spravochnik* (Leningrad, 1950), p. 11.

21. A fascinating study of *Virgin Soil Upturned*'s impact among factory workers (and also of how Communism uses literature) may be found in V. Echeistova and A. Lebedev, *Vecher rabochei kritiki po "Podnyatoi tseline"* M. *Sholokhova* (Moscow, 1934).

22. *Sobranie sochinenii*, VIII (Moscow, 1959), 88.

23. *Ibid.*, p. 96.

24. A. Serafimovich, "Mikhail Sholokhov," in *Mikhail Sholokhov, Literaturnokriticheskii sbornik*, ed. S. G. Lipshits (Rostov n/D, 1940), p. 8.

25. *Sobranie sochinenii*, VIII, 105.

26. The term *"ocherk,"* which has no exact English equivalent, signifies an essay that contains fictional elements. Sholokhov's "Word on the Homeland" is an example. The term is comparable to English "sketch" as it was understood in the early nineteenth century and practiced, for example, by Washington Irving. Probably the "interchapters" of Steinbeck's *The Grapes of Wrath* exhibit the form to best advantage in contemporary American literature. Truman Capote's *In Cold Blood* also has similarities. See Alexander Ninov, "Literary Form and Content," *Soviet Literature* (December 1965), pp. 143-49.

27. Lezhnev, "Molodoi Sholokhov," pp. 55-56. Cf. M. Kokta, *Publitsistika Mikhaila Sholokhova* (Kiev, 1960), p. 37.

28. V. Zakrutkin, *Tsvet lazorevyi: Stranitsy o Mikhaile Sholokhove* (Rostov n/D, 1965), pp. 28-29. See also A. V. Kalinin, *Veshenskoe leto* (Moscow, 1964), pp. 84-85.

29. B. S. Emelyanov, "O *Tikhom Done* i evo kritikakh," *Literaturnyi kritik* (November-December 1940), p. 185.

30. *Don, Kuban i Terek v Vtoroi Mirovoi Voine: Istoricheskaya povest o vtoroi voine kazachestva s bolshevikami, (1941-1945)* (New York, 1960), pp. 20-21.

31. This happened despite the fact that Sholokhov worked on the scenario along with S. Ermolinskii and Yu. Raizman. But the same thing occurred when he worked with I. I.

Dzerzhinskii on the opera version of *The Quiet Don.* This is the "work" that Stalin and Molotov praised when they saw it in Leningrad (January 17, 1936). In the final act Grigory leads the fight against the aristocrats and gains vengeance over Evgeny Listnitsky for seducing Aksinya. The opera program states: "Grigory calls the Cossacks and peasants to unite in the struggle for a better life. On to Novocherkassk! Day breaks. The Don glitters. An elemental, mighty song dies away into the distance: 'From boundary to boundary, from sea to sea, the laboring people take arms. For land, for freedom, for a better lot—let us fight to the death.'" This opera and also Ivan Dzerzhinsky's *Virgin Soil Upturned* are described in V. M. Bogdanov-Berezovskii, *Sovetskaya opera* (Leningrad, 1940), pp. 203-25.

32. See D. H. Stewart, "The Textual Evolution of *The Silent Don,*" *The American Slavic and East European Review,* XVIII (April 1959), 226-37. Cf. Radovan Lalić, "Zur Textkritik an Scholochows *Stillem Don,*" in *Michail Scholochow, Werk und Wirkung,* pp. 79-88.

33. For a translation of this passage, see Appendix B, pp. 214-15.

34. *And Quiet Flows the Don* (New York, 1946), pp. 479-80.

35. Lezhnev, *Put Sholokhova,* p. 383.

36. Chronological entries about his article on Stalin, "Father of the Working People," (*Pravda,* December 20, 1949) and the obituary he wrote for Stalin (*Pravda,* March 8, 1953) that appear in Abramov and Gura (1958), pp. 168 and 170, are removed from the second edition, pp. 203 and 205. It is interesting to remember that Stalin called Sholokhov soon after the war and urged him to finish *Virgin Soil Upturned.* V. Petelin, *Gumanism Sholokhova,* p. 481.

37. *Mikhail Sholokhov, Kritiko-biograficheskii ocherk* (Moscow, 1952), pp. 110-19. Also see V. A. Alekseev, "O nekotorykh osobennestyakh publitsistiki M. A. Sholokhova," in *Mikhail Sholokhov, Sbornik* (1956), pp. 98-118. The trend to convert Sholokhov into a mere journalist was continued by I. V. Rybintsev, *M. A. Sholokhov-Publitsist* (Drogobych, 1958), which is a poor precursor to the major study by M. Kokta, *Publitsistika Mikhaila Sholokhova* (Kiev,

1960). This is a detailed analysis of Sholokhov's expository prose, worthwhile in every respect except the inflated value which Kokta places on a minor aspect of Sholokhov's work.

38. The entire debate was printed in *The Current Digest of the Soviet Press*, III (April 1951), 12-14.

39. See note 32 above.

40. "Das Schicksal eines Kosakenromans, Michail Scholochow und *Der Stille Don*," *Der Monat*, No. 90 (March 1956), p. 13.

41. *Pravda* (January 22, 1963), p. 2.

42. V. Koroteev and V. Efimov, "Na Donu," *Izvestiya* (July 1, 1956), p. 3.

43. P. Gavrilenko, S. *Sholokhovym na okhote*, pp. 16, 20, 36.

44. *Voices in the Snow* (New York, 1962), p. 58.

45. *Sobranie sochinenii*, VIII, 283-84.

46. Reported in *Literaturnaya gazeta* (April 10, 1958), p. 1. See *The New York Times* (May 11, 1958), p. 26.

47. Professor Gleb Struve noted in a letter to the editor of *The New York Times* (December 12, 1965, p. E-11) that the insulting remarks about Pasternak and Solzhenitsyn that Sholokhov made at a press conference honoring his Nobel Prize were not printed in *Literaturnaya gazeta* for December 2, 1965, though they appear in *The New York Times* account, December 1, 1965, p. 13. Here, as again at the twenty-third Party Congress, Sholokhov's vanity and boorishness—or contentiousness—very likely embarrassed moderate Communists who are trying to inhibit Khrushchevian, as well as Stalinist, bullies.

48. *Literaturnaya gazeta* (April 2, 1966), p. 1; partly translated in *The New York Times* (April 2, 1966), p. 4. The full text is in *Soviet Literature* (July 1966), pp. 118-24).

49. *The New York Times* (November 14, 1966), p. 5.

50. V. Zakrutkin tells the story of Sholokhov's influencing the Party Central Committee to release Alexei Bibik, who had disappeared during the thirties. *Tsvet lazorevyi: Stranitsy o M. Sholokhova*, pp. 29-32.

51. *Literatur und Revolution* (Köln, 1960), p. 93.

52. Petelin, *Gumanism Sholokhova*, p. 16.

53. Zakrutkin, p. 13.

54. N. Maslin, *Roman Sholokhova*, p. 93.

55. V. G. Vasilev, *O "Tikhom Done" M. Sholokhova*, p. 201.
56. "Peking Paper Brands Sholokhov as a Traitor," *The New York Times* (May 14, 1956), p. 7. Also see Jürgen Rühle's remarks in *Literatur und Revolution*. A recent Chinese publication in English, *Some Questions Concerning Modern Revisionist Literature in the Soviet Union* (Peking, 1966), contains two scathing indictments of Sholokhov's hypocrisy and pascifism: Chang Chun, "Selected Statements by Sholokhov, the Renegade Author" (pp. 30-55) and Tsai Hui, "The True Features of the Renegade Sholokhov" (pp. 56-64). A favorable interpretation of Sholokhov's anti-war sentiment may be found in Wladimir Borstschukow's "Das Kriegsthema bei Scholochow," tr. G. Warm in *Michail Scholochow, Werk und Wirkung*, pp. 131-41.

In the 1950's, Soviet editors liked to print testimonials from Chinese peasants endorsing Sholokhov's books. In the 1960's, he became a goodwill ambassador, not to China, but to Japan and East Germany.

Appendix B

1. In 1936 an English edition of 3100 copies was issued by the Co-operative Publishing Society of Foreign Workers in the U.S.S.R., edited by Naomi Williams, who stated: "The present translation is fundamentally the same as the one published by Putnam, London. Certain passages omitted in the English edition have been retored and slight inaccuracies in the translation have been corrected." It is much more complete than Putnam's but still flawed. E.g. Timofei's diary (Part iii, Chap. 11) is omitted.
2. *Mikhail Sholokhov, Sbornik statei* (1956), p. 265.
3. *Ibid.*
4. All page numbers refer to *The Silent Don*, tr. "Stephen Garry" (New York, 1946), 2 volumes. In Russian the work was published in eight parts, distributed in four volumes that correspond to the English translation, which I enclose in parentheses, as follows: Volume I, Part i (I, 3-83), Part ii (I, 83-171), Part iii (I, 171-279); Volume II, Part iv (I, 280-402), Part v (I, 403-554); Volume III, Part vi (II, 10-311—Chapter 1 in the translation is actually

the second chapter); Volume IV, Part vii (II, 311-78), Part viii (II, 581-777).

5. A dog's head and a broom were attached to the saddles of the Oprichniki, the notoriously brutal armed forces of Ivan the Terrible, as a symbol that they would sink their fangs in the tsar's enemies and then sweep them away (Sholokhov's note).

6. The entire document, of which this was the first paragraph, was deleted from Soviet editions during World War II and only partially restored since.

7. This passage, too, was deleted from Soviet editions—by 1936.

Bibliography

To date, the best edition of Sholokhov's collected works is *Sobranie sochinenii*, 8 volumes (Moscow: Goslitizdat, 1956-60), but this is being supplanted by a nine-volume edition (1965-67) which will include the first part of *Oni srazhalis za rodinu* (*They Fought for Their Country*). Surviving manuscripts are preserved at the Gorky Institute in Moscow. Because revision and emendation are almost continuous, it is always valuable to compare recent with early editions. For example, each of the following editions of *Tikhii Don* (*The Quiet Don*) contains significant differences: (a) the serialization: *Oktyabr*, Nos. 1-10 (1928); Nos. 1-3 (1929); Nos. 1-8, 10 (1932); *Novyi mir*, Nos. 11-12 (1937); Nos. 1-3 (1938); Nos. 2-3 (1940); (b) portions of the book, published separately in 1928 by "Roman-gazeta," which included titles for individual chapters, omitted from subsequent Russian editions but preserved by H. C. Stevens in the English translation; (c) the first separate edition of each volume: I-IV (Moscow, 1928, 1929, 1933, 1940); (d) the deluxe edition of the first three volumes, splendidly illustrated by S. G. Korolkov (Moscow, 1935-37); (e) the first single-volume edition (Moscow, 1941); (f) the bowdlerized "Stalin edition" (Moscow, 1953).

Podnyataya tselina (*Virgin Soil Upturned*) has received far less editorial attention; hence, the text of Volume I remained almost unchanged from serialization in *Novyi mir*, Nos. 1-9 (1932), to the bowdlerized version in 1952. Volume II escaped mutilation: compare the three serialized texts [*Oktyabr*, Nos. 5-6 (1955), Nos. 2-4 (1960); *Neva*, No. 7 (1959),

No. 1 (1960); and *Don*, No. 7 (1959), No. 2 (1960)] with the first separate edition (Moscow, 1960).

Revision also occurs in the short stories between journal versions and those in collections. Important separate editions are *Donskie rasskazy* [*Don Tales*] (Moscow, 1925, 1926), *Lazorevaya step* [*Azure Steppe*] (Moscow, 1931) and Volume I of *Sobranie socheninii* (1956). The war stories and essays are easiest obtained in the eighth volume of *Sobranie sochinenii* (1960).

There is no definitive biography of Sholokhov in Russian. Four books contain almost all available information: Viktor V. Gura and Fyodr A. Abramov, *M. A. Sholokhov, Seminarii* (Leningrad, 1958, rev. 1962); V. V. Gura, *Zhizn i tvorchestvo M. A. Sholokhova* (Moscow, 1955, rev. 1960); Isai G. Lezhnev, *Put Sholokhova* (Moscow, 1958); and *Mikhail Sholokhov, Literaturno-kriticheskii sbornik*, ed. S. G. Lipshits (Rostov-on-Don, 1940). Three recent works add interesting details, the first about Sholokhov's boyhood, the other two about his activities since the thirties: A. Palshkov, "Molodoi Sholokhov," *Don* (August 1964), pp. 160-71; Pyotr P. Gavrilenko, *S Sholokhovym na okhote* (Alma Ata, 1965); Vitalii A. Zakrutkin, *Tsvet lazorevyi: Stranitsy o Mikhaile Sholokhove* (Rostov-on-Don, 1965). Additional information may be gathered from published interviews, of which three of the most revealing are: V. Ketlinskaya, "M. Sholokhov," *Komsomolskaya Pravda* (17 August, 1934); M. Neznamov, "Beseda s pisatelem," *Bolshevistskaya smena* (Rostov-on-Don, 24 May, 1940); and V. Koroteev and V. Efimov, "Na Donu," *Izvestiya* (1 July, 1956). A collection of interviews would be most valuable, especially if it included Sholokhov's remarks abroad as well as at home.

Criticism of Sholokhov's work has passed through three phases: (1) reviews and polemics (1926-34), (2) critical evaluation (1935-50), (3) scholarly investigation (1950-). Soviet bibliographies deal adequately with the last two (e.g., Gura and Abramov, pp. 228-327, is by far the most complete) but tend to slight the first. Thus, it is virtually impossible to find references since the Second World War to the collection of essays by S. Dinamov, A. Selivanovsky, E. F. Nikitina, and

I. Mashbits-Verov in *Mikhail Sholokhov, Sbornik statei,* ed. E. F. Nikitina (Moscow, 1931) or to "Stalinist" works such as I. Makarev, *K proshlamy net vozvrata: O romane M. Sholokhova "Podnyataya tselina,"* (Moscow, 1934) and I. I. Chekhovskii, *O "Podnyatoi tseline"* M. Sholokhova (Kursk, 1936). Current bibliographies ignore almost entirely the critical controversy which first greeted Sholokhov's books, when he was accused of insufficient class consciousness, inadvertant pantheism, and excessive sympathy with White Guards, Cossack nationalists, kulaks, and other enemies of Soviet power. This controversy echoes in Veniamin T. Goffenshefer's *Mikhail Sholokhov, Kriticheskii ocherk* (Moscow, 1940), but for a more complete survey than any in Russian, we must turn to Charles B. McLane's unpublished M. A. thesis *Sholokhov and the Soviet Critics* (Columbia, 1948). This too is incomplete, as can be seen by consulting the bibliographies in Chekhovskii's book or in P. Kisilev's, *O romane "Podnyataya tselina"* M. Sholokhova (Moscow, 1934). All major journals in Moscow and Leningrad carried articles about Sholokhov's work, but the most interesting journal is *Na podyome* (Rostov-on-Don) for 1929 through 1931. Here the controversy was most intense and the issues clearest.

Of greatest importance among the growing number of critical and scholarly books are: Anatolii F. Britikov, *Masterstvo Mikhaila Sholokhova* (Moscow, 1964); Mikhail D. Kokta, *Publitsistika Mikhaila Sholokhova* (Kiev, 1960); Yury B. Lukin, *Mikhail Sholokhov, Kritiko-biograficheskii ocherk* (Moscow, 1952, rev. 1962); Isai G. Lezhnev, *Mikhail Sholokhov* (Moscow, 1948); Vasilii M. Litvinov, *Tragediya Grigoriya Melekhova: "Tikhii Don"* M. Sholokhova (Moscow, 1965); Nikolai N. Maslin, *Roman Sholokhova* (Moscow, 1963); Viktor V. Petelin, *Gumanism Sholokhova* (Moscow, 1965); M. I. Soifer, *Masterstvo Sholokhova* (Tashkent, 1961); Veniamin G. Vasilev, *O "Tikhom Done"* M. Sholokhova (Chelyabinsk, 1963); Lev G. Yakimenko, *Tvorchestvo M. A. Sholokhova* (Moscow, 1964); *Mikhail Sholokhov, Sbornik statei,* ed. B. A. Larin (Leningrad, 1956); *Tvorchestvo M. A. Sholokhova, Sbornik statei,* ed. P. I. Pavlovskii (Moscow, 1964). Of special interest is the pamphlet on Sholokhov and the cinema: A. Vlasov and A. Mlodik, *Geroi Sholokhova na ekrane* (Moscow, 1963). In addition, numerous works have been published by university presses, but these are not generally available outside the Soviet Union.

Almost all of Sholokhov's works are available in two translations: Mr. Henry C. Stevens (pseudonym: Stephen Garry) has translated the major works for Putnam and Co., Ltd. in London (reprinted by Alfred Knopf in New York); Mr. Robert Daglish has both revised Stevens and translated independently for the Foreign Languages Publishing House (FLPH) in Moscow. Thus, *The Quiet Don* appeared in England and the United States in two volumes (abridged by approximately 25 percent), entitled *And Quiet Flows the Don* (1934) and *The Don Flows Home to the Sea* (1940)—Knopf's two-volume, boxed edition is called *The Silent Don* (1941); the FLPH edition in four volumes (uniform with recent Russian editions) is called *And Quiet Flows the Don* (1960). *Virgin Soil Upturned*, Volume I, appeared in England and the United States in 1935 (retitled *Seeds of Tomorrow* in the Knopf edition), an earlier, inaccurate Soviet translation having been mercifully forgotten; Volume II, entitled *Harvest on the Don*, in 1960. The FLPH edition in two volumes is called *Virgin Soil Upturned* (1961 and 1964). Although fragments of *They Fought for Their Country* appeared earlier, the most accessible translation is in *Soviet Literature* (July and August 1959), pp. 3-56 and 3-72. "A Man's Fate," retitled "The Fate of a Man," translated by Mr. Daglish, appeared in *Atlantic*, CCIV (November 1959), 41-45; but it was published earlier as "A Man's Lot" in *Soviet Literature* (May 1957), pp. 3-30. Mr. Stevens translated a substantial selection of Sholokhov's early stories in *Tales from the Don* (London: Putnam; New York: Knopf, 1961) and added another volume in 1967, entitled *One Man's Destiny*, which includes essays and speeches (unfortunately abridged) as well as stories. Mrs. Miriam Morton translated "The Colt," "The Rascal," and "The Fate of a Man" in *Fierce and Gentle Warriors* (New York, 1967). The dust jacket erroneously claims that "Mrs. Morton is the first American translator of Sholokhov. . . ." Mrs. Assya Humesky and I translated "The Colt," "The Brat" ("The Rascal"), and "The Chairman of the Revolutionary Soviet" in *The Dalhousie Review*, XXXIX (Winter 1960), 529-33; XLI (Autumn 1961), 324-46; and XLIII (Winter 1963-64), 507-11.

Outside the Soviet Union there is no extensive study of Sholokhov's life or work. More valuable than the brief accounts in book reviews and standard histories of Soviet literature are to be found in: Willi Bredel, *Sieben Dichter* (Schwerin, 1950); Olga A. Carlisle, *Voices in the Snow* (New York, 1962); Jürgen Rühle, *Literatur und Revolution* (Köln, 1960); Ernest J. Simmons, *Russian Fiction and Soviet Ideology* (New York, 1958); *Michail Scholochow, Werk und Wirkung* [Papers from a symposium at Marx University, Leipzig (March 18-19, 1965) celebrating Sholokhov's visit to East Germany], ed. Erhard Hexelschneider and Nikolai Sillat (Leipzig, 1966); and the following essays: Herman Ermolaev, "Sholokhov Thirty Years After," *Survey*, No. 36 (April-June 1961), pp. 20-26 [an excellent study of the two volumes of *Virgin Soil Upturned*]; Rufus W. Mathewson, "The Obscene Tattoo, New Notes from the Soviet Underground," *Columbia University Forum*, IV (Winter 1961), 31-40 [on *Virgin Soil Upturned*, Volume II]; Helen Muchnic, "Sholokhov and Tolstoy," *The Russian Review*, XVI (April 1957), 25-34. A dissenting note, amid the small chorus of praise, was sounded by Mikhail Koriakov, "Soviet Literature: Dictatorship of Mediocrity," *Thought* (Spring 1951), pp. 77-102. Frequently, essays and informative notes about Sholokhov have appeared in *Soviet Literature* (formerly *International Literature*), *Soviet Press Translations, The Soviet Review*, and *The Current Digest of the Soviet Press*.

Index